TRY IRONWOOD,
AN EDITOR REMEMBERS

Michael Cuddihy

Introduction by Robert Hass

ROWAN TREE PRESS
BOSTON, MASSACHUSETTS 02108

ACKNOWLEDGMENTS

Cover design by Rita Daly of Daly & Daly, Brookline, MA.

Poems reprinted by permission of the author:
"For Kayak Magazine," Lou Lipsitz; "La Tâche," Bill Matthews; "Abortion,"
"Cuba, 1962," Ai; "August, Quiet," Peter Nelson; "Hard Rain," Tony Petrosky;
"Escape Hatch," Bruce Andrews; from "The Book of Job," by George Oppen,
reprinted with permission of Linda Oppen Mourelatos; "Anna Grasa," Bruce
Weigl; "Blake," Linda Gregg; "A Milk Truck Running into a Crazy Maid . . . ,"
Frank Stanford; "The Closet," Bill Knott; from "A Separate Notebook: the
Mirrored Gallery," and "Inscript," Czeslaw Milosz; "Blue Horses," Susan
North; "Broken Pantoum for Three Voices," Laura Mullen; from "The Ecstatic,"
Fanny Howe, "Jury Selection," Lucia Perillo; from Book Four of "A Reading,"
Beverly Dahlen; from "Piecing Emily Dickinson," Lynn Sukenick; "He Will
Not Leave a Note," Alberto Ríos; "Silence," Gregory Orr; from *T & G, the
Collected Poems (1936–1966),*" Lorine Niedecker.

Letters and Reviews Reprinted with permission:
3 Oppen letters reprinted by permission of Linda Oppen Mourelatos; Oppen
letter, from *The Selected Letters of George Oppen,* edited by Rachel Blau du
Plessis, Duke University Press, North Carolina, 1990, reprinted by permission
of Rachel Blau du Plessis; from "Introduction to Eskimo Poetry," Richard
Lebovitz; Review, *Ironwood* 7/8, Michael Cuddihy; Review *Ironwood,* 23;
from James Wright's review of Robert Penn Warren's *Promises, Kenyon
Review,* Vol. XX, No. 4, Autumn, 1959; Review of *Ironwood* in *Library
Journal,* Dec., 1972.

Rowan Tree Press
124 Chestnut Street
Boston, Massachusetts 02108

For George Cusick—
the "great-hearted"
a rock and a soft place

and my brother Lester,
generations of love, support,
being there

Speed bonny boat
Like a bird on the Wing
Over the sea to Skye—

AN INTRODUCTION

Ironwood: my memory of the magazine alights on a weekend in the middle of winter in Vermont. The year must have been 1978, and I was teaching in a two week course at Goddard College, days crowded with poetry workshops, lectures on poetry and poetics, readings of new poetry and fiction. Having no other time in which to do it, I locked myself in a dormitory room on a Friday afternoon, like a student doing a term paper, and worked until Sunday night churning out an essay on Tomas Tranströmer's "Baltics" for one of the special issues of the magazine. I remember long nights, deep snow outside drifted into mounds, the pine woods creaking and snapping in the cold, occasional sounds of laughter from the parking lot, whispers and laughter in the hall—throaty laughter, one thinks, working alone at night in a dormitory room, whispers and little cascades of secret, amused laughter against which one hunches and bears down toward the translated winds combing out the lives of generations on a Swedish archipelago and its artifacts, from which—an old church, a hut, a water tap, bladders of seaweed in the surf—Tranströmer's singular and lucid imagination had made emblems of human fate.

I have some memory of making a call to Tucson, Arizona midday on Saturday when it appeared that I was actually going to get the thing written to tell Michael Cuddihy that the piece was as good as on its way. Michael's level, dry, somewhat gravelly voice suggested that he'd believe this somewhat plausible proposition in the event. No expression of amazement or gratitude at my heroics. I think he asked me whether I thought it was any good, about how long it was, and what day it would arrive. Walking back to my room, feeling, as I often did where prose was concerned, like the Raskolnikov of deadlines, I thought about the singlemindedness of good editors. Michael was already well known for pressing famous poets for new work and then rejecting it if he didn't like it. He was also well-known for giving young poets encouragement. If they sent him five poems and he thought one was promising, he'd keep the one, send the four back with a note of brief praise, and ask to viii

see more. One older writer remarked to me that no one had worked with young poets this way since Marianne Moore was poetry editor of *The Dial*. Sometimes the procedure would lead to the publication of a poem or two and sometimes it wouldn't. One of the younger poets at Goddard had worked up a parody of the technique, a purported Cuddihy letter that began, "Dear Sir: Thank you for sending me your life. It is a very interesting life, despite its beginnings. If you have four or five other lives which you could show me, it's possible that one of them would be more interesting than the one you sent or, taken together with it, would reveal contours less tedious . . ." Etc.

Back at my desk there would have been the matter of a baptismal font in a medieval church on an island in Sweden, into the stone of which scenes of warfare and violence had been cut, martyrdoms, plagues, the faces of gargoyles. "Nowhere the lee," the translation said: whatever faces outward suffers. But inside was the blessed water, tranquil, clear. Another emblem, this one of poetry and history, perhaps of spirit and flesh. I would have been absorbed again in the work, another day and a half of composing sentences to my head, muttering to the wall, typing. It is what magazines can give writers, work to do and a place to do it.

The first issue of *Ironwood* appeared in February 1972 and the last in November 1988. During the seventeen years of its life it was probably the best magazine of its kind in America. Though, in fact, there was nothing else quite like it: it published only poetry and prose about poetry and appeared twice a year. Its readers came to know the format that had evolved. One issue each year would gather Cuddihy's version of the interesting new work in poetry, and the other—the special issue—focussed on a particular writer, occasionally two writers, and rarely, a theme.

The adventurousness of the special issues and their aesthetic border crossings gave the magazine its character and its excellence. There were issues on American poets—James Wright, George Oppen, Robert Duncan, among them; on European poets such as Tomas Tranströmer and Czeslaw Milosz; one issue was devoted half to work by and essays about Linda Gregg, a poet who at that time had not yet published a book, and half to H.R. Hay's translations, collected for the first time, of the great Peruvian poet César Vallejo; another issue was divided between a group of new essays on Emily Dickinson, including a large piece of Susan Howe's remarkable *My Emily Dickinson,* and half to essays about the relatively little known and seminal work of Jack Spicer; still another issue focussed on the impact of the translation of classical Chinese poetry on American work. It was always in its orientation a writer's, rather than a scholar's, magazine, keeping a conversation going about the state and future of the art.

This quality of *Ironwood* came, of course, from Michael Cuddihy, so it was very interesting to me to read in this memoir his account of his discovery of poetry and of the founding of the magazine. It's a wonderful story and admirable of him to tell it with so little embellishment. Translating Maritain, plowing through works of metaphysics and aesthetics and political science, work his undergraduate education at Notre Dame had prepared him for, he hires a typist who happens to be a poet, falls in love with her, and is stung by her suggestion that he's too rational. "I was hungry for personal experience," he writes, "anxious to get close to my feelings. Poetry might be a way. I began writing, spending hours with poetry, or alone in the desert or along dry riverbeds listening."

A conversion! It has a remarkably clear echo in that famous passage in John Stuart Mill's autobiography in which Mill describes how, working very hard at philosophy and political economy under his father's tutelege, he falls into a terrible depression, comes across a few lines of Wordsworth's poetry which stir his feelings, and undergoes an intellectual and spiritual re-birth. The similarity isn't coincidence. The time that Cuddihy writes about, the time of the founding of his magazine, was a particular moment in American poetry. The generation of poets who had begun publishing in the late fifties and early sixties had broken through, and the direction of their work was visible, its energy in the air. It was described at the time as a resurgence of modernism, a revolt against the technically and thematically conservative procedures associated with the New Critics. And it was that, but it was also, perhaps primarily, a wholesale resurrection and reformation of some of the central impulses of romantic poetry. This was clear not only in Allen Ginsberg's frequent evocations of Blake and Shelley, but also in the way that Robert Bly and James Wright borrowed from Wordsworth and Coleridge the *plein air* naturalness of their titles. An insistence on experiential knowledge—*O Taste and See;* a new nature poetry—*The Back Country;* an insistence on spontaneity and surprise—*Meditations in an*

Emergency; on imagination and inwardness—*A Coney Island of the Mind;* a general sense of defiance and of the demotic—*Not This Pig;* all this was in the air, as the titles of characteristic books makes apparent, and so was the theme of quest, the search for values—*Diving Into the Wreck.* There was, in addition, the sense of extremity and instability at the center of private life which had been dramatized with a new intimacy by Robert Lowell and John Berryman and Sylvia Plath among others; and all of these tendencies were being cross-fertilized by translation of the experimental traditions—German expressionism, French and Spanish surrealism—that Anglo-American poetry had not absorbed.

Meanwhile, a younger generation of poets was emerging and beginning to take its bearings among these currents. Robert Pinsky's *The Situation of Poetry* appeared at about this time, and it is also not a coincidence that it begins with a meditation on Keat's "Ode to a Nightingale." Romanticism was what needed to be thought about. I know that I first became aware of *Ironwood* when the first of its two issues devoted to George Oppen caught my attention in a bookstore. It surprised me because I had glanced at the magazine before and thought I had it pegged as one of the many that were springing up just then in imitation of Robert Bly's *The Sixties.* They were full of imitations of Bly and Wright and W. S. Merwin and Galway Kinnell, occasionally of Frank O'Hara. For good reason—all of these poets were writing arresting poems. But George Oppen was another matter. Like many of the younger poets, he wrote a spare free verse, but he came to his style from quite a different direction. He was a modernist, derived from Williams and Pound, for whom technique, because it had to do with perception, was an ethical issue. He didn't think it followed easily on the heels of inspiration and in this way and others, his modernism was a critique of romantic poetry, just as much of the new poetry was a critique of the obliquity and high-mindedness of modernism. I didn't know then that George Oppen, who had set his poetry aside for twenty years while he did political work, found himself writing poems again in the late fifties when he began to read a book about aesthetics by Maritain. Cuddihy and Oppen, it turns out, were crossing in opposite directions to the same place.

I stood in the bookstore reading the issue and thinking that the editor of this magazine—from Tucson of all places—was a more complicated person than I had imagined. *Ironwood* was always faithful to its originating impulse, the opening to feeling, but it was the complicated, continually evolving curiosity about where poetry was heading that made it so interesting and lively.

Michael Cuddihy mostly lets these issues speak for themselves in his memoir. The story that he has to tell—plainly and crisply—is the story of getting the magazine out, and he tells it with the disarming and characteristic attention to detail that makes an editor. Readers will also find that the narrative is full of glimpses of some writers, now dead, who are very much alive in these pages—Wright and Oppen and Duncan and Raymond Carver, among them. Finally, there is the matter of Michael Cuddihy's tenacity and courage. He speaks about his situation quite matter-of-factly, but for the whole life of the magazine, he was severely disabled, his health precarious. Working with him it was something one was hardly aware of. Ironwood: it thrives in the desert and they say it's tougher than oak.

Robert Hass
Berkeley, California, 1990

HAZEL: A PRELUDE

I was sitting in on some printmaking classes taught by Andrew Rush, a wiry, intense man my own age. He stressed the physical side of printmaking, known since the Sixties as media. I wasn't studying art in order to create, simply observing what went into the etchings, dry points, lithographs, and woodcuts I had admired for a good while. I had been struck by how many sculptors, accustomed to working in stone, turned to lithography when it came to trying their hand at graphics. Somehow, a quality inherent in the stone entered the lithograph, just as the sharper, more splintered outlines common to wood marked most woodcuts. One day, Andy asked me whether I knew Hazel Archer. The name was unfamiliar. He quickly told me about her Black Mountain College background and her reputation as a photographer, recommending her classes in photography, perception and design at the Tucson Art Center. Before the week was out, I had found my way to the Art Center where I introduced myself and got permission to sit in on her photography class.

Hazel sat erect in a wheelchair, looking very much like a Buddha with a beautiful, smiling face. She would pause before speaking or simply sit, allowing the moment to expand like a raindrop. Her photography classes stressed vision; students with technical questions were told to ask them after class. Hazel would often say that 50 people, each with the same kind of camera and facing the side of a barn, would wind up with 50 different pictures. What made the difference was who was behind the camera. Because I could not handle a camera myself, she gave me my own assignments. One that stuck in my mind involved looking at photographs of the Civil War dead, then comparing them with photographs of the World War I and World War II dead. Hazel wanted me to observe the processes involved in photography without allowing emotions or ideas to manipulate my responses. That the same restraint that marked the Civil War photographers did not prevail during World War I and World War II led to widespread manipulation of public emotion, the majesty and terror of death lost under the gruesome, bloody surface. The class devoted several weeks to the early years of photography, the evolution of subject matter as well as forms. We saw certain early photographers imitating the formal oil portraits of their day, others whose work looked very much like lithography, etchings or drawings. Obviously, the work that resembled oil paintings owed some of this to the hours-long exposure time required in the early days so that time actually entered the process. At length, with Alfred Stieglitz, photography found its own way and began to inherit much of painting's traditional subject matter while Stieglitz, the gallery owner and impresario, arranged for the showing of new forms of abstract painting, including cubism.

Of Stieglitz, Hazel would often relate exemplary tales or anecdotes. Two that come to mind involved his second gallery, An American Place. Stieglitz refused to take out a single ad or even have the gallery listed in the Yellow Pages. Those who cared would find their own way there, alerted by word of mouth. The other story involved visitors to the gallery who, when they asked the man standing silently nearby how much a painting or photograph cost, were invariably asked: "What is it worth to you?"

As much for the pattern of their lives as for the depth and relevance of their ideas, Hazel required us to read and discuss certain gurus or visionaries, as she called them, whose names recurred with some frequency: Maria Montessori, Buckminster Fuller, Martin Buber and J. Krishnamurti. More often than not, these people had not attended primary or secondary schools, but stayed at home, with a tutor or some member of their own family directing their studies. People like Margaret

Mead, Luther Burbank or Stieglitz himself would be cited here. Since perception usually involved shutting down our conceptual apparatus or putting it on hold, it might seem extremely self-limiting. But the faculty of perception was not restricted to vision or recognition. It could include ethical decisions such as putting oneself forward in a human situation where something cried to be done. Among the hindrances to perception Hazel mentioned were what she called the polarities: good and bad, right and wrong, the beautiful and the ugly and so forth.

While she rarely criticized friends or people she knew in person, she had an uncanny ability by a simple laugh, a tilt of the head or subtle shrug of the shoulders, to consign someone to the further reaches of Limbo. This form of communication was in keeping with the aura of quietness that surrounded Hazel: even when speaking, there were long pauses. It was part of an attitude of patience, passive waiting, which may have grown out of her years in a wheelchair, the result of polio contracted at age 10. When she started Hidden Springs School, Andy and Jean Rush, along with Hazel and myself, made up the school board. I remember how, at our first meeting, we all sat for what must have been half an hour until Andy finally ventured a few words.

Among the valuable things Hazel taught me was that you could find almost everything in your own backyard rather than having to travel to Europe or some recognized cultural center. She was pointing toward the culture we make rather than the one we venerate because we are its heirs. Her remarks propelled me in the direction of the culture we make. It was as if a light switch had been thrown inside my head. Impossible now to avoid the conviction that this helped turn me toward poetry, the writing of it. Here she spoke in the authentic accents of Black Mountain College where painters, architects, craftsmen and poets pursued their independent routes to a "home-made world."

poetry or alone in the desert or along dry riverbeds, listening. Without realizing it, I was incorporating parts of a female persona. Slowly, slowly, the poems came. I promised myself I would not let her know I was writing poetry until I had published at least one or two, a promise I kept.

Not surprisingly, most of my poems concerned love and death, often linked. Almost every respiratory polio I had known or heard of had died by the age of 40 to 42, most in their twenties or thirties. One friend, an occupational therapist, told me optimistically that I would live to the age of 34. At the time, I was 23. With luck, I thought, I could make it into that charmed 40 to 42 circle. It seemed doubtful I could go beyond that.

The following January, I sat in on Dick Shelton's U. of A. writing workshop. How much I had to unlearn from my English classes in the early '50's. For one thing, I had little sense of natural speech rhythms. Each week religiously, I read two or three books from our list, along with several others. Another side to the workshop was the problem of students' criticism. I was often confused by the way students demolished different parts of a manuscript until there was practically nothing left. Not all these manuscripts seemed worthless, but once they became fair game, students kept piling on negative comments. The process was reversed with poems the class tended to like—everyone signed up to praise a line or two. Good poems wound up being praised even for their bad lines—all the good lines had been taken. While Shelton maintained a hands-off attitude with students, his own criticisms were quick, surgical, leaving their targets in markedly better shape. Almost the first thing Dick Shelton said when we entered his workshop was, "I can't teach you how to write but I can get you published." Shelton's remark was more modest than it might sound. I suspect he had in mind the techniques and tone that were currently in favor, acceptable to magazine editors and book publishers such as Wesleyan, rather than his connections. Even so, it seemed to make poetry a bit too much like advertising. One valuable thing Shelton taught us was the practice of automatic writing, introduced in the '30's by the Surrealists. It required emptying the mind as best you could, then writing down whatever came into it. The aim was to induce a trancelike state. At the time, I found it extremely useful and still resort to it occasionally. After one or two semesters, I dropped out and kept working on my own. I had a few things published and was lucky enough to land a half-dozen poems in *Kayak*, a magazine known for its generosity to relative unknowns, its surrealism and the general excellence of its issues. The name was synonymous with vision and daring, the kind of poetry that dealt with politics, the world, things. The following lines of Lou Lipsitz spoke eloquently "For *Kayak* Magazine":

> Our poems, shining and deadly, dense with emptiness
> represent the dark interior
> —the hearts of multitudes like factories at night
> full of silent, black machinery and the smell of oil
>
> But our poems also rave at dusk, burn secretly in fields,
> mad, nativistic, like hope's Ku Klux Klan
> obsessed with reconstruction.

> (from *Cold Water*, Wesleyan, 1967)

Many of the best poets in America sent their best work to *Kayak*. The list included W. S. Merwin, Philip Levine, John Haines, Gary Snyder, Charles Simic, James Tate, Sharon Olds, Mekeel McBride and others. The magazine's tone was jaunty, irreverent, full of gumption and energy. Its reviewers were as likely to attack *Kayak*'s own favorite poets as they were other writers. While poets like Dick Shelton and W. S. Merwin, with *New Yorker* contracts, had to give that magazine first refusal on all poems, many of their best still wound up in *Kayak*.

My experience of poetry did not begin with *Kayak*. Twenty years before, in 1950, my freshman year at Notre Dame, I heard Dylan Thomas read. Even from the back of the auditorium, I could see he was drunk. Still, the voice held me in thrall, so musically rich was it, ringing "like the echo inside the thin iron of blackened bells." I remember being specially moved by "Fern Hill", "Poem on his birthday" and "Do not go gentle into that good night". A fellow student whose room adjoined mine let me borrow his volume of Thomas's poems. It turned out I had already read a few of them since my brother Jack had the same book.

By 1954, a year out of the hospital, I went with a girl friend to hear Dylan Thomas read. Months later, we saw him again, reading from contemporary Welsh poets. So erratic were his speech and behavior that one never knew what might happen next. A few months later, we went to see the first production of *Under Milk Wood*, with Thomas acting as narrator. Within a few months Dylan Thomas was dead.

The YMHA was only five blocks from our house—easy to reach in my wheelchair. That year and the next, I must have attended five other readings, including, I think, e. e. cummings and William Carlos Williams. One time I was so bothered by the poet's voice that I left early. Readings were still rare then and few poets had mastered the art. That year, the courses I was taking at Columbia University included one on modern American poetry taught by Babette Deutsch. Here, we read and discussed Jeffers, Sandburg, Frost, Dickinson, Marianne Moore, Rexroth, Edward Arlington Robinson, and above all Whitman, Williams and Hart Crane. I remember a final exam, given orally, where Deutsch asked me about Whitman's rhythms, particularly those in "Out of the Cradle, Endlessly Rocking." Unable to respond positively to those rhythms at the time, I had to admit I didn't like them. Try as she might, reading me portions of the poem, I stood my ground. I could not honestly agree with her. We must have spent two long minutes speechless, literally eyeball to eyeball. Finally, she blinked. I wound up with an "A" in the course.

The best of my poems were gone. My *Kayak* acceptances had depleted my reserves. For the next year or two, I published no more than a handful of poems. After I had been writing close to a year, I got in touch with Brother Antoninus, a Dominican monk I knew from a lecture series I had run for the University of Arizona's Newman Center. Antoninus had nearly won the Yale Younger Poet's award for 1937. He was a disciple of Robinson Jeffers and a World War II conscientious objector, his tightly-strung lines revealed an intense inner life and powerful sexual feeling, powerful to the point of obsession. Well over six feet, rangy, he had little of the gut one expects in a man who has recently turned fifty. Antoninus was reluctant to take me on as a student for the summer. For one thing, he had never taught poetry; for another, such a task would require an enormous effort to shed himself of his own work and get inside the poetry of another, only to leave it again. When at length he relented, agreeing to see me once or twice a week, I'd visit him at his ground-floor apartment in the Kentfield Priory. He'd get out a jug of

10

red wine and we would talk of poetry, there or out under the trees. I listened as Antoninus spoke of Pound and Williams and Whitman. He loaned me his copy of the *Cantos*. When I showed him my poems, he would look them over, then hold them for review until our next meeting. He felt that I needed to put myself into my poems more than I had. I was grateful for his advice and determined to follow it. When we'd pick him up for dinner Friday nights, he would bring along a record or tape of Pound reading from the *Cantos*. You could see and feel excitement in his eyes. Although he was already beginning to be known among his fellow poets, Antoninus, or Bill Everson as he was then called, had really drawn the spotlight of publicity during the Beat era when he found himself grouped with the Beats. For all their sexual daring and raunchiness, it was Everson, the Catholic lay brother, who often wound up getting the most publicity. An expert printer like his father before him, he produced a superb limited edition of the Psalms which today is worth a small fortune, esteemed by libraries and collectors. Although Everson's ties tended to be with the Beats and Black Mountain poets, he followed closely the careers of leading mainstream poets, particularly Catholics like Robert Lowell and Thomas Merton. As a reader, he developed a style of pacing the floor, silent, charging the room with latent energy until he had audiences on the edge of their seats, hungry for his words. Those who were put off by these maneuvers would slip from the halls, leaving him relieved, assured the place had been delivered of negative feelings and vibrations. The idea for such showmanship, he once told me, came from watching JFK and his own father, the bandmaster in a small California town. His immersion in Jung enabled him to justify his adopting this persona. What amused and delighted me was how down to earth he was, full of bawdy humor and anecdote. The night we picked him up on our way back from Point Reyes, he had just received and read the text of Pope Paul's encyclical on birth control. Referring to the Pope, he commented: "I didn't think he'd have the balls." Then, more reflectively: "What better place to take a stand than at the entrance to the womb." Although he didn't teach me much craft, I felt he had given me something important: the sense of belonging to an ancient and honorable fraternity with its traditions, its myths, its rituals, and a good deal of interesting gossip and anecdote, particularly concerning the more prominent West Coast poets. I was not too surprised a few years later when he took off his Dominican habit after a reading and announced he was leaving the order to marry a woman half his age.

* * *

One thing that made the University of Arizona important for poetry was the Ruth Stephan Poetry Center, located on the edge of campus. Not only did it house an impressive collection of poetry books, it included complete sets of recent and contemporary American poetry magazines. An adjacent building was home to visiting pets who stayed anywhere from a day to a week or longer, usually while reading or visiting classes. Like others before and since, I was able to meet and talk with poets whose work really mattered to me: Charles Simic, James Tate, Allen Ginsberg, John Haines, Bert Meyers, Mark Strand, Diane Wakoski, Sandra MacPherson, and Galway Kinnell. Twice a week, I would drop in at the Poetry Center, reading books off the shelves and exploring the magazines. When I found one like *Kayak* or the *San Fransisco Review*, I went back over previous issues, savouring the contents, including even letters to the editor. As the son and grandson of publishers, I had a kind of hereditary interest in books and magazines. My father's study held a five-foot shelf reserved for weeklies, monthlies, and quarterlies. As a boy, I read *Life*, the *Saturday Evening Post* and *Collier's* but was intimidated by the bold print and pictureless rough paper of *Commonweal*, *The Christian Century* and *America*. What I didn't realize at that age was that those magazines gave my father a better grasp of what Catholic or Protestant clergy were likely to read. *Harper's* and *The Atlantic* I took up as a junior in high school, enjoying the stories and an occasional article. Funk & Wagnalls, the firm headed by my grandfather and later my father, each year sold thousands of *The Pulpit Commentary*, used by roughly one-third of America's Protestant ministers. While grandpa wound up a Knight of Malta and a Knight of St. Gregory, he got away with publishing these things, along with a similar compilation for rabbis. At a time when the Catholic Church was much stricter than it is today, Grandpa Cuddihy managed to be both unorthodox and acceptable.

The magazine I spent most time with was Cid Corman's *Origin*. The library must have had 60 issues at least. Associated for almost a decade with Black Mountain College, the magazine printed work by Creeley, Olson, Duncan, Levertov, and other Black Mountain poets. In addition to those poets, there were poems, features, and sometimes whole issues on other poets such as Zukofsky, Niedecker, John Logan and H. D. Important translations appeared there first, as well as work by Antonin Artaud, inventor of the Theater of Cruelty. Another issue was devoted to Joseph Albers who left Black Mountain to head up Yale's prestigious School of Design. Much of this work was at least a decade ahead of its time.

Another magazine that caught my imagination was Robert Bly's *The Sixties*. I liked much of the poetry, particularly the translations. Almost every issue carried blocs of French, German, Spanish, Norwegian or other poetry in translation, Bly's way of opening up American poetry to the unconscious and the emotions as opposed to the poetry of the mind favored by the English tradition. Essays on Louis Simpson, Donald Hall and W. S. Merwin saluted these poets for their contemporary subject matter and feeling but pointed out the contradiction inherent in their continuing to use older forms. Later issues included essays on Levertov, Ignatow, Creeley, James Wright, Logan, Dickey and Snyder. Bly pushed surrealism, particularly the Spanish and Latin American varieties, which he considered more deeply rooted in their own cultures than was that of the French. *The Sixties* and The Sixties Press exuded the fervor of the early Methodist circuit riders and tract writers. It was the kind of magazine you could not afford merely to leaf through. I quickly became a subscriber.

Choice and *Lillabulero* were other magazines that appeared more erratically, heavy with first-rate poetry and provocative essays and reviews by writers I found congenial. John Logan edited *Choice*, Bill Matthews and Russell Banks *Lillabulero*. The first printed a great range of good poetry, tending to arrange poets by cities and regions: poets like Bly and James Wright, Bill Knott, Dennis Schmitz, Naomi Lazard, W. S. Merwin, Galway Kinnell, Kathleen Fraser and others. Early on, Bly contributed two lengthy, controversial review-essays to the magazine. *Lillabulero* printed a certain amount of short fiction, normally selected by Russell Banks, whose own perspectives paralleled orthodox Black Mountain ones. The poetry was carefully chosen, normally underwritten, with an emphasis on craft. It had the air of an elite magazine in the

best sense of the word. There were, of course, others, but these were
the ones that drew me, heart and head.

Among the poets I met at the Center, John Haines stood out for his
bearing and character. The son of an admiral, he had spent several years
as an abstract painter in New York City before leaving for Alaska where
he homesteaded for over a dozen years in the wilderness, killing his own
game, living alone, trying to explore as far as possible his own depths
and the Alaskan wilderness. A healthy corrective to the more superficial
types with their vision of easy success, Haines had the dark, brooding
outlook of an Old Testament prophet. In conversation, he mentioned
Bly's axiom that a poet should spend at least two hours in the field for
every hour spent at the desk. As I remember, he himself thought the
ratio should be more like six to one, unless I have reversed the names.
The original statement obviously referred to deep listening or the process of sharpening awareness, preferably in nature.

One poet Haines brought to our attention was Wendell Berry, whose
Openings and *Findings* contained marvelous sequences. Berry was a
Kentucky writer with a successful academic career who left a teaching
post at Cornell to take up farming in his home state. In his poetry, art
and life reflected one another. His strong moral stance and do-it-yourself
attitude obviously spoke to what was deepest in Haines. With the publication of several novels and an imposing array of books on farming,
nature, and ecology, Berry became one of the intellectual godfathers of
what would later be called "the counterculture." I immersed myself in
both collections.

Another poet I found engaging was Charles Simic. A refugee from
Yugoslavia, he was jolly, whimsical, a good listener. His knowledge of
wines embraced both Europe and California. Over the years he would
pass along a number of good tips, particularly when it came to Zinfan-
dels and Petite Sirahs. Simic had a down-to-earth manner which he
combined with a taste for the finer things, including wonderfully powerful Yugoslavian coffee. He was a sympathetic if critical observer of
his peers, elders. I remember his remarking of one distinguished poet
that he was afraid of suffering. Of another, he pointed out that most
of his recent books had been written several years before. The vehe-
mence of his remarks on the fifties poets really surprised me at the
time.

* * *

During this period, my poetry had stalled. It was not a question of craft, more like a failure of energy. What poems I wrote appeared thin to me, not rooted enough in my life, my body. By the spring of 1971, I decided to see if I could sit in on Bill Matthews's summer workshop at Cornell. He was married to Marie Harris, my second cousin. If all worked out, I could learn a thing or two about poetry and get some expert advice on editing. This was not mere idle curiosity. If I was ever going to start my own magazine, it had to be soon. I was nearing forty. My father and grandfather had been publishers, running Funk and Wagnalls. Grandpa Cuddihy had even started *The Literary Digest*, a forerunner of *Time* and *Newsweek*, which reached a circulation of two million in the early '30's. My oldest brother Lester who, shortly before World War II, had tried unsuccessfully to start a nationwide chain of newspapers located in the state capitols, had been asked by Bill Mauldin to help him put out a daily on the troopship carrying the 45th Division to Alexandria, and later, Palermo. The newspaper helped amuse and distract thousands of GI's for the three crucial weeks. There was no getting away from it, it was in my blood.

So I wrote Bill, enclosed a few poems and got back a nice letter. I made plans and had my rocking bed towed up to Ithaca where we rented a house thirty yards from Lake Cayuga, some twenty miles in length. It was a warm, rustic place with a kitchen as big as the living room, a bathroom larger than the room where I put my bed. We would spend much of that summer in the kitchen. After several days of getting used to the house and exploring the nearby countryside, I gave Bill and Marie Matthews a ring and invited them for spaghetti dinner. They were a most attractive couple, intelligent, sophisticated, very easy to be with. Among other things, we shared an interest in wine, including the newer Chardonnays and Rieslings from New York State. As a Yale upperclassman, Bill had worked for a year in a New Haven wine shop. He told how visiting alumni would uncork the older clarets as much as six hours in advance of a dinner at his Yale club. Bob Bachen, whose spaghetti we were eating, had just driven me through the Finger Lakes country to Hammondsport, the wine capital of New York State, a green landscape, whose lovely rolling hills reminded me of Brueghel. We had our usual share of adventures, asking directions of a lovely woman who invited us to her house for tea. Editor of the wine industry's newsletter, she used her position as a bully pulpit for Konstantin Frank's attempts to grow Chardonnay and Johannisberg Riesling, both white varietals. Later, we had driven over to Frank's modest home and tasted his wines. Delicate yet strong, they had won gold medals at tastings all over Europe and America. Still, at six dollars a bottle, they cost roughly twice the average good quality California varietal. Frank was a Russian-German whose ancestors had been invited by Peter the Great to settle in the Ukraine. Like thousands of his fellows, he had come west toward the end of the war and wound up in America.

Together with his poems and first-rate editing, Bill's provocative essays and reviews had earned him a place in the bustling small press world. He seemed equally at home with established publishers, where his Ivy-league background didn't hurt him. That summer, he was working on translations from Jean Follain, a contemporary French jurist and poet.

For half the summer, I sat in on Bill's workshop. The classes lasted between two and three hours five afternoons a week. My fellow classmates were intelligent and serious. After a week or two, I realized that a group of intelligent women, veterans of Bill's workshops, tended to set the tone for the class. Good poets themselves, they had a favorite male poet who was probably the best writer in the class. That summer there was much discussion of Sylvia Plath, Diane Wakoski and Erica Jong. Bill ran his workshop fairly casually; Friday afternoon classes often took place in a local pub.

A number of Bill's ideas from that summer stayed with me. For one, he considered line length a measure of the poet's confidence, how far he or she was willing to go from home base before returning to the margin, like a child skipping ahead of her parents, excited by her sense of daring. Another idea that recurred with some frequency was Bill's notion that a poem should not take itself too seriously as a poem. Though I responded positively to this, in my own seriousness, I never totally absorbed it. What impressed me most was his sense of how to end a poem, particularly the kind of ending that seemed to continue even after the poem was finished. I had been accustomed to poems that announced their ending well in advance and began to have a better sense of how many successful poems only discovered what the poet was saying through the act of writing itself. A fair number of these changed direction well after the poem had begun. Bill's notion of the unconscious differed markedly from Robert Bly's. For Bly, the unconscious was a link to instinctive life, to the body and the animal world. While Eliot and Pound feared the unconscious as the Puritans had, the French poets were right in trusting it as a source of spiritual energy. For Matthews, the unconscious resembled a junkyard, full of outworn images, notions and scraps, some of which could indeed be useful, though hardly a prime source of energy.

Going to class and back was a pleasant drive, 15 miles each way, through rich dairy-farm land. We soon discovered a house that sold wonderful, homemade bread. I had already spoken to a neighboring farmer about buying unpasteurized milk. Reluctant, the farmer let himself be persuaded. Every four days, we would pick up a three-gallon can, stopping to chat. Norwegian-born, the farmer was just my age, had one or two degrees in agriculture from Cornell and was a great admirer of Thomas Jefferson and his ideals. We became friends, visiting back and forth.

The first time we drove to the Matthews to pick them up for dinner, Bill was outside, doing a series of jumpshots about twenty feet from a basket fixed to his house. He sank 13 in a row before he broke off and went in to get Marie. We enjoyed a terrific evening together but what stuck in my head were those 13 consecutive baskets. Anyone else would normally have stopped at an even dozen. Not Bill.

I had at least one impromptu lunch with Bill and Marie. We ate off a large wooden table with all sorts of manuscripts piled here and there on smaller tables. They had nearly finished restoring their late 18th century house to its original lines, including stairs that closely resembled step ladders. Their two sons, Willie and Sebastian, were quick, handsome and impulsive. Marie was already doing her own research and writing in her part of the house and tended to keep to herself when not eating meals or serving drinks.

One Sunday, I drove over about noon and found John Logan down from Buffalo for the weekend. John looked much like a middle-aged rabbi, studious, scholarly even, glasses well off the bridge of his nose.

He knew hundreds of his contemporaries personally and in detail, including their latest poetry manuscript. For him, the boundaries of his own family and the even larger family of students and *Choice* contributors grew until they reached from one ocean to another. He had come to Notre Dame the very fall polio prevented my returning. He taught in the small Great Books program known as the General Program of Liberal Education, where I had been enrolled in the first class a year before.

While I prepared for the workshops by polishing older poems instead of breaking new ground, Bill Matthews loaned me a large box of literary mags. Together with issues I hadn't read of *Choice*, *Lillabulero* and *The Sixties*, I was introduced to several important magazines, including *The Tennessee Poetry Journal*, *December* and *New: American and Canadian Poetry*. I should mention as well *Apple* and *Pebble*, two small but lively and well-edited magazines from the mid-west. I was impressed by *TPJ*'s special issues and its zeal for integrating Southern poetry with what was going on in the Northeast and other centers. Along with consistently good poetry, *December* contained first-rate features on film, and hard-hitting political analyses. Many evenings and mornings were spent examining the things in that box.

By the second week in July, it was time to get started. I got together with the two young men helping with the wheelchair and asked their suggestions for a magazine title. We came up with 20 names, which were reduced to three: *Kettle*, *Pulse* and *Ironwood*. Of these, *Ironwood* appeared to have the edge. Reading over my own poems, I came to realize, rooted as I was in a wheelchair, how deeply I felt drawn to trees, themselves deeply rooted yet reaching well into the sky. It seemed an apt metaphor for my kind of poet. In fact, I felt closer to cottonwood trees but there was already a *Cottonwood Review*. Like a great many small magazines, the name summoned up contrary elements, in this case mineral and vegetable, dead and living. Ironwood was the second heaviest wood, with the greatest density. Local to Arizona and the desert, it could be found elsewhere in America. Finally, in an almost subliminal way, the word suggested the image of the cross with the iron nails going deep into the wood, the horizontal contradicting the vertical, history and eternity in a single image, central to a 2000 year tradition.

18

*   *   *

I got hold of a typist through student placement at Cornell and arranged to dictate letters to poets whose addresses I got mostly from Bill Matthews. When I asked him one day after class, he rattled off fifteen or twenty in a virtuoso feat of memory. The others I had myself or got through their publishers. Bill had promised me my choice of the Follain translations he and Mary Feeney were doing. The people I wrote to in preparation for the first issue included Charles Simic, Diane Wakoski, George Oppen, Donald Hall, Bill Meredith (an old acquaintance from New York), David Ignatow, W. S. Merwin, Wendell Berry, Dennis Schmitz, Andrei Codrescu and John Haines. I also wrote to Dick Shelton, Peter Wild, Steve Orlen and William Roecker, all at the University of Arizona. My letters named those in the issue as if they had already sent work. Beyond a blind optimism, I had no assurance that they would. As it turned out, almost everyone on my list honored me with poems.

One poet whose work I was drawn to was C. K. Williams. A copy of his latest manuscript lay on a small table in the Matthews' dining room. After I had thumbed through it with some care, Bill offered to let me take it home for a week or two. I would spend many hours going over the poems until I came up with two that seemed wildly exciting, full of rhythmic energy and charged language. They would go at the beginning of the issue.

With July drawing to a close, replies began to arrive each day or two, more and more poets sending work or pledging it within the next few months. As I finished writing to those on my list, I was already able to assure them that we had at least seven or eight groups of poems on hand with others promised. Diane Wakoski sent a 14-page poem whose subject was Sylvia Plath as her alter ego. Through much of its length, the poem was powerfully sustained. The problem was, it seemed to allege that Hughes had killed Sylvia Plath, and a second wife, as though he himself had stuck their heads in the oven. Even granting poetic license, the poem struck me as libelous. It would certainly have put the issue on the map. If not technically responsible for what could be considered signed opinion, I felt responsible. I must have spent two or three weeks

of mostly sleepless nights, going over this and over. At length, I passed
up the poem and settled on three modest lyrics.

*   *   *

When Mary Cusick flew to Ithaca from Boston, we had already decided that she would join me in Tucson in the fall. It was a momentous
step for both of us. Next day, we drove up to Lake Ampersand near
Saranac Lake to spend a couple of weeks as guests of my friend Ted,
who had worked for me in Tucson. It would be a kind of honeymoon for
Mary and me, who had known each other since she came with one of
her brothers to visit me in the hospital sixteen years before. Ted's
grandparents owned this enormous place in the Adirondacks, with two
lakes, one of them over a mile long, overrun with deer, bear and other
wildlife. Before the Civil War, the property had belonged to Ralph Waldo
Emerson, Louis Agassiz, and a group of Cambridge philosophers. A
photograph shows the fourteen men standing on an island in the lake,
complete with vests, suitcoats and ties. They have twenty guides min-
istering to their needs.

*   *   *

By the time I left Saranac for New York in a one-engine plane, I was
glad to be heading back to Tucson. First, though, we drove from New
York City to Water Mill. There I telephoned H. R. Hays and arranged
a meeting. He got hold of David Ignatow and we all met at the Hays
place in East Hampton. A dapper man with a crisp voice, Hays had an
air of quiet authority that reminded me of my own father. Ignatow was
warmer, more gregarious, with a steady flow of energy. His more than
30 years editorial experience made him a natural choice as the first editor of the new poetry tabloid APR. Hays had published over 20 volumes
of fiction, anthropology, sociology and poetry, including translations from
the Spanish and German. Mrs. Hays brought out a tray with coffee.
Much of her time was spent selling real estate; the same was true of
David Ignatow's wife, the artist Rose Graubart. In each case, the couple
lived in their own house during the winter and rented it to members of

the wealthier summer colony, as it was called, during the three summer months. During this period Ignatow was teaching at Southampton College, only 20 miles away. We talked about poetry and poets. I showed them a poem I was thinking of taking and both men reacted unfavorably. There was far too much ego in the poem, they felt. I was grateful for their advice. They talked bitterly of the '40's and '50's when the ubiquitous influence of W. H. Auden had prevented their work from being taken by most of the good little magazines. Ignatow had already sent me work and Hays loaned me a manuscript from which I selected a couple of poems. He also let me borrow his Vallejo translations. When after a week with them, I asked if I could print some, he responded with some bitterness that Vallejo's widow had forbidden it.

My nephew Les was spending a few weeks at the family house in Water Mill and loaned me a couple of books dealing with typefaces. I spent hours, whole days even, thumbing through a large looseleaf directory of typefaces. Mostly the sizes ran from six or eight points in small quantum jumps up to 36 points until you looked at the large page opposite, full of 60-point caps. I acquainted myself with the contemporary-looking sans-serifs, the kind of clean face that reminded me of Swedish modern furniture, what a nephew called "that Bauhaus look". My own taste ran to older faces, or what were called transitional faces: Goudy Old Style, Caslon #540, Garamond, Baskerville, and Palatino. By the time I caught the plane for Tucson, I was leaning toward Goudy or Baskerville.

After a week to get my ground legs and reorganize the house, I designed a slip small enough to fit five to a page. A friend at the University offered to stencil 200 copies, which we cut into a thousand slips and mailed to Hitchcock, Logan and Matthews. As the weeks passed, I found letters in our new mail box from poets whose names I had seen in *Kayak*. I spent a good deal of time going through their poems, trying to answer within a week or two. Week after week, the task simplified itself in most cases; some poets I had read in *Kayak* or elsewhere, others were totally unknown. Right off, I realized that my preferences involved more than mere opinions: they represented commitments I would have to stand behind.

Before leaving town after Bill Matthews's last class, I had located the best wine shop in Ithaca and found a bottle of La Tâche, an extraordinary red Burgundy. Years ago, I had been given a case of this heaven-sent wine. La Tâche was an unforgettable experience and Bill and Marie just the persons to appreciate it. Along with a thank-you note, I had a bottle delivered to them before returning to the house to pack. Three weeks later, in Water Mill, I received the following poem:

La Tâche 1962

for Michael Cuddihy

Pulling the long cork, I shiver with a greed so pure it is cu-riosity. I feel like the long muscles in a sprinter's thighs when he's in the blocks, like a Monarch butterfly the second before it begins migrating to Venezuela for the winter—I feel as if I were about to seduce somebody famous. Pop. The first fumes swirl up. In a good year the Domaine de la Romanee-Conti gets maybe 20,000 bottles of La Tâche; this is number 4189 for 1962. In the glass the color is intense as if from use or love, like a bookbind-ing burnished by palm-oil. The bouquet billows the sail of the nose: it is a wind of loam and violets. "La tâche" means "the task." The word has implications of piecework; perhaps the vineyard workers were once paid by the chore rather than by the day. In a good year there would be no hail in September. Work every day. Finally, the first pressing of sleep. Stems, skins, a few spiders, yeast-bloom and dust-bloom on the skins. . . . Now the only work is waiting. On the tongue, under the tongue, with a slow breath drawn over it like a cloud's shadow—, the wine holds and lives by whatever it has learned from 3½ acres of earth. What I taste isn't the wine itself, but its secrets. I taste the secret of thirst, the longing of matter to be energy, the sloth of energy to lie down in the trenches of sleep, in the canals and fibres of the grape. The day breaks into cells living out their secrets. Marie agrees with me: this empty bottle number 4189 of La Tâche 1962 held the best wine we have ever drunk. It is the emblem of what we never really taste or know, the silence all poems are unfaithful to. Michael, suppose the task is to look on until our lives have given themselves away? Amigo, Marie and I send you our love and this poem.

Grateful as I was for the poem, the editor in me failed to acknowledge its overwhelming merit. Perhaps I was embarrassed by having presented such an extravagant gift. I had visions of my fellow poets queuing up, each with his own rare vintage. I didn't quite realize that the poem was being offered to me for *Ironwood*. Stanley Plumly, poetry editor for the *Ohio Review*, quickly took the poem when Bill offered it to him. The experience confirmed my belief that it is often harder to receive than to give. When Richard Howard reviewed *Sleek for the Long Flight* for APR, "La Tâche" was the poem he singled out for special praise.

When I first wrote to George Oppen, I mentioned that my own perspectives were related to what I called 'Kayak surrealism.' I might have told him he was connected in my mind with Alfred Stieglitz, the great American photographer and champion of the Post-Impressionists. Looking back, I realize that this remark might more accurately have been directed to Dr. Williams. Oppen's response was challenging:

(("Kayak surrealism"? Yes, but what, by now, does the word mean? if one calls a law-brief Surrealist it seems to be so
        I believe I may just now inadvertently have written a defense of the word and the school Hadn't meant to

Oppen added that he would make some decision about sending me two or three poems after returning to San Francisco early in September. Weeks later, he sent "Poem About the Garde," which, by his own admission, was atypical. When I wrote back returning the poem, I expressed my readiness to print it, provided he include one or two more representative poems. Oppen responded promptly:

Dear Michael,
        alright: a serious editor   One can't object to that
                George Oppen [a huge beautiful signature]

Another letter concerning the poem says, "the poem faulted from the start in that the last line is "revelatory' and wrongly 'Arranged'." A later paragraph adds "Depth, the possibility of learning from ones own poem— nb, the fact of having learned—all of this that can be called *music* is, one hopes, in other poems."

Most of the return letters I was getting were enthusiastic but few drew me as Oppen's did. Mostly, they dealt in gossip or "Po Biz", a somewhat derogatory reference to the gregarious, extroverted side of poetry with its readings, conferences, organizations, workshops, and poetry-in-the-schools: the whole tissue of bureaucracy that had grown up out of the conjunction of federal funds with a renewed American interest in poetry. While immediate in their diction and syntax, in their look on the page, Oppen's letters spoke from and to the depths of poetry, living and other things. For all their sophistication, they were rooted in a thoroughgoing value system.

Thinking of typing, rough and smooth paste-up, design and the whole spectrum of things to be done, I began seeking out those who could help with the magazine. Andy Rush, my printmaker friend, offered to help with rough pasteup and do the design work on the cover. A poet and fiction writer who had interrupted a teaching career to go through the University's MFA program, Rita Garitano helped me to process and answer incoming mail. Ron Mahka, a Peace Corp veteran who had worked three years on the Navajo reservation, spent his evenings helping me go through the day's *Ironwood* mail. Mary Cuddihy, who had recently come west to share my life contributed in many important ways.

When it came time to paste-up the first issue, Marilyn Huggins and Marcie Holbrook offered to help. While rough paste-up involves setting the individual poems in proper order on facing pages, in our case it included making sure the relation of the poem to its surrounding white space became integral to the poem. That way, the person doing final paste-up would not need to make those decisions. It allowed time to select the most coherent and forceful arrangement of the magazine's contents. While one or two people read one set of galleys for typos and misspellings, someone else could quietly proceed with rough paste-up. Well in advance, I made a point of going to the typesetters with the best local reputation, Tucson Typographic Services. I had hoped they would have the Goudy Old Style typeface. Joe Holderman, who ran the shop, shook his head. It would cost him five or ten thousand dollars to add the font to what he had on hand. Since my own health was uncertain and little magazines notoriously mortal, I didn't feel I could guarantee anything, nor would he have taken my assurances at face value. When he gave me the addresses of two first-class California printers, Holmes Typography of San Jose and Mckenzie Harris of San Francisco, I sent them both xeroxes of the same poem and, within a fortnight, I had received samples of both printers' workmanship. While Holmes did a good job, McKenzie Harris's version of Goudy was literally breathtaking. The rub was the price. Given that, I decided to go with Tucson Typo, and use Baskerville. Then I checked to see how long the offset printers would take once we had presented them with the final paste-up. The answer was two to three weeks, but we were told to allow two extra weeks to cover unforeseen difficulties, like having one of the machines break down, losing a spare part, or having a delay in getting the right paper.

When I went with Andy Rush to Shandling Lithographing, I let him select the paper. As a printmaker, he was accustomed to looking at all kinds of paper and had even gotten to see how homemade papers were fashioned in modern Italy. Though the paper selected was described as ivory, I was too much of a greenhorn to know that ivory was an offwhite, not too far from a yellow. For me, it was still the ivory of Ivory Soap, 99-&44/100% pure and therefore snow-white. Later, with the issue in our hands, I saw how brown the print looked and switched to a lighter color, choosing Warren's Oldstyle, with improved results. Apart from this, the paper was a good choice and so was Shandling.

Through a mutual friend, I got the telephone number of Florence Ogawa. She was already starting to use Ai (Japanese for "perfect love") as a *nom de plume*. When I told her of the magazine and mentioned well-known contributors, including locals like Steve Orlen and Dick Shelton, she sounded somewhat diffident about her work but at length agreed to send me something. I had read a few of her published poems here and there, plus a few from old workshops. But however well made, those student poems were polite, restrained, academic. When her current poems arrived, I began reading them right off. What I held in my hand was alive: Fierce, raw, they struck home. One had a sense of the way poor people live. Again and again I went over them, these poems, feeding on them, their life. I wound up taking four and returning the others. Here's one I took:

ABORTION

Coming home, I find you still in bed,
but when I pull back the blanket,
I see your stomach is flat as an iron.

You've done it, as you warned you would
and left the foetus wrapped in wax paper
for me to look at. My son.
Woman, loving you no matter what you do,
what can I say, except that I've heard
the poor have no children, just small people
and there is room only for one man in this house.

Another poet who had been given one of our slips by John Logan was
G. E. Murray, a man of astonishing imagination and a good, overall
command of craft. I was too inexperienced, too close to American neo-
surrealism, to be as aware as I might of his shortcomings. As it was, his
poems crackled with a kind of electric energy. Murray had taught here
and there but was now making a living as a free-lance journalist and
book reviewer, soon to become the first person with a weekly poetry
column in a major American newspaper. When I asked him and Florence if they would inaugurate our chapbook series, to begin in fall '72,
they agreed.

One impressive thing about the *Tennessee Poetry Journal* was the
quality of their interviews with featured poets. David Ignatow, Robert
Bly, and others revealed little-known aspects of themselves and their
habits as writers. Whether it was the ebullience of the poet or the interviewer's skill in eliciting responses was hard for an outsider to tell.
Perhaps having the same interviewer made for a comfortably predictable
relationship. Certainly, Scott Chisholm did his homework without seem-
ing academic. I had been hoping for an interview with James Wright
but geography and timing were against it. So we put that off until our
next issue. Chisholm sent me a rough outline of an interview with Donald Hall, covering his years as an editor and interviewer for *Paris Review,* and his joint editorship of the 1961 anthology *New Poets of England and America.* Honest, openly repentant even, about his "careful"
ignorance of poets like Creeley and Ginsberg, Hall's admission was the
kind of ecumenical gesture among schools of poetry which represented
the direction I wanted *Ironwood* to take. While I wasn't prepared to
print just anybody, by soliciting George Oppen and William Meredith
among others, I had gone outside the typical neosurrealist poets to include one of the better fifties poets and a giant of the numerically small

but important Objectivists, a group that numbered Louis Zukofsky, Charles Reznikoff, Basil Bunting and, in some measure, William Carlos Williams himself.

In dedicating the first issue to three editors, George Hitchcock, William Matthews, and John Logan, I was careful to link each one with the basic thrust of the magazine he edited. With Hitchcock, I specified his generosity and daring, the encouragement *Kayak* had given to "a poetry of vision and perception." With John Logan it was his catholicity, the extent of his embrace, that especially drew me to *Choice*. With Bill Matthews and *Lillabulero* it was the concern for moral seriousness and poetry rooted in a sense of place that stood out. Furthermore, *Lillabulero* impressed me with the way the magazine handled paper and print, with how the white space of the page entered mysteriously into the creation of the poem. You didn't lightly toss an issue of *Lillabulero* into the wastebasket.

After Thanksgiving, satisfied I had enough good material for an issue, I set about getting copy ready for the printers. For one thing, I didn't have more than a foggy notion how to mark. Here, Andy Rush was a help. By a simple fraction, 10/12, he showed the type size as 10 points (numerator), and the figure below (denominator), the amount of space between lines. If the copy was poetry, the phrase "line for line" indicated how it should be set; if prose, a phrase like "24 picas" would show how long you wished the lines, and the word "justify" tell the printer to make the right margins even. Other marks specified paragraphs and other differences in the way print was to be handled. Andy marked up much of the first issue while I followed suit. This issue and the next were actually set with hot type on a linotype machine. Altogether, it took ten days for the rough galleys of the poems, reviews, and interviews to come back from the typesetters. In those days, we picked up and returned our galleys; they were not delivered by messengers. Bill Matthews had suggested that a self-respecting literary magazine owed it to itself and its contributors to send them proofs and we followed this procedure each time. By the time we were into the new year everyone, to the best of my knowledge, had responded.

Everyone, that is, except Bill Matthews. In Ithaca that summer, Bill had promised me a review of Mark Strand's *Darker*. A book that had captivated me as well as hundreds of other poets, young and not so young, Bill had been using it in his regular workshop. Every three or four weeks, I would drop him a line or mention it over the phone. Busy, he kept reassuring me. I had, incidentally, written Mark Strand, telling him of the impending review and asking for poems. While he didn't promise any poems, he promised me translations—good ones—by Thanksgiving. In the event, those translations never arrived. When the review of *Darker* did arrive, it was decidedly ambivalent, its irony aimed at Strand's blurbs. As I was to learn a year or two later, when the lone issue of Bly's *The Seventies* appeared with a jibe at "reviews of Mark Strand's *Darker*," Bill Matthews found himself beset by conflicting loyalties, given Bly's and Strand's rival claims to sponsor the young, brilliant Gregg Orr. Now the conflict seemed to center on Charles Simic, with one blurb quoting Strand very favorably on Simic's work. The blurbs cited in the review bore indirectly on questions of conflicting sponsorship and poetic turf. For some years, Matthews had acted as a loyal defender and spokesman for Bly and many, though not all, of his ideas. Although at the time I was enamored of *Darker*, the book probably deserved most of the criticism Matthews leveled at it.

*   *   *

My wish to start another poetry magazine had brought me my share of incredulous looks and comments. Although my background and reading had prepared me, there was much I had to learn about poetry, both traditional and contemporary. Still, with *Lillabulero* planning a leisurely demise, the *Tennessee Poetry Journal* recently defunct and *Sumac* going belly up, there was room for at least one more. Twice I had had poems taken by *Sumac* and admired its breadth of taste. For one thing, it printed George Oppen and Ezra Pound, along with a wide range of Black Mountain poets. I wanted a magazine that was inclusive in the kinds of poetry it printed yet succeeded in printing the best of each. A magazine, too, that kept aloof from cliques or factional disputes, and avoided the power politics of New York City or the narrow provincialism of the western regions. A magazine with a clean, clear, uncluttered format that would make it easier for poems to maintain and heighten their immediacy, easier for poems to happen on the page rather than being hung there like notices on a bulletin board. A magazine, too, that would print relative newcomers without their having to be "sponsored" by some name poet. A magazine that would reflect the era in which we live both formally and with respect to content. Yet *Ironwood* had no program, open or covert. If I felt that an attitude of openness toward the future and the unknown was crucial, it was partly because my own views were not yet fully developed but remained largely inchoate.

When it came time to begin smooth paste-up, Rita Garitano and Marilyn Huggins recommended Frances Curtis, who had had valuable experience running high school newspapers and magazines. Because these surfaces were the ones to be actually photographed by our offset printers, smooth paste-up required more care than did the rough. Apart from the text, only light blue pencil or crayon could be used since they would not be picked up by the cameras. In 1972, we did not have access to waxed proofs, or if we did, were unaware of it. Consequently, there was lots of shifting proofs around. The thing was to do it quickly before the glue hardened and keep it thin enough to avoid lumps. Given her teaching schedule and the demands of private life, Curtis was available only on weekends which usually meant Sunday afternoon, and I was grateful for having begun the process well in advance. I tried to center poems left to right and made sure they were pasted up a bit lower than most magazines did them. The job was done on a magnificent black walnut table that a painter friend had made for me. Although Frances Curtis would measure things very carefully, I developed the habit of eyeballing the proofs to see if they tilted upward a little on the left or right side. If I thought they could be off a little, Frances would check again and frequently wound up having to make changes.

For the cover, Andy Rush adopted a simple graphic design: a single column of names on the left side with IRONWOOD in large optima sans serif capitals across the middle and the issue number 3/4 of the way up and well right of center. With only the color of the cover changed, this format was maintained through the next three issues. The first issue had a very light gray cover with a dark gray numeral designed and drawn by Hazel Archer.

It was January 25th when we took the issue to the printers, all 86 pages. A week later, we were told to pick up our blue line proof, which enabled us to check if poems were level and straight, or set too far right or left. More importantly, it gave us a last chance to correct misspellings and typos, the more egregious ones especially. The blue line proof contained the complete text of the magazine in light blue ink on a pale yellow waxy surface, the pages separated into unbound 16-page signatures, lying one inside another. We returned the proof next day with whatever changes were needed. Three weeks later, mid-February, we had our issues, 1156, well beyond our print run of 1000.

Through a friend who worked for Cody's Bookstore in Berkeley, we got Bookpeople to distribute the magazine in the Bay area. Altogether, they sold over a hundred copies. In New York City, stores like Gotham Bookmart and the Eighth Street Bookshop took ten copies each. By the time we were finished, they had sold 35 copies apiece.

The response to our first issue was almost universally favorable. A number of contributors and editors compared it to the first issue of *Field*. Several claimed it was the best new magazine to appear in the past decade. Only Ted Weiss of *Quarterly Review of Literature* grumbled and that was about the "three editors" of my dedication. Clearly, we had done a few things right. There seemed few if any typographical errors. The issue sold for two dollars, with a one-year (two issue) subscription costing three dollars. At the back of our first three issues, we enclosed a page with three subscription cards, and soon found ourselves with fresh subscribers. On the last page of the issue were three one paragraph reviews I had written myself. The first was of a Beacon Press edition of translations from Pablo Neruda and César Vallejo, done by James Wright, John Knoepfle and Robert Bly, the second a small pamphlet of prose poems by Vern Rutsala, from Greg Kuzma's Best Cellar Press and the last a chapbook of Bly translations from Tomas Tranströmer, issued by Lillabulero Press. Though I had not asked Robert Bly for poems, this page made plain some of my own leanings.

Early in March, what I imagined was a response to our first issue arrived from George Oppen:

Michael
    Michael   ____it's difficult to put gently enough, or with sufficient circumlocution And so I've delayed writing you, tho I have intended to write
what you sent was .thru a fumble of hands in

your shipping 'department'   — an empty envelope
           O K   O K   Stop blushing   Try
again
      Regards

           George

Mary, Ron, myself—we looked at each other with incredulity before relaxing into a long laugh and sending off ten copies of the issue. It was the first and last time this ever happened with anyone, although, given the state of the U.S. mails, many issues failed to reach their destinations for one reason or another. Unfortunately, there is no Bermuda Triangle where one can picture them awaiting the resurrection.

In response to the first issue, Robert Bly wrote, "The magazine is clear and solid, and has a mood like wood." He singled out Ai's poems, especially "Abortion", for special praise and offered to send me Machado translations he was working on. We wound up printing a couple of them in issue #3.

Since the new year, we had been getting an increased flow of poems as the magazine found its way to the various islands of poets strung across the nation. Richard Hugo, Ai, Philip Levine and W. S. Merwin were the only poets I solicited for the second issue. By now, I was working on G. E. Murray's chapbook which we changed to *A Mile Called Timothy,* rather than the more predictably surreal *The Bandaged Mirror.* Ai's manuscript had been taken by Houghton Mifflin, who were rushing it toward publication. They were understandably reluctant to have a smaller book of the same poems competing with theirs. Still, she soon let me select three fine poems from the manuscript, including "Cuba, 1962":

> When the rooster jumps up on the windowsill
> and spreads his red-gold wings,
> I wake, thinking it is the sun
> and call Juanita, hearing her answer,
> but only in my mind.
> I know she is already outside
> breaking the cane off at ground level,
> using only her big Indian hands,
> I get the machete and walk among the cane,
> until I see her, lying face-down in the dirt.

Juanita, dead in the morning like this
I raise the machete—
what I take from the earth, I give back—
and cut off her feet.
I lift the body and carry it to the wagon
where I load the cane to sell in the village.
Whoever tastes my woman in his candy, his cake,
tastes something sweeter than this sugar cane;
it is grief.
If you eat too much of it, you want more,
You can never get enough.

Much of the power of this poem derives from its music, especially the superb last five lines. Here, the repetition of long a and e sounds makes of our reading itself a kind of feast for the mouth, culminating in the consonantal rhyme of "grief" and "enough."

Within two months of our first issue, Phil Levine read in Tucson and came for dinner. He and Fran made an engaging couple. I liked their energy, his bluntness and his poems. We had in common a fondness for obscure Spanish wines and other things Spanish, hard as it was to fathom how someone with Phil's political stance could feel so at home on the soil of Franco Spain. Phil told us how much he had enjoyed having George Oppen read at Fresno. Whenever they went up to San Francisco, usually twice a year, he and Fran would visit George and Mary. He pointed out how rarely he spent time reading poetry magazines. It was the younger poets who kept up with them, particularly the newer magazines. They were more likely to be our audience. One quality he valued in an editor was loyalty. George Hitchcock of *Kayak* had helped him get started but, more importantly had stood by him when he was in a slump, and managed always to print something. This kind of editor made all the difference. Another who had been very important to his career was Fred Morgan of *Hudson Review*. Phil spoke of Studs Terkel, a Chicago journalist turned oral historian, whose most recent book, *Working*, he had recommended to his writing students. Since the best of his own early poems had dealt with sweeping floors and other menial jobs in Detroit, he obviously felt that their poems could benefit from the kind of realistic, concrete details given in Terkel's interviews. At a relatively late age, when he had already published four or five collections, Phil had achieved his reputation. It had been a long wait but he was almost grateful now that it hadn't come sooner. He described being taken up, finally, by Eastern critics like Richard Howard and wined and dined all over New York. While he had loved it, it had made him somewhat uncomfortable. He spoke well of Robert Bly's *The Sixties* but warned that printing Neruda now was not the fresh thing it had been when Bly did it. He also pointed out how few American poems Bly had printed in all those years. Paying closest attention to his remarks on loyalty, I took his words to heart. After we had had an exuberant early supper, he gave a generous and spirited reading. Before the week was over, Ai threw a party for the Levines in her downtown apartment and everyone had a good time. Within a fortnight, Phil sent poems, including "Grandmother In Heaven," with which we began our second issue. Dick Hugo mailed us a fine letter poem which we printed across from his "A Snapshot of 15th S.W." Both Hugo poems wound up in the second edition of *Naked Poetry*, the superb anthology of open form poetry edited by Steve Berg and Robert Mezey. In our first issue, I had included two zany poems of Nicanor Parra translated by W. S. Merwin, but now Merwin favored us with his own poems, one of which we took. Other work just showed up in our box or came at the suggestion of someone like John Logan. One was James Moore who, with Patricia Hampl, had started *The Lamp in the Spine*, an iconoclastic magazine coming out of Iowa which opened its pages to talented newcomers, particularly women with something fresh to say. Along with Moore's own brand of literary iconoclasm, the magazine printed provocative essays, particularly on sexuality. One essay took on W. S. Merwin, Galway Kinnell and James Wright in one swoop. In addition to taking a poem, I asked Moore to review *Down at the Santa Fe Depot*, an anthology of Fresno poets edited by David Kherdian. I liked what I had read and thought Moore might feel the same, having written warmly of Kherdian's poems. The review trounced the anthology, conveniently dividing it into workshop poems and the poetry of childhood, which Moore felt was the only subject these young poets were equipped to write well about. In the process, poems like "They Feed They Lion" were ignored. I was bothered but intrigued. Phil Levine exploded in a letter to me, drawing a parallel with *Genesis* and *Job*. Moore was unruffled. He was teaching me something.

Another poet to write was Lew Hyde, who sent translations from Neruda's *Residencia*. I printed four with the Spanish facing but turned down
an essay on his translations, not knowing it had been written by Robert
Bly. The essay showed up later in APR, along with a large selection of
translations. Ai's poems were also featured by APR about the same time.
I was soon to realize that their 28 associate or contributing editors gave
them unparalleled access to commercial publishers, writing programs
and ambitious poets, older and younger. Whatever their errors of commission or omission, they nearly always included good poems or great
translations, along with important if long-winded essays. Although most
poets I knew badmouthed them, the same persons jumped at the chance
to be printed by them.

APR's 28 associate editors suggested a comparison with the European
feudal system at the time of the Crusades. The kings of various countries
called on their dukes, who summoned the next in rank, the process
repeated to the level of squire and vassal. With APR, directors of writing programs, leading poets, prominent essayists and influential publishers, all had something to get and something to give, while the sheer
multiplicity made it easier to turn down someone's work. Because APR
had 26,000 subscribers and appeared six times a year, it could offer a
commercial publisher space to print one fourth of an entire book of
translations, say 16 poems, with a potential audience wider even than
the book was likely to draw, but with a real potential for significantly
widening that audience. In an earlier era, those 16 translations might
have been divided between four to six of our leading poetry magazines
while today's small magazine editors were often faced with the dilemma
of standing in line for translations APR had chosen to pass up. Fortu-
nately, with Follain, with Supervielle, with Neruda, with H. R. Hays's
Vallejo translations, we were there first, but the chances of this happening again were bound to shrink. The same was true with strong ethnic
poets and women writers. APR could make their names and faces familiar to tens of thousands which would, among other things, make it easier
for them to get readings. Given their tabloid format and circulation,
they could come on as democratic and populist while printing John Ashbery and James Merrill.

Clearly, operating a little magazine in the age of APR would mean
more emphasis on special issues and special features. It would also suggest increased attention to the neglected or forgotten poet, the one who

shunned the limelight. And it might suggest as well more attention to the truly experimental, which APR normally neglected but could in fact embrace if they so desired. It might even mean a relative neglect of certain ethnic poetries simply because APR could sweep up so many of such poems, including the best work. If you were seeking to print such work, you would have to be there first or develop a different slant. In *Ironwood*'s case, another reason for concentrating more on special issues was the documentary aspect of such issues, their importance for posterity. Perhaps our emphasis on the white space of the page as participating mysteriously in the creation of the poem was something APR could never even approach. Some of our best poets hungered for those beautifully chaste pages. Finally, one had to be the first to discover new or neglected poets, even if it meant caring for them in ways that went beyond printing their work.

In our second issue, the person who most excited me was Peter Nelson. He sent us three poems: "Between Lives," "The City in Winter" and "August, Quiet". Peter had studied with John Logan and wrote with a quiet intensity. His poems felt relaxed, natural, with a perfect pitch. He seemed of the same cloth as Merwin or Galway Kinnell. Here is the shortest of the three:

AUGUST, QUIET

—After reading American Indian speeches

They are the words of betrayed lovers.
My own letters used to lie on the desk like that.
I have lost track of this life.
At the window insects press in, take up positions
Like markers on a war map. Signals pass along the webs;
A spider revolving in the awesome
Intelligence of its legs.

In seven lines, the poet had cut to the bone, revealing himself and his subject. The single image as a metaphor provided an instant replay of American expansion westward with the Signal Corps and the Seventh Cavalry the real "legs" of the American war machine, though often they may have acted as the instrument of the railroads.

Two others who sent me work were Heather McHugh and Lyn Lif-

ginning with *Sanctuary* and *The Wild Palms*, which enabled me to finish at least seven novels in four months, including *The Sound and The Fury* and *Light In August*. I've been grateful to him ever since.

Marty enjoyed going through manuscripts with me. One criterion he regularly championed was integrity of line, by which he meant a line's ability to stand by itself, ending preferably with a noun, a verb or the kind of adjective that could double as a noun, as opposed to an incomplete phrase like "of the." Without being aware of the term, I already shared his views on integrity of line. In the Black Mountain view, as propounded by Charles Olson, line length was related to the poet's breathing so that, correctly broken, a new line began simultaneous with the breath. Some of the best poets combined integrity of line with maintaining the connection to the breath. A few years down the road, I came to realize that a poem was more than the sum of its parts. Like an auto mechanic checking off tires, suspension, plugs and points, I got so busy I didn't pay enough attention to whether the car ran. In this case, whether the poem honestly worked. I would pass on all its parts and lose sight of that larger thing that was supposed to go on in poems as it does in people—one's constitution, temperament and so forth. Obviously, I shouldn't exaggerate the harm done here. Still, in each issue, it may have proved decisive in a handful of cases.

For Marty, another test was, in Pound's words, "language charged to the utmost"—meaning that not only should words be accurate, they should be used with a sense of their roots, connotations, and latent energy. From my standpoint, this kind of poem suggested ego anxiety in the poet; for all its brilliance, such a poem, like a fancy French restaurant, could shut people out rather than inviting them in with its intimate tone and the interior space it created. Marty was receptive to my objections. In fact, he may have secretly welcomed them. I often had the feeling it was not his own view so much as the aesthetic program of *Poetry Northwest* he was half-attempting to convert me to. Of all the magazines I had read, this was the one I disliked most—for its format, its slick paper and the poetry they printed. I had read many poorer magazines, of course, but of the respected ones, this was the one that most rubbed me the wrong way. Still, they had their virtues. For one thing, they printed a good number of women poets, including beginners, at a time when this was rare.

Acutely aware of the sound qualities that distinguished germanic words

38

from Latin-derived ones, Marty singled out the germanic diction of poets like Robert Lowell and Richard Hugo as opposed to the more latinate vocabulary of, say, David Ignatow. In creating a harsher music with more stress on the consonants, the germanic words came across as more physical. They also proved a more appropriate vehicle for breaking the pentameter, conforming as they did to the rhythmic patterns of contemporary American speech.

Dick Shelton's poetry-writing workshop led me initially to accent whenever possible the first and last syllables of a line. Here, accenting the first syllable was more important. With experience, I came to see how often other values might conflict with this goal. For one thing, a poet could be so intent on convincing himself that he had a strong line that he could lose touch with his own experience, his own feelings, as expressed there. The vocabulary itself, which called a final stressed syllable masculine and an unstressed a feminine ending, betrayed this archetypal link. I came to regard such lines as so many barbells, steel rods with a heavy weight at either end. Workshops, particularly the University of Montana's, turned out reams of poetry with a disproportionate share of these masculine stresses. For all their restless energy, a number of Hugo's own poems, nearly always those with the most final stressed syllables, seemed out of touch with the feeling, the deeper meaning of those very lines, as if the poems were running on automatic pilot or cruise control. As an editor, I noticed how *Choice*, John Logan's magazine, tended to print the highest percentage of poems with flexible, relaxed yet complex rhythms, the kind of patterns the mind and will could not invent or arrange. For me, the whole subject of rhythm and rhythms became so obsessive that, every time I turned to a novel or even a work of non-fiction, I found myself arranging and rearranging the rhythmic patterns of the sentences.

*   *   *

Looking back over correspondence from this period, I find the great majority of our contributors required several exchanges of letters at least before the issue with their work appeared. Often, such exchanges involved proposed revisions and these could bounce back and forth as much as a good tennis volley. Frequently, I would ask poets to drop the final line, or even the final two or three, or else find some other way to leave things open so that the poems, in ending, did not close off all formal possibilities. Here, I was much influenced by Bill Matthews though I may have carried the tendency to an extreme. A good number of poets accepted my suggestions regarding their last lines or other changes; just as many stood their ground. In most cases, I would try to obtain at least a couple poems but not at the cost of quality. In spite of our first issue's containing a good percentage of multiple poems, I was not conscious of this until later, after our fourth issue. By multiple poems, I mean two or more by the same poet printed in sequence. It is usually hard to get an idea of an unknown poet's work from just one poem. Most editors would, I suggest, consider two poems a minimum and three ideal. Should you print four or more it is probably going to look as if you are featuring that poet. Still, one could do a very good issue with four or more poems by each of thirty poets. The problem is, most younger poets are anxious to accumulate magazine credits and therefore tend to spread their best poems a bit thin. Their concern is multiple magazines, ours, multiple poems. As year followed year, I was always on the edge of having a form rejection slip with enough space to add a comment below, or my initials, should the manuscript warrant. Meanwhile, our submissions grew slowly. I read each one with some care and wrote short notes of three to ten lines to at least a quarter of them. These I dictated to one of the young men helping with the wheelchair and so forth. Briefest and most perfunctory were the rejection slips I wrote by hand. They had to be brief precisely because such an effort taxed my limited reserves. I would write something like "None of these. Sorry. M. C."

A month before our second issue, the December *Library Journal* carried the following brief review of our first:

A substantial new little mag which differs from most in that it is expansive (86 pages), is letterpress, and is meticulously edited. It comes closer, in fact, to feeling like a well supported university item, but nothing indicates that Cuddihy is getting that kind of help. The first issue is dedicated to "three extraordinary editors; George Hitchcock (*Kayak*), John Logan (*Choice*), and William Matthews (*Lillabulero*). Obviously, *Ironwood* will not be a carbon copy of *Kayak, Choice,* or *Lillabulero*." Perhaps not, but the editor has the touch of his "extraordinary" three. There is a nice balance between the known poets such as David Ignatow and Diane Wakoski, the predictable, Donald Hall and George Oppen, and the relative beginners. An exciting, rewarding, and, for the most part, successful first time out. Let's hope the editor can keep it up. If he does, this promises to be a major new voice in the little mag world.

Of the three presses cited above, two published their own books. One of five presses awarded an unsolicited $10,000 grant by the NEA, Kayak Press's books and chapbooks were remarkable in their use of color and imaginative artwork. Using good quality paper and print, our own early chapbooks resembled those of Lillabulero Press, whose books were largely unadorned. Such a series would certainly attract good manuscripts, thus helping the magazine. I was doing it for its own sake as well, seeking to create a haven and support for those poets I most believed in.

Late in November, 1972, we issued our first chapbook, G. E. Murray's *A Mile Called Timothy*. Before settling on fourteen poems for the chapbook, I had gotten the author to send me almost everything he had written. Steve Romaniello, a sculptor from an artist's commune north of Tucson, did the cover drawing. A man with many friends, Murray sent all of them a special form and the orders came flooding in. Half the 500 copies we had printed were gone within the year. After the withdrawal of Ai, we filled the gap in our publication schedule with Thomas Johnson, a young Cornell graduate whose best poems, rooted in his native South, combined intelligence and verbal inventiveness. He was an editor and we wrote back and forth, comparing notes on magazines, poets and translations. For the spring issue, I chose four Johnson poems and scheduled his chapbook for a few weeks later.

For all our disappointment at not getting a James Wright interview, we were able to print a pair of his poems: "To the Saguaro in the Desert Rain" and "Discoveries in Arizona." Meeting James Wright and hearing him talk, however briefly, in the faculty lounge of the University of Arizona was a memorable experience. Stocky, greying, looking several years older than his age, Wright answered a number of questions from his student audience, many of them undergraduates. Detecting critical references to the police in Wright's poems, one student asked him what

he thought of the police. After pondering for a moment, Wright told us
the following story. A few years earlier, he had returned to his birth-
place in Martin's Ferry, Ohio and went to look up an old high-school
chum, now a policeman. When he reached the small station and looked
inside, the friend wasn't there. There were only two policemen, one of
whom sent the other to the hospital for help and asked Wright if he
could hold up a prisoner who had just tried to slash his wrists. Wright
stood facing the man, his hands holding him. He looked down and, next
thing, he was on the floor. He had fainted. The point of the story, Wright
explained, was that, if he were ever to become a cop, he would have to
harden himself because the nature of the job forced you to live at the
extremes of crime and danger.

Another poet I met for the first time was William Stafford, who read
that May at the university. Disarmingly modest, with a warm smile, he
was someone who made poetry sound easier perhaps than it is. We had
him to the house one evening and before we knew it were all talking
about families, childhood, things the average visiting poet would soar
above or ignore. One discordant note occurred when I showed him the
latest *Harper's* with a poem by James Wright, "The Young Good Man",
which I very much admired. Clearly, he didn't feel it deserved its place
in the magazine. His tone hinted at what, in another man, I would call
condescension. For all the imagination in his poems, Stafford was clearly
a rooted man, in many ways a throwback to the fifties. Where most
visiting poets adopted some form of clothing associated with the alter-
native culture or else dressed like the academics they were, Stafford was
more like an ordinary man in a tan sweater, someone who made you
forget about categories. Yet this man, accepting and accepted, had been
a conscientious objector during World War II. He had even, at the publisher's request, written a biography of his fellow C.O., William Everson, later known as Brother Antoninus. There was a whole lot more
there than met the eye, but it was an extra relief that, for all his candor,
he felt no need to have it meet the eye.

Stafford showed me the latest *Northwest Review* with two featured
poets and a strong group of translations. He felt a magazine made a
stronger impression with this kind of focus. I was weighing his remarks
against Scott Chisholm's description of us as a strong, gimmick-free magazine. For his part, Stafford praised the group of Neruda poems from

the *Residencia*, along with Ai's poems and Peter Nelson's, in our second issue.

Perhaps the most significant work submitted during this period was written by Frank Stanford and Tony Petrosky. Stanford sent us fat envelopes with brief notes written in brown ink with an old-fashioned pen, possibly a quill. What impressed me was that his first submissions made no mention of publications, just the names and dates of manuscripts from which they were taken. Since some went back to the early sixties, I thought him a much older poet, possibly black, given the amount of rural southern dialect he used. Curious, I wrote proposing revisions and asked for more poems, also inquiring about his age. Frank welcomed my suggestions. Other letters told of hunting and fishing, working in the garden, friends in jail for murder, taking groups of underprivileged kids camping. He turned out to be 23 years old and had been writing since he was seven. At the age of 13 he had written an enormously long poem: *The Battlefield Where the Moon Says I Love You.* He wound up sending me the manuscript. It was endless, shot through with brilliant passages echoing Beowulf, Dante, the Troubadors, and others, yet rooted in Frank's own history, set within the Civil Rights movement of the Sixties. Other letters spoke of managing an art film house with his wife Ginny, a promising painter. He had also made a few short films himself and received an award for one of them.

Tony Petrosky wrote to me in October, 1973 at the suggestion of John Logan. The poems he enclosed spoke from the heart with great power and a moving tenderness. Much of his strength came from the realistic yet reverent way he identified with his grandfather and struggled with his parents; the way, too, the poetry dealt with coal mining, distilleries, things another era had dismissed as unfit for poetry. Within a fortnight, I was writing to let him know that I had taken four of his poems for our impending issue. Already leaning toward a chapbook, I asked to see more. Here's one of the original poems:

HARD RAIN

Your lips are cold.
They should be, you're dead;
solid as the heart of a stone
drinking nothing but rain—
even in the brilliant sun.

I ask myself what I'm doing here
kissing the lips of a dead man.
What is this place?

The earth, dressed like a man,
holds what I wanted most. Left behind
with a fire pawing my soft insides
I still feel the violent black flower,
the other women who sipped a little of you.
Bastard. Naked.
In the middle of the night
a long length of ruby-colored rope burns
in my stomach. I wrap it round,
and round my fingers, feed it anything but love.
That's all I owe.

I tell my dreams
grant every claim, slowly,
deliberately. In my own good time
I'll answer the rain.

*　　*　　*

Our third issue had been delayed several times and would shortly go
to the typesetters. Reviewers had held us up only to announce, after I
rejected their poems, that they were unable to write their reviews. Much
as I treasured continuity and reliability, I decided that quality was more
important. I decided to pay for poems, essays and reviews as a means of
attracting more and better quality poems and to make it more attractive
for reviewers to write for us. In the small press world, reviews tend to
be written by free-lance reviewers rather than at the request of magazines. All too often such reviews are celebrating an already well-known
poet who happens to be their teacher, or a promising newcomer who
happens, in this instance, to be the writer's prize student. Much of this
writing is sincere, even ingenuous, but it misses its mark more often
than not.

Another poet who would figure in our third, fourth and fifth issues
was Bruce Andrews. A Ph.D. candidate in Political Science at Harvard,
Andrews was interested in the sounds of words in much the way abstract
expressionists were interested in the surface of the paint for its own

sake, rather than for the sake of any particular meaning. He wrote several elaborate, fascinating letters on the poetics of his own poems, tracing their ancestry back through Zukofsky to Gertrude Stein. His neat, intelligent handwriting gave these letters the quality of historic documents. Here is "Escape Hatch," the first Andrews poem I accepted for *Ironwood*:

ESCAPE HATCH

I could crevice
this bag of tricks wind
goes through.

Or on a hill
woodshedding.

The zeal of the animals.

A new skein of
notes, blues,
give them away the agate.

Carpenters glow

A fleet of swag-bellies
or mole breath
cyclone.

Rob a brocade.

Mesh them up:
alto, tenor,
broken-down pollen.

Take the new
bones and the trunk,
voltage,
handful of bolts.

Lady knew me in
bandages.

A wrist, too.

Bituminous mouthpiece.

A bow hoists the sax.

Notes fly,
come apart.

Flats rivet high.

Get inside metal
one pickpocket.

air—tool marrow.

wind.

#3 reed, #2 reed,
#2½ reed, getting my
map and high temperature.

Anti-mithradatism.

Tinsel up.

All in splinter, flex, once
and for all get my arm
from the sling.

Metal banquet.

Playing like a catalept.

Scott Chisholm had been unable to get anything short of a 70-page interview from Louis Simpson, and with Simpson proving recalcitrant with poems, it seemed too overwhelming a commitment. Our second issue contained instead a good-sized interview with William Matthews. Matthews proved a perfect subject: fluent, articulate, relaxed in a way few younger poets seemed to be. He had interesting things to say on workshops, chaos versus order in poetry, irony, tonal range, the sense of place, political poetry, and other subjects. Another feature was "Locating American Literary Establishments", a chapter from Richard Kostelanetz's *The End of Intelligent Writing*. Kostelanetz explored the nature, role, size and behavior of American literary cliques as they came to dominate the national scene for a decade or two before being supplanted by competing groups. The piece felt accurate, even though the writing lacked distinction and avoided more substantive issues such as quality. I printed it not only for its general interest, but to send a signal regarding my own independence. At least a couple of important poetry honchos must have gotten the signals because their behavior toward me cooled. Our third issue included a selection of Eskimo poetry in translation by Richard Lebovitz. Here he discusses the origin and character of these poems:

It was partly this wide-eyed wonder at the world, a world that still retained a sense of mystery, that attracted me to the songs of the Eskimo. It was obvious that the Eskimo had not yet been separated from the physical world by material civilization. His songs therefore represented for me poetry close to its primal source. I have since learned that the Eskimo words for "to breathe" and "to make poetry" are the same. The Netsilik Eskimo Orpingalik called his song "my breath." And Kilime, an Angmagssalik Eskimo, spoke thus: "All songs are born out in the great wastes . . . Without our knowing it they come with our breath, words and tones which are not daily speech. . . ."

Instinctively, I shared Lebovitz's response to this primitive communal poetry. Our readers, by and large, would feel the same way.

That March ('73) Sandra McPherson came to Tucson for a reading. I arranged to take her for a drive to the riverbed just below the first foothills north of town. It remained dry all but a few weeks a year. As we drove along the desert foothills and neared our destination, Sandra began asking pointed questions. Her hunger for precise details was intense and infectious. She would ask us to stop the car, get out and crouch before some tiny plant, twig, or flower, fingering it ever so gently. We had lunch overlooking the riverbed. This had become my favorite part of Tucson, in great measure because of the huge cottonwoods that lined both sides of the river bank, one every 50 yards or so. In the wind, the leaves rattling sounded like typewriter keys and looked incandescent in the sunlight. Usually, this area was deserted but now and then a dune buggy would go by or someone on horseback. It was a day when time stopped and things stood lit from within. We returned with a good deal more energy than when we had come. I would see Sandra several more times when she and her husband Henry Carlisle and her daughter spent Christmas in Tucson.

During her visit, Sandra and I discussed how many of James Wright's poems I should take. He had asked Dick Shelton to send me whatever poems he considered worthwhile. Of the three, I was very much taken by "To the Saguaro in the Desert Rain," less so by "Discoveries in Arizona". The third poem I found disappointing. Since Sandra had written a somewhat critical piece for *Iowa Review* pointing out how often Wright had used words such as "dark", "darkness" and "darkening," I counted on her being fairly hard-nosed. To my surprise, she said that, at the time she edited *Poetry Northwest,* she would have taken all of them from such an important poet. When I asked Steve Orlen the same question, his answer had been pretty much the same. Feeling easier about taking the first two, I returned the third. Interestingly, it showed up a few months later in *APR* but does not seem to have been included in any of Wright's subsequent collections.

*   *   *

Mary and I spent the summer of '73 in Mill Valley, California, a small town nestled in the mountains across the bay from San Francisco. It was part of Marin County, our summer headquarters from then on. We set out to get in touch with George and Mary Oppen, whom we knew only through correspondence. The Oppens were spending the summer at their Polk Street apartment in San Francisco instead of Little Deer Island, Maine. We arranged to have them over for lunch, and it was a brisk, sunny day when they arrived. We were struck by how wonderfully different they were: Mary with her shy, endearing smile, warm blue eyes taking you in; George with his gift for symbolic anecdote and understated humor, his soft voice easy on the ear. For all their 65 years, they retained much of the aura of youth, the look and feel of explorers. But they were getting on in years, too, and knew it, even if they could still spend nights sleeping on the floor of their tiny sailboat. We moved to the terrace for lunch, drinking soup and eating cold cuts, enjoying the motions of the huge pines behind the garage. The Oppens, while no longer Communists, were still people of the left, intrigued by the Chinese experiment in housing and feeding a billion people, but making it clear that they wouldn't want to live there.

At some point, loud rock music began blasting next door. George mentioned a near neighbor who, for several months, had played hard rock for hours on end. While they enjoyed the music in moderate amounts, they had found the endless strident repetitions at such high volume difficult to bear. Then George told of their going to the rock festival at Atlamont in the East Bay. Even before the violence occurred in which one or two spectators were killed by the Hell's Angels, they could sense it. The occasion is commemorated in the first of Oppen's *San Francisco Poems* which ends: "obscured by their long hair they seem / to be mourning," It was the end of an era.

With a week left of summer, I tracked down Brother Antoninus. He had left the monastery, married a woman in her twenties and was working as a caretaker for the Big Creek Lumber Company, a few miles from Davenport, in the Santa Cruz Mountains. He met us at the general store and led us slowly in his jeep along twisting, rutted roads. Finally, deep in the woods, we reached the clearing with its splendidly isolated cabin. He had two buildings, actually, one for living and the other for his manual printing press. His wife was visiting her parents for a week. We sat under two immense redwoods which he called his refrigerators. How cool it was sitting there, only a few miles from the blazing freeway. A stream where he was able to catch salmon and steelhead at various times of the year ran thirty yards behind his cabin. The cabin walls were covered with skins and he wore an imposing grey beard along with several American Indian necklaces. Everson, as he was now called, taught printing and poetry at Santa Cruz. He was also completing a couple of books on Robinson Jeffers. As we left, he excused himself for a moment and came back with a beautifully-printed edition of *Tendril In The Mesh*, his first major work in six years. It was after reading it for the first time in public that he stripped off the religious habit he had worn for over eighteen years and returned to private life as William Everson. The copy he inscribed to us was signed with that name but below he had written "The Feast of St. Augustine."

Another poet we got to see that summer was John Logan. Bill Matthews had told me they always took John to Italian restaurants when he stayed with them, so Mary and I decided to have him out for spaghetti. Since Peter Nelson was visiting John at the time, he joined us for supper. I was already corresponding with Peter about a chapbook, *Between Lives*, to be the third in our series. John exuded energy and warmth. He had an encyclopedic knowledge of the American poetry scene and could name a score of poets he knew in your town, whether it was Tucson, Arizona or Kalamazoo, Michigan. In fact, Much of John's accumulation of poems for *Choice* took place on the road, as he went from city to city, manuscript to manuscript. He often wound up with the best poems a poet had, partly because they loved and respected him, even more because he got to examine entire manuscripts before much of the work had been seen by other editors. Before the night was over, I had a chance to hear John read a few poems; he enjoyed reading other people's work as much as his own. He had a way of slowing a poem down, accenting each word, each syllable, in a loving way that opened up the word, the line, the poem. When I read aloud, I did it like a man with shoes on trying to ford a shallow stream on a few rocks without getting wet. John somehow entered the poem from the inside and made it available as speech, song. He loved Mary's dinner, we all did, but John with a special gusto which he fueled with generous pulls from his own glass of whisky along with hearty samplings of our red wine. By 2 AM, I was doing my best to move the wheelchair out of John's way when he seemed on the verge of falling. I got to bed a little before 3 AM. When I phoned next day, Peter Nelson answered. He sounded exhausted but was more concerned for John who he said would kill himself if he kept on drinking like this. Yet it turned out John had been up since nine, working on poems.

We saw Peter himself several times that summer, going over poems, talking and getting acquainted. The fact that Peter wrote with an old-fashioned fountain pen was, in this case, a clue to a finely-honed sensibility and perfect taste. He had stayed in touch with the boy in himself, which may account for the good-natured, innocent humor that found its way into some of his poems. An instinctive familiarity with Jungian archetypes added a dark resonance to others, many of them rich and musical. Peter had spent a week at Robert Bly's farm, and a couple of his best poems came out of that experience.

Robert Bly had sent me another note about our second issue, singling out a few poems for negative criticism, especially Richard Hugo's letter poem. He had good words for Ai's poems, Michael Benedikt's Apollinaire translation and Lew Hyde's Neruda translations. He felt I should not be at the mercy of those who sent work but should go out and find work I liked. Stung, I wondered aloud why Bly could find good things to say about his erstwhile disciples and not others. Looking back now, I think he was at least partly right in his general criticism if not always in the specific instance.

We were falling behind in our schedule, having trouble obtaining reviews on time. A good deal of energy had shifted to the press. The chapbooks I was publishing could have been published much as submitted. In most cases, however, I worked to see more poems, struggling to get the strongest possible group for each book. The same was true of individual parts of poems. With many poets, I suggested changes and secured them. Even if a poet did not like my suggestions, the process often challenged him or her to come up with better alternatives. I viewed the press as a means of getting a wider, deeper flow of quality manuscripts for the magazine. To some extent this proved true. When it came to advertising or marketing them I lacked aggressiveness, skill, even the taste for it. It was easier to perfect individual books and produce them well than to ensure a wide readership and distribution. Still, the problem was endemic to the small press world and if we did somewhat better than most, it was owing to the quality of the work itself, along with the poets' connections.

*   *   *

By the time we had returned from California and begun pasting up our third issue, I was thinking ahead to issue #5, which I wanted to be a special issue concerning the work of George Oppen. No one had ever done such an issue in spite of Oppen's having won the Pulitzer Prize in 1968. For all the depth and power of Oppen's work to that point, it was the newer poems that drew me. Like W. S. Merwin, Oppen had taken to beginning sentences, thoughts and phrases in the middle of a line. The result, apart from a certain difficulty, was a dramatic increase in energy, surprise, complexity. The lines needed to be read backward and forward. Phrases moved like elements in a Bach fugue, creating all kinds of contrapuntal effects. The frequent use of long dashes and ellipses created breaks in the text which served to invite the reader to plunge deeper into the meaning and the void out of which meaning rose. Eliot had written in *Four Quartets* that "old men should be explorers . . ." and Oppen was showing the way, venturing well ahead of the pack, but not for merely technical reasons. The way he could string disparate nouns along a line created the kind of energy transfer the surrealists strove to obtain but without violating the identity or otherness of objects:

> Rooted in basalt
> Night hums like the telephone dial tone blue gauze
> Of the forge flames the pulse
> (from "The Occurrences")

These poems, like much of Zukofsky's *A*, liberated Oppen and Objectivism from what had become in many instances too static a posture. Oppen's friendliest critics, such as John Taggart and Rachel Blau Du Plessis, were only beginning to explore the revolutionary nature of this work.

When I finally contacted him, Oppen's response was characteristic: "as for the special issue: I could only be pleased by it. But somehow I have become incapable of handling these things, of thinking about them— I have made only messes, confusion. . . ." And later: "If you don't want to undertake some or all of this, I surely will see every reason why you might not want to. . . . But also, I can assure you that, if you undertake it, I will NOT cavil at any decision that you do make." Finally: "I'm far from urging you to undertake this, Michael. Maybe you should give the time to your own work."

Having gotten the go ahead from George, I wrote to James Laughlin, his publisher at *New Directions,* asking for advice and suggestions. I wanted to try to get statements at least, if not something longer, from Reznikoff, Zukofsky and Carl Rakosi. Laughlin sent the addresses but warned me against writing Zukofsky: "The last time I mentioned George to him, he nearly bit my head off." Laughlin also suggested I write to Hugh Kenner and mentioned in addition Charles Tomlinson, an English poet and critic close to Oppen. I wrote to each of these people and awaited results.

When *Ironwood 3* appeared, it included a letter from Philip Dacey, an editor of *Crazy Horse,* criticizing James Moore's review of the Fresno anthology. His letter concentrated on a single poem which Moore felt had become unnecessarily rhetorical, projecting the poet's (P. Everwine) own feeling of weariness onto nature in order to universalize it. Both Moore and Dacey may have exaggerated but the exchange served to focus readers' awareness on a critical issue, underlining the genuine values at stake in small, seemingly unimportant word choices. One thing at stake was whether Everwine was exploiting nature rhetorically as manufacturers did the environment. If so, then the same lack of respect for the otherness of nature informed the attitudes of poet and industrial polluter.

For our first issue, I had written a paragraph on *Night Vision*, a brief but compelling collection of Tomas Tranströmer's poems. A few weeks before *Ironwood 3*, Tranströmer read at the University of Arizona. A lean, quiet figure just short of six feet, he seemed a bit defensive regarding the number of his publications. Perhaps the smaller number or size of his collections marked him off from his fellow Swedish poets. From my standpoint, his restraint in having work published was an index of his basic seriousness. Here in America, we were not used to seeing that much of a foreign poet's work in English, so we liked Tranströmer just as he was. In conversation, he was sparing with words. I sensed an ambivalence toward his translators and American sponsors. True, they made his work available to a much wider audience, but like a blind man with a seeing-eye dog, he could never be totally sure it was *his* work people were reading. His English was good enough for him to have his doubts.

January brought Adrienne Rich to Tucson for the Poetry Center's reading series. Fresh from the National Book Award for *Diving Into the Wreck*, Rich was decisively turning to feminism and lesbianism as the axes of her work, her life. Mary had sat in on the class Rich spoke to and enjoyed the give and take. Rich agreed to come for dinner and proved a sympathetic and attractive person. Unfortunately, my stomach was acting up that night and I was forced to flee to the bathroom every 15 or 20 minutes. Since this required Mary's help, we kept leaving our guest stranded at the table.

*   *   *

For months I had been getting good poems from poets as various as Bruce Andrews, Lyn Hejinian, Nathanial Tarn, Robin Magowan, Kathleen Fraser, James Moore, Nils Nelson, Sandra McPherson and Russell Edson. Although individual names could pass unnoticed on the covers of that era, a lengthy correspondence lay behind each one's appearance in the magazine. For me they were part of a complex whole, even if the poet's focus was inevitably and necessarily his or her work. So, initially, was mine. It had to be.

An important feature of *Ironwood 4* was the interview with Denise Levertov. Although it took months for it to be transcribed and revised, I was satisfied with what I was sent. The interview was serious, relevant, spirited. Levertov herself, it later developed, had been unhappy with much of the transcription and editing. Apparently, she would have preferred that flaws in diction and syntax, inevitable in conversation, be erased, or minimized. Accustomed as I was to identifying Black Mountain poets by their attachment to the rhythms of natural speech and to a preference for the process, I was surprised. Because the interview was already on videotape and had been transcribed and edited in New York state, I assumed it had been okayed. So there was no small degree of chagrin on my part for what must be considered an oversight. I had been in touch with Levertov herself, hoping to include at least one or two poems but what she offered me had, or would, appear in the *New Directions Annual*. The fact that Levertov hated the picture of her we used only deepened my sense of failure.

June saw Mary and me returning to California for the summer. This time, we rented a house in Kentfield, eight miles from Mill Valley, surprisingly cheap for such a well-to-do neighborhood. Much of that summer's correspondence concerned the chapbooks we were publishing. By now, Tom Johnson's *Footholds* had appeared and was attracting favorable comment and good reviews. I had gone through nearly 200 poems before settling on 16 for the book. Johnson's poems were quiet, but with sudden leaps of the imagination. The diction was physical, the better poems rooted, but certain poems did not feel as grounded in a body as they might have. One problem was that Johnson, an extremely prolific writer, had chapbooks springing up all over the place. I counted at least four within a year of *Footholds*. Peter Nelson's *Between Lives* had just come out. It was a book I was proud to have published. Singly, and together, the poems exuded a sense of rich, psychic life. One wanted to know more of this person. The poems did not have designs on their readers, they floated in their own deep space, charging the page around them. If one could imagine such a place, they belonged somewhere between the work of W. S. Merwin and Galway Kinnell.

When Tony Petrosky's chapbook, *Waiting Out The Rain*, finally appeared, it came as something of an anticlimax. We had been over the poems so many times, and I was still exhausted from pneumonia. Still, I was grateful to Tony for his support during my illness; grateful, too, for the poet's restraint, for his immersion in the world, his family, the landscape. He revealed himself by this love, by the intensity of perceptions born of it. Even the occasional awkwardness here bespoke his authenticity. Petrosky took his place alongside Berry, Ignatow and Snyder, poets with a deep-seated sense of place. The book deserved the good reviews it got and would have sold even more had I possessed the kind of marketing skills and energy required.

With Miriam Levine's *Friends Dreaming* there was more of a problem. A single poem, 10 pages or more, occupied two-thirds of the book and threw everything out of kilter. A rich, hallucinatory poem, it lacked a deep relationship to the other poems in the collection, and lay there like a tuna with a handful of minnows. Though the long poem had been my reason for doing the book, Levine would have been better served by my printing it all by itself, eliminating it from a collection which could have included at least 12 or 14 poems when these were ready, or else making it part of a book with twice as many pages. She was and remains a sensitive, capable poet.

*   *   *

One morning toward the end of July, we woke to find the house already warm, something rare. By ten o'clock, it was in the mid 90's and climbing. After breakfast, I phoned John Logan who was in San Francisco for the summer, and we agred to meet for lunch at the Caravansary, a block north of Lombard. Anxious to escape the heat, we were in the city by noon where we spent some time looking at wine glasses from West Virginia before discovering the Museum Shop, a place with museum-quality stones, rugs and other folk art from all continents. At length, we found our way to the Caravansary. John was with Morton Marcus, visiting for the day from Santa Cruz. I had read his poems in *Kayak* for years. Large, solid, his brown hair and beard beginning to gray, he was smoking a pipe he kept busy all through lunch. John had a way of relaxing everyone without hogging the spotlight. He was trying to lay a review of his latest book on me while I did my best to ignore him. The food was delicious but my glass of milk oddly lukewarm. When we got up to leave, Mary excused herself and Dave Ewing and I headed for the street. We were standing in the sun, or Dave was, when it slid behind clouds, and a strong breeze blew from the Bay. I was beginning to feel just a bit cold when John and Morton joined us for a moment before going on their way. I wanted to put on my scarf but had left it with Mary. For the next five or ten minutes, I kept hunting sunny places, but there was little sun and most of that only in the street. Then Mary emerged and I could don my scarf. My throat was beginning to feel sore. It was amazing how quickly the temperature had dropped, though the weather was still not what you would call cold. It would be too hot to return home for three or four hours so we strolled over to Union Street. Out of nowhere, like a "familiar compound ghost" came Jack McCarthy, a friend from New York whom I hadn't seen in a dozen years. After chatting for some minutes we went our separate ways, finally entering Minerva's Owl, a small, brightly-lit bookstore. Browsing through poetry books, we struck up a conversation with an attractive young couple, Phil and Juanita Dow. He turned out to be a friend and former student of John Logan. He was amazed to find that we had just had lunch with John. After awhile, they drifted off and we drove down to the Marina and looked out at the water and the Golden Gate Bridge. With my throat a bit sorer now, I kept trying to drink enough water to throw off the soreness but it didn't work. We looked along Lombard for a place to eat and wound up at *Monroe's*, an English-style restaurant with a French menu. Good as the food was, I couldn't shake that soreness. It was close to nine when we got home but the air was still warm. The mercury had reached 108 degrees in Kentfield that day with no air conditioning in the house.

Next morning, I woke with a terrible sore throat, lots of mucus, a fever of over 102. Mary called a doctor whose name had been given us. I was so terrified of letting the infection get off to a running start that, when I didn't hear from him within four hours, I took two tetracycline capsules from my airplane bag. I was using an intermittent positive-pressure breathing unit to reinforce an extremely weak cough. The results were less than satisfactory, the mucus hard to bring up. When we finally got hold of the doctor, he decided to continue the medication rather than start me on something of his own. The weather was a carbon copy of the day before. In fact, the mercury hit 108 degrees for ten consecutive days.

Days passed and my fever remained the same. After four or five days, I noticed that the view from my rocking bed had changed. Where formerly I had seen green grass and brown tree trunks with green pine needles and blue sky, now everything appeared black and white. Some change in perception had been brought on by physiological change, my lungs perhaps. When the doctor called, he pretended that what I had was simply a bad chest infection but told Mary otherwise. I was 42, the maximum age I had hoped to reach and the doctor was convinced I would lose hope if he shifted me to a hospital. It was time for him to go back east—summer vacation. Another doctor, totally new in the county, was supposed to take over but the baton seemed to get dropped for a couple of days. Convinced I had pneumonia and was on the verge of dying, I made a will, dictating it one afternoon to Dave Ewing, along with final letters to Mary, to a favorite nephew, and to Nils Nelson, a young poet. I was unable to sign the will, much less write it, so it would have been worthless except as an indication of my wishes.

What followed was extraordinary. I began chanting lines as they came to me. I felt I was dying and about to rise while simultaneously the world itself came to an end. The experience involved a new religious vision where the polarities, death and life, good and evil, male and female joined within the framework of traditional Catholicism. It lasted at least five hours, so intense I even neglected sips of water. For a couple of hours, I convinced Mary to rock with me and she was pulled almost totally into my vision. It was dark outside by the time the whole thing was over. I was left much more peaceful, ready for death, but still prepared to struggle.

Next day, we did our best to get in touch with Dr. Margolin, the young chest man who was taking over for Dr. McCrumb. It took more than a day to run him down and another for him to see me. I had been receiving oxygen through a Bird valve for days now. When Dr. Margolin showed up, my bowels had been impacted for more than a week, a situation he quickly, if painfully, remedied. By the next day, Margolin had arranged for my rocking bed to be moved to Marin General Hospital while I was taken there in an ambulance. As the crow flies, we were only 400 yards from our house. Almost at once, I was placed in intensive care where, on and off, I would spend the next six weeks. There were only 13 beds and a staff of bright, capable nurses. I felt wide awake on arrival and found myself cracking jokes with the nurses, something they may not have appreciated. My rocking bed was something of a distraction, easy to bump into.

By my second day, I was having bouts of delirium. Both lungs had collapsed. In order to reinflate at least one lung and explore the blockage, I was given a bronchoscopy with a general anesthetic. This meant inserting a slender instrument by way of a rubber tube lowered through the mouth and into the bronchial tubes. No cutting was involved. As I regained consciousness, I could hear doctors debating where to insert a needle with the fluid needed to restore blood pressure. Obviously, I could not be sure what they had in mind, it sounded so urgent. Having regained consciousness, I felt desperate to get through to them, but was unable to communicate my state of mind. Whether it would have made any difference I don't know. Weeks later, we speculated that had the anesthetist been aware that the rocking bed was normal for me, even during sleep, they might have switched it on once the operation was over. As it was, they blamed the anesthetic, 50 milligrams of Demerol. Before I left the hospital, one or both lungs would collapse twice more. The third bronchoscopy was performed by my own doctor without anesthesia on my rocking bed. It turned out to be the easiest and most successful of all.

During my time in I.C.U., my bed was almost always next to one with a prisoner from nearby San Quentin. Nearly all these prisoners had been shot by guards or stabbed by other inmates, and all but one were black or Chicano. At least one of these I.C.U. cases survived, they were usually strapping young men. A policeman on 24-hour duty looked through a thick square window at the prisoner. It was next to impossible for him to avoid staring at me or my rocking bed—enough to induce paranoia in a healthy person.

My oldest brother came out from New York for a visit. So did my best friend, Mary's brother, George Cusick. The visits were a real boost to my morale. Mary's meals, cooked by her or brought in from good restaurants, were also a substantial help. Often, she would eat the hospital supper while I devoured what she brought. I found myself cracking more than my share of jokes. Frank Stanford and Tony Petrosky wrote me regularly and kept in close touch with Mary by phone. Their letters were a genuine pleasure. Another correspondent was Nils Nelson who spent the last week or two of my pneumonia sorting through *Ironwood* mail and returning with a note those manuscripts that didn't need further reading. As I began slowly to get better, I would put in an hour a day working with him. Finally, my legs heavy as stone pillars, I was able to get out of bed. It was a slow process but by the time I was allowed to leave, I could go in my wheel chair. It would be six months before I totally recovered. We were forced to rent a nearby house for an extra five weeks, at which time I was strong enough to fly back to Tucson. George and Mary Oppen had returned from spending the summer on Eagle Island in Maine. Before having to leave California, Mary and I were able to see them once or twice. I remember the way Mary Oppen looked at me that last visit. Deep down, she was convinced she would never see me again. Sensing that, I swore to myself that she *would*. I will never forget that look in her eyes.

Weak as I was, I got to witness my first California wine harvest that fall. I had my wheelchair parked near the ends of two rows of grapes. Singing in Spanish, the pickers moved in a group using small knives, their hands dropping clusters of dark grapes into wicker baskets. They moved as if under a single impulse, the white foreman looking somewhat strained and distant compared to the faces that shone with such energy. I spent some time talking with a few of the pickers who knew some English. Most were from Mexico but the group included one or two Guatemalan students who had studied in Mexico City. For lunch, they ate sandwiches and fruit. Later, I followed some of the gondolas, as the vehicles were called, back to the Sebastiani Vineyard where they dumped their clusters onto a conveyor belt which ferried them to an immense steel tank. How exciting it was to watch as bees and yellow jackets swarmed over the dark clusters, lit here and there by patches of yeast-bloom and dust-bloom.

*   *   *

On our return to Tucson, I had to work almost simultaneously on two issues. One was #4 and the other #5, the special Oppen issue. Almost a year behind, I could not afford more slippage. Oppen's fellow Objectivists, Carl Rakosi and Charles Reznikoff, had both responded to my letters, Reznikoff enclosing a brief but touching reminiscence and Rakosi giving me permission to reprint an equally-moving memory of his own first meeting with Oppen after a lapse of 30 years. Oppen sent me a copy of *Grosseteste Review*, an English literary magazine with a special feature devoted to his work. Charles Tomlinson offered to let us reprint his excellent brief essay from *Grosseteste*. Going further afield, I asked Bruce Andrews, the most avant-garde poet we had printed, if he was interested in writing on Oppen. He jumped at the idea, producing a brilliant, complex, but ultimately convincing series of notes that addressed the formal and thematic concerns of *Discrete Series*, Oppen's first book. Diane Wakoski, whose own writing was closer to deep imagist poetry, volunteered an essay on "Route". The closest this special issue came to a purely scholarly effort was Rachel Blau DuPlessis's long essay on "Of Being Numerous" which she titled "What Do We Believe To Live With"? It was Rachel who first told me about Mary Oppen's unfinished autobiography, suggesting I ask her to let me use some of it for the issue. Shy as she was about it, Mary agreed to send me the section about France and another one. I was delighted with it. In addition to the touching details of living in their own house near the French Alps, the memoir covered visits to Pound and Brancusi, and details on Two Publishers, the Oppen's own small press in France, which published the original *Objectivist Anthology*, a novel of Williams and Pound's *A B C of Reading*. Still, I wanted some changes, mostly questions of syntax and the use of the hyphen. Mary's response was to pull back, standing firmly behind what she had written. I had to decide which was more important, printing the piece or having it appear closer to my way. I gave way. Like the book later on, the chapter captivated a good many readers. Owing to the more than 40 year lapse of time and the distance from Europe, Mary Oppen's memoir of their years in France gave the issue its emotional center as well as extraordinary resonance. Across from Mary's first page, I put two old snapshots, beautiful ones of George and Mary, and another of George training their horse Pom-Pon. There were other photographs, and two drawings of George by Jim Sloan, a good friend who had met the Oppens at our house. Finally, a short essay by Theodore Enslin concentrated on George as a person while a series of Oppen's letters to a French editor and translator presented his conception of Objectivist Poetics. A brief Oppen bibliography was my contribution.

Shortly before our deadline, John Taggart got in touch with me about writing for the issue. Though he had been careful to avoid getting involved with details, Oppen himself may have suggested it. Over the phone, I asked Taggart if he had read Donald Davie's piece in *Grosseteste Review*. Characteristic of Davie, it had been critical, casting a cold skeptical eye on Oppen's apparent turning of his back on the past, on all rhetoric or at least the older rhetoric. It was George's comments explaining or occasioned by the poems that seemed to rub him the wrong way. Between the lines, a sensitive reader could detect Davie's admiration for the poems. Still, Taggart had been bothered by the essay, as I was, and agreed to write a critique. When it arrived, his essay seemed like a classic case of overkill, out of all proportion to the original provocation. I phoned George to ask what he thought about printing something that came on so strongly. Taggart may already have written him about the piece, possibly even mailing him a carbon. As I later discovered, George was clearly bothered because he had been asked by Oxford University Press to write a blurb (preface?) for Davie's *Collected Poems*. Though he managed a sentence or two, his ambivalence was palpable. Davie obviously wanted or expected more and a painful correspondence ensued. Were we to print this attack on Davie, it would make it look as if he, George, had engineered it, or given his tacit consent. Relieved on my own account, I offered to phone John. A minute or two after I hung up, George phoned me, because, as he said, it was really his moral responsibility to call John. As so he did.

The most exciting part of the issue was George Oppen's poems. There were eight in all, and three, "The Book of Job and a Draft of a Poem to Praise the Paths of the Living", "Myth of the Blaze", and "The Speech at Soli" took up 13 pages. "The Book of Job" was written to honor Mickey

Schwerner and two other civil rights leaders in Mississippi in the Sixties
who had been neighbors and friends of the Oppens in Brooklyn. The
poem ran eight pages, with the parts loosely connected. Here are its
final lines:

> mid continent iron rails
> in the fields and grotesque
> metals in the farmer's heartlands sympathy
> across the fields
> and down the aisles
> of the crack trains
> of 1918 the wave
> of the improbable
> drenches the galloping carpets in the sharp
> edges in the highlights
> of the varnished tables we ring
> in the continual bell
> the undoubtable bell   found music—in itself
> of itself speaks the word
> actual heart breaking
> tone row it is not ended
> not ended the intervals
> blurred ring
> like walls
> between floor
> and ceiling the taste
> of madness in the world   birds
> of ice   Pave
> the world o pave
> the world carve
>
> thereon.

The other poems were equally powerful: "Myth of the Blaze" drawing
on Oppen's experience of being wounded in Alsace during World War
II and "The Speech at Soli" dealing with issues raised by Pound in the
last *Cantos*. Of 82 pages, 18 were devoted to poems and a few more to
a brief interview. Oppen wrote me half a dozen letters concerning these
poems.

The first poems were received in mid-October, '73, and the second group in April, '74. In between my asking him and their arrival, George vacillated about sending the "long poem". Once he was convinced we were going to devote an entire issue to his work, he was much more inclined to let us have it. After that, I suspect the problem lay in the poem itself, whether it was truly 'finished' and whether our printing it in its present form would inhibit further development. Since James Laughlin at New Directions had finally agreed to an Oppen *Collected*, George wanted to know if we would be bothered by further changes in the poem after we published it. I assured him we wouldn't. Except for small changes in the first couple of pages, we wound up with a version nearly identical to the one printed in the English *Grossteste Review*.

Mention of New Directions brings me to the design of our Oppen cover, the first I did myself. With Oppen's New Directions books in mind, I set myself to visualize a fresh cover. What struck me right off was that they were black and white, with or without photographs. I would avoid images, using only type plus a signature. Given Oppen's age, his austerity, a smooth black cover with his huge signature slanted across the front should carry maximum impact. The economy of means would speak to what was most characteristic of the man, his poems. The rub was, George rarely signed letters with his last name, and those he did were often done with a lead pencil and therefore difficult to reproduce. He agreed to send us specimens in black ink. Stan's assistant, Lanny Rosenbaum, took one and kept enlarging until everything felt right. The result was a striking cover whose force the years have not diminished. On the back, we placed a note on poetics from an Oppen letter to Rachel Blau DuPlessis:

. . . The process by which sometimes a line appears, I cannot trace. It happens. Given a line, one has a place to stand, and goes further____
It is impossible to make a mistake without knowing it, impossible not to know that one has just smashed something. Unearned words are, in that context, simply ridiculous—tho it is possible to be carried astray little by little, to find oneself, quite simply, trying to deceive people, to be 'making a poem'. One can always go back, the thing is there and doesn't alter. One's awareness of the world, one's concern with exis- tence—they were not already in words—And the poem is NOT built out of words, one cannot make a poem by sticking words into it, it is the

poem which makes the words and contains their meaning. One cannot reach out for *roses* and *elephants* and *essences* and put them in the poem——the ground under the elephant, the air around him, one would have to know very precisely one's distance from the elephant or step deliberately too close, close enough to frighten oneself.

When the man writing is frightened by a word, he may have started. . . .

Shortly before our deadline, John Logan sent "Poem For My Brother", a moving, evocative elegy of his lost childhood and the rivalry and love of two brothers. To help structure the poem, John used his own system of seven-and-thirteen syllable lines. Perhaps it served him as a kind of net in Frost's sense of the word, generating freedom in the writing since the restrictions are so obvious and external. John started the poem with blue and brown, one color for each brother, and his buying a ring for his older brother. The day of our luncheon and the onset of my pneumonia, he had been in the Museum Shop just before us. He may even have bought the ring then. I took the poem and it led off the issue.

With five poems apiece, Tony Petrosky and Frank Stanford were the real stars of *Ironwood 4* which appeared just as 1974 gave way to 1975. There was a line drawing of Frank by his wife, Ginny Stanford. The special George Oppen issue materialized six weeks later. Because of the way the two issues crowded each other, *#4* got shunted aside in the bookstores. Because of its design, pages of luminous, moving poetry, and the mix of other material, the Oppen issue received a good deal of acclaim. *Ironwood* was helping make something happen.

Dr. Margolin had warned that the six months that followed my long bout with pneumonia were crucial to my recovery. In January, I came down with what turned out to be pneumonia. This time, the right antibiotic brought my fever down within a day or two and I recovered quickly. Three weeks later, I celebrated my 43rd birthday. I had survived the odds. Each additional year I have come to regard as a gift. My obsession with death has largely relaxed. Up close, death looks a lot less fearful. I have pneumonia to thank for that. As always, anxiety lies in the between.

Within a week or so of sending George Oppen his copies of the special issue I received the following letter:

64

Dear Michael:
    the meaning of the book, the value of the book (and I think it is very
high value) is your own love of poetry—
        what shines even from the cover of the book is your love of
poetry, I become almost dizzy to find myself playing a part in it

and another step into beauty beyond belief with the photo on the page
where Mary's eyes look across the page to Mary's prose, eyes and prose
in the same light, reflecting the same light, everything becomes clear at
this moment The light that *matters*.

        Michael, no way to thank for this labor of love   A love that
picked, among other things, me. But it's your love, Michael, it's yours   A
lot of praise for me in the book, but I blush sheepishly; what shines, is
Michael's capacity for love, and care, and I thank you   Tho it is impossible to thank you.

                    George

    There is more, dealing with each contributor's part of the issue, giving
even the disaffected Zukofsky credit for his early help and example. Altogether, it is the most grace-full letter I have ever received. In the
world of poetry, it is rare for someone to perceive exactly what you are
doing. Over the years, in moments of discouragement, that letter has
helped sustain me.

                    *   *   *

    That spring brought poems from a Vietnam veteran, Bruce Weigl.
Just as Vietnam was not a war you could usefully compare with any
other, so Weigl's poems did not resemble any war poems I had previously seen. Their tone was low key and honest without any of the hard-
boiled quality you get reading Hemingway, say, or Mailer on their own
wars. Instead, there were occasional bits of understated humor and a
fair amount of ambivalence. Drugs, sex, jungle rot, exploding mines,
hand grenades tossed into hootches, these and a disconcerting amount
of turmoil are evoked and made vivid in his best poems. I took three for
our sixth issue and we began corresponding about a chapbook. Here is
one:

ANNA GRASA

I came home from Vietnam.
My father had a sign
made at the foundry:
WELCOME HOME BRUCE
in orange glow paint.
He rented spotlights,
I had to squint
WELCOME HOME BRUCE

Out of the car I moved
up on the sign dreaming
myself full.
The sign that cut the sky,
my eyes burned.

But behind the terrible thing
I saw my grandmother
Beautiful Anna Grasa.
I couldn't tell her tell her.

I clapped to myself,
clapped to the sound
of her dress.
I could've put it on,
she held me so close,
both of us could be
inside.

One possible consequence of having done the Oppen issue was a definite turn toward the experimental. An Oppen disciple, John Taggart sent us 17 pages from Part One of Dodeka where most of the short individual poems were enclosed within perfect squares, roughly 2½ inches a side. The poem had its source in the Pythagoreans, in Plato's *Timaeus* and Plutarch. Taggart was attempting to reduce the Greek words to their physical, often animal ancestors. On the last two pages, many of the lines, indeed whole four-line poems are repeated in different contexts with others broken up, some lines shifted or indented. The result is a startling work: the language physical, compressed, pulsing with energy, reaches beyond itself, with the final pages creating a more fluid, random-seeming medley of the separate poems. Leslie Scalapino's nine brief narratives from *The Woman Who Could Read the Minds of Dogs* were, if anything even more startling. As I was to write a year later in *Ironwood 7/8*:

> Her world is in motion, slow motion most of it: people riding taxis or airplanes, circling on their bikes, walking, loping, swimming. We inhabit their perceptions, and, just as important, the way they speak, interrupting themselves, presuming the listener already shares their whole store of experiences. While she seldom obeys Pound's dictum about composing according to the sequence of the musical phrase, most of us at our typewriters, with all the interruptions a day brings, will feel the rightness of this speech, these "segments," just as we do hearing a hall clock at night, watching it drop back a minute in the act of moving forward.

Mark Linenthal sent a six-page "Poem For my Brother Michael", remarkable for its immediacy, the diction shaped perfectly to bear the freshness of the perceptions—a poem of honesty, courage. These poems continued the practice of having at least one long poem per issue begun by Bill Meredith's "Hazard the Painter" in # 1, Lynn Lifshin in # 2 and Jane Lippe in # 4. It would help mark *Ironwood* off from most other little magazines, particularly the mainstream ones. There was much discussion of "workshop" poems at this time and I found longer poems less likely to become obsessed with mechanical details and a kind of empty perfection. This was even true of poems that took half or all of a second page. Often, it was an indicator of urgency, the poet at the service of his material even while he strove to order it. One unforeseen consequence of this was an increasing flow of such long poems. Some version of supply and demand seems to operate with poets and magazines so that a small increase in supply (space) leads in short order to a far steeper increase in demand (long poems). Here, the editor is faced by an embarrassment of riches, or else merely embarrassed. If you increase the number you print, the flow will mount drastically, and so on. The worst part is, writers with brief lyrics may start looking elsewhere.

Before we even had time to get settled into our summer rental for

1975, the San Francisco Book Fair had begun. This year it was held in the basement of the Veterans Memorial of the Civic Center. We had registered in advance and made the trip across the Golden Gate once or twice a day, bringing copies of the first five issues. Part of a huge small press contingent, for the next three or four days, we got to meet or stare at many "stars" of the small press world—poets, novelists and publishers. We found ourselves stationed next to John McBride of *Invisible City* and the Red Hill Press, which specialized in Italian poets and relative newcomers, particularly Bay Area poets. *Invisible City* was a tabloid using high, quality paper and often stunning graphics to heighten the reading and reception of many of these writers. John was brilliant, ebullient with a mouth as quick as his mind; at 18, he had been a Marin County delegate for McGovern at the New Politics Convention.

Though we sold two or three times as many books as our neighbors, we were barely able to cover the cost of renting the space and paying for parking, tolls, sandwich lunches. It was a great place to look, compare notes and make contacts, but if you judged the fair by its ostensible purpose, it had to be deemed a failure for almost all participants, apart from a few near-commercial presses such as Capra. Still, the Oppen issue sold well at the fair and brought a number of interested and interesting poets to our booth.

John and his co-editor Paul Vangelisti were both Oppen enthusiasts and John had been some help in getting the Oppen issue together. In our third issue I had included a couple of Paul's poems. *Invisible City* had just brought out a new issue with 11 sections of Leslie Scalapino's *hmmm*. Mary and I were taken with this poem and set about trying to learn more of the author. A couple of weeks later, John brought Leslie over to our house in Corte Madera for lunch. It was cool and sunny that Saturday, and we ate out in the garden. A beautiful young woman with enormous dark eyes and thick brown hair falling to her shoulders, she appeared preternaturally shy. In attempting to fill the gaps in conversation, I found myself struggling not to speak too much. Leslie had a way of nodding and smiling when she could agree wholeheartedly with something. She had spent much of her life in places like Taiwan or exotic regions of the Third World where her father's career as the chairman of Berkeley's Political Science Department had taken him. That summer and the next, we saw more of Leslie. She had an ancient car which she kept going with spit, love and baling wire. With my own predilection for aging wheelchairs and automobiles, I was naturally a sympathetic observer.

Sometime in late spring or early summer, Robin Magowan had written to me about our doing a book of his poems involving his relationship with Nancy Ling Perry of the Symbionese Liberation Army, killed with most of her fellow members in the police assault on their Los Angeles refuge. He sent me the manuscript: a gripping prose narrative that encompasses a series of brilliant, intensely felt poems. Perry was a sometime member of Magowan's writing workshop at Berkeley. Robin and Nancy Ling Perry spent several weeks in West Marin and along the Russian River making love, doing acid and other drugs. At the time I received the manuscript, the few surviving S.L.A. members were waiting to go on trial in Sacramento. Were I to publish Magowan's account as it stood, some of the things he quoted her as saying could have prejudiced anyone who read them. I would have felt less need to be careful had he ever shown in writing that he shared any of her views, but there was no indication of that. In the afterword that followed the poems and closed the manuscript, he spoke of her needing to borrow $500. With the FBI looking into precisely this kind of detail, he didn't want their names together on a check, but suggested a comparable sum for a few of her watercolors, which was done. Since Magowan had already made clear that he would help pay for the book if I did it yet wanted to make at least $500 from sales, I wondered about *those* checks. In a nervous time, immediately after Watergate, I was leery of doing the book, though fascinated by the chance to play a role in such an affair. One thing that left a particularly bad taste in my mouth was Magowan's closest attempt to deal with the politics of the situation. He wound up the book asking: who would you rather spend the night with, Nancy Ling Perry or the Los Angeles Police? While I didn't feel comfortable printing the poems by themselves, given their obvious association with drugs, I was much more uncomfortable providing ammunition for the enemies of Ling Perry and her S.L.A. associates in a case I knew very little about. The very origins of the S.L.A. remain suspect, shrouded in mystery, possibly even an invention of our intelligence services. Perhaps we will be permitted to know in a few more decades. Magowan took the manuscript we had

Michael Cuddihy   *Mary Cuddihy*

Ai (Rebecca Ross)

George Oppen (Charles Amirkhanian)

Frank Stanford (Ginny Stanford)

Tony Petrosky

Susan North

Czeslaw Milosz (B. Piotr Urbanellis, Poland)

Linda Gregg (Betty Sheedy)

wrote to me about doing a piece on Simic's more recent *White*, which New Rivers had issued. It was a book I was particularly fond of but could never find in a bookstore, here or in California. Charlie had worked for a time as business manager of *Aperture,* an astonishingly pure quarterly of photography with superb reproductions and critical appraisals of comparable value, clearly the best magazine of its kind in the country. He mentioned a photograph of himself in the Hartford railroad station by Siegfried Halus, a young photographer whose work had been printed in *Aperture.* The Halus print turned out to be our first cover photograph. When Simic proved unable to come up with more than the four poems he gave us, I decided to limit the appreciation to the two pieces we had. The feature was printed near the beginning but the issue wound up a double issue, # 7–8, our first so far—176 pages compared to an average of about 100.

Where #6 represented a turn toward the experimental, # 7/8 moved more decisively back into the mainstream with a section of ten Tucson poets, plus a score of relative newcomers. Here, the magazine was clearly opting for youth and relative inexperience. Interestingly enough, Book People's catalog compared #6 unfavorably with an issue of *Painted Bride Quarterly,* a Philadelphia magazine, citing our preference for established poets and neglect of the experimental. True, Charlie Simic, whom they criticized for machismo, led off the issue (#6) with three poems, but here was Leslie Scalapino from their own Berkeley, following immediately with nine poems and John Taggart ending the issue with 17 pages of his most experimental work to date. This kind of response was enough to make a hyena weep.

David Ignatow was one poet whose response was really worth the attention you put into his work. If you wrote him far in advance of an upcoming issue, he would send you work without much delay and, whenever possible, would have more at hand to send you if the first poems were returned. It was as if the initial exchanges were preliminaries where each party took the measure of the other's seriousness. At some point, as if responding to a hidden signal, a group of new poems would emerge, rife with possibility. If you could point out a place to cut which served the overall purpose of the poem, Ignatow was ready enough to take your suggestion. Perhaps it was his long experience as an editor, 20 years with the *Beloit Poetry Journal,* 16 or more with *Chelsea,* and the last five or so with APR that enabled him to welcome others into his work. Indeed, Ignatow had made a habit of writing poems out of the obstacles to poetry, what most writers would rather shut out in order to "hear myself think."

Ironwood 7/8 included intense, often visionary poems by David Romtvedt, John Haines, Marjorie Sinclair, Ignatow, Kristina McGrath, Ray Amorosi, Christopher Buckley, Mari Nakamura and Christine Zawadiwsky. Phyllis Hoge Thompson's "The Candle In the Woods" and "The River" were rhythmically complex, rich in archetypal associations. Among the Tucson contingent, several darkly brooding lyrics by Steve Orlen stood out, along with exciting work by Stephanie Hallgren and Boyer Rickel. Ai's three poems included an amazing Marilyn Monroe persona poem. When she appeared reluctant to let go of them, I made her an offer she could accept. After Ai had moved back to Tucson with Lawrence Kearney, we saw a good deal of them. A substantial poet already, Lawrence grew in stature during his association with Florence (Ai). She was an omnivorous reader who had read all the books on the lists but concentrated now on the novel, particularly newer work from Japan, India and the Spanish-speaking world. She read as well the historian of religion, Mircea Eliade, and the anthropologist Claude Lévi-Strauss.

In addition to its 35-page section on Charlie Simic, *Ironwood* 7/8 published four reviews, including Kathleen Fraser's scintillating tribute to James Moore's *The New Body*, Eric Torgersen's article on Faye Kicknosway, Doug Blazek on Gregory Orr and my own page on Leslie Scalapino. Finally, there was a small but powerful group of charcoal drawings by Charles Littler. Of the seven artists in or near Tucson whose work I was reasonably familiar with, his was usually the most abstract or the most difficult. In order to amplify the local presence in the issue, I decided to reproduce these, giving Charles the kind of break that always seemed to elude him.

In mid-October of '76, Mary and I flew to visit her favorite brother George and his wife Pia at their farm outside Leeds, Alabama. George had been my roommate at Notre Dame and I considered him my best friend. We had two wonderful weeks, filled with enormous, succulent dinners, endless toasts and three exhilarating drives through Georgia and into Tennessee. Grabbing the chance to tour the Civil War battlefield of Chickamauga, I was moved by the scrupulous recording of each participant's role—where they fell, which acre of ground—both officers and men. Hard to imagine an unknown soldier in this context, with each of the dead identified by name, regiment, company, state. This part of the South, the further you got into the small rural towns, the more formally the black couples appeared to dress. We saw them coming from lunch at the unbelievably good barbeque places that dotted those mountain towns. The air was crisp with Fall and I felt I had had a glimpse of another, more complex mixture of people and landscape than I had hitherto run across. On our return to George and Pia's after one such trip, there was a message asking me to call the printer, in this case Lanny, an assistant to Stan. When the magazine was partially plated, Lanny had begun to notice disconcerting numbers of typos in several places. Once everything was plated, it would cost more than twice as much to do over. The situation required our immediate attention, which meant returning to Tucson.

Lanny's worst fears were confirmed. Scores, possibly hundreds of typos, were involved. As I remember, two or three plates had to be reshot and all kinds of repro pages slowly corrected one at a time. In spite of the massive cleanup, it is hard to glance through a copy of that issue without running across several typos. Whatever praise the issue earned, the multitude of errors remained in our minds, even into sleep.

For the summer of '76, we returned to Corte Madera, to the same house, which belonged to an English professor at San Francisco State. While a spacious barn out back made for a quiet retreat, bookshelves in at least six rooms held more than 3000 volumes and hundreds of classical LP's. Our first week there, we discovered that Paul Metcalf was reading from his just-published *Apalache* at the Unitarian church in Berkeley. That Sunday afternoon, we drove over to Berkeley and found our way to the church. Dustmotes hung in the shafts of sunlight. A tall, husky man with cheeks as large and red as fresh apples stood before us. His voice rang almost too heartily, occasionally approaching a roar. As he neared his sixtieth birthday, this great-grandson of Herman Melville retained a head of straight blond hair. Although Metcalf's accounts from America's early centuries did little to flatter the colonists, it held little comfort for the Indians. The audience of about 25 people were polite, friendly, restrained. During the intermission, Mary and I purchased a copy of *Apalache*, noticing to our chagrin that it was the only one sold that day, unless others had bought copies before our arrival.

That summer, we arranged for the West Coast Print Center to do the printing and typesetting for Steve Orlen's and Bruce Weigl's chapbooks. Ever since meeting him shortly after I began writing poems, I had liked Steve Orlen. Friendly, he combined humor with a blunt, outspoken manner. He had a good reputation as a teacher, someone who expected a whole lot from his students. His wife, Gail, was a first-rate painter whose work bordered surrealism and photorealism. When I sent Steve a bunch of my poems early in Spring, 1975, I got them back several months later with a powerfully incisive critique. What took me by surprise was the interest he expressed at the end of the letter in doing a book with us. Still smarting under his criticism, I cursed him softly to myself. Before I could write him, declaring my readiness to look at a manuscript, several weeks elapsed. I was going to make damn sure that his own collection adhered to my sense of the best he could do. While I liked much of what he initially sent, I held out patiently, month after month, while he continued to write more poems. After 14 months of this, we had what looked to me like a strong collection, enriched by two or three profound poems dealing with painting where the experience of poet and painter, husband and wife, reflected and deepened one another. I asked Gail Orlen if she would do the cover and include one or two drawings on the inside pages. After she had shown me a number of interesting possibilities, we agreed finally on the cover and one drawing.

Made up mainly of poems about Vietnam and its aftermath, the Weigl chapbook was smaller. Here was a fresh sensibility dealing with fresh material, an original contribution to what was then a relatively small amount of poetry published on the war. Gail Orlen's Weigl cover was more surreal, reflecting the fractured sensibility brought on by the Vietnam experience. These were two solid additions to our chapbook series. That summer, I found myself driving to the West Coast Print Center at least once a week to check with Don Cushman or whoever might be in charge of the manuscript at the moment. Given its subsidy, the Center represented a real savings for us, though it took some adjusting on my part to deal with its unfamiliar procedures.

The third book we printed at this time was Nils Nelson's *Chicago*. Earliest of the three, I had been working on it with Nils for something like a year and a half. In the four years since he first submitted poems, Nils Nelson, then a Tucson resident, had become a close friend. I was his chief booster and most severe critic. While my endless editing probably helped those poems some, they took a toll. The basic energy was his, something I could never provide. If the net effect of all my efforts was to diminish that energy, then it was probably wasted. As it is, I suspect that without me, the result would have been a somewhat different, though not inferior, book to the one we published. The poems were painwracked, wrestling with the problems created by loss and perfectionism. We printed Nils's chapbook in Tucson just before #7/8. At the end, our only problem was what to do with the cover. Since Nils wanted to call his book *Chicago*, Mary dug up her old birth certificate, which had been signed in a very large hand by Richard J. Daley, then County Clerk of Cook County. Exposed carefully on a plain background, the fragments made a sepia-colored collage.

Before going to Alabama to visit George and Pia, I had received an envelope from Frank Stanford, thick with poems. There was such a sense of urgency about them that, thinking Frank or Ginny had died or been injured, I tried to reach them by phone. As it turned out, each telephone had a recorded message referring me to the other. I felt like a kid trapped in a mirrored labyrinth, unable to retrace his steps. I had hoped to see Frank while in Alabama. Only after returning did I try the Benedictine monastery where he had gone to high school, since he had kept in touch with some of the monks. I reached a woman who said the monks were at dinner. When I told her the details, she announced she was Frank's mother and ran the monastery's guest house. As far as she knew, Frank was all right, living in Liberal, Missouri, just north of the Arkansas border, on a farm that belonged to Ginny's parents. When I reached him there, he reassured me that everything was OK. I told him how moved I had been by the poems, and how worried. I proposed a book with these poems at its core, hoping as well to include three of them in our next issue. After that, he would send me additional poems as they were written or found, a process that would go on for another year or two.

I asked Steve Orlen to review Tess Gallagher's *Instructions To The Double*, and wrote to the author. Gallagher responded by sending me a group of poems, from which I selected "The Ballad of Ballymote," "Woman-Enough," and "Women's Tug Of War at Lough Arrow." Perhaps my having taken the long poem, "Terra Cotta," by Michael Burkard, made a difference, though I wasn't sure. Tess was extremely loyal in her loves and friendships. Altogether, issue #9 contained first-class work by a remarkable collection of poets. Thomas Masiello, a disciple of John Ashbery, gave us four poems. James Moore, Dick Hugo, William Kloefkorn, Sharon Olds, Lynn Strongin, Norman Dubie, Pamela Stewart, William Bronk, Steve Orlen, C. D. Wright and others equally good. Karen Brodine had several frightening poems dealing with women in the new work place of word processors and computers. As I look over the poems and contributors, this issue seems quite likely the strongest one, poem for poem since our first.

When we were almost finished with the final paste-up of #9, an envelope arrived with a long poem from George Oppen: "If It All Went Up in Smoke." It was quarter to one. Trying to keep calm, I raced through the poem. Then we headed for the car and drove to Tucson Typographic where I asked how soon we could have a proof. With luck, they would have it by four o'clock. When I let George know, he sounded pleased. Then he phoned back 15 minutes later to say that David Gitin had told him the poem had been printed in APR, and so would not be eligible for reprinting. I had had poems from at least three poets reprinted there without acknowledgement. I tracked down the issue of APR, and discovered the poem in question was only one of seven in this sequence, albeit the longest. When I said that I would acknowledge the printing of that section immediately below it in the text, George agreed. By four that afternoon, a galley proof was on its way to him. Two or three days later I had his corrected galleys in my hand. Not much needed changing, and the final paste-up was completed a day or two later. What to me was an extraordinary poem may have been lost on many of our readers. Still, a number who read it in *Ironwood* think the result more fully achieved than later, when this poem was broken up to supply nearly half the poems in *Primitive*, Oppen's last book. It was Oppen's tendency to develop poems as he went along, but always he went from smaller to larger. Given the shortness of the collection, I can understand why a publisher might have preferred having these shorter poems contribute their separate energies to the larger book.

Though the largest of its kind, the last-minute entry was typical. Each issue was a fortress that had to be made impregnable. Gary Cooper in *Beau Geste* comes to mind: Commanding a besieged fortress for the French Foreign Legion, he keeps propping up the dead and wounded against nearby parapets, then fires from behind to make it look as if they were alive and functioning. After one last assault, the Arabs finally withdraw and melt into the desert with only Cooper alive, literally holding the fort. For better or worse, I had enough of those elements in my character to make me more than a little uncomfortable.

Not long after the appearance of *Ironwood 9*, I received a letter from C. W. Truesdale, the publisher (New Rivers) of *White*, which had been the subject of James Carpenter's essay on Charles Simic. Although he had described it as a page-by-page analysis of the poem *White*, Carpenter had quoted the entire poem verbatim in *Ironwood 9* and I didn't have the foggiest. For one thing, all his page numbers were odd numbers. Since I had never been able to purchase a copy in California, New York or Tucson and was reduced to borrowing Peter Wild's copy in order to read the book, I did not have it with me when we put the issue together. The main thing that infuriated Truesdale was our failure to mention New Rivers at the very moment we were reproducing the full text, albeit with chunks of prose sandwiched between quotations. When I asked him if the book was out-of-print, he answered that it was. We would print an apology on the very first page of our next issue, I assured him. Perhaps I could help drum up interest in a new edition. The thing, I decided, was to make a virtue of necessity, using my apology as a springboard for saluting the small presses for nurturing so much extraordinary talent in poetry and fiction, as well as for the quality of their editions. I pointed out that Simic's first book for Braziller was actually made up of the poems in his two Kayak books, give or take a poem. On the last page, I recommended some 80 current small press titles.

For the cover, I used a photograph of sculptor Ruth Asawa taken by Hazel Larsen when both were students at Black Mountain College. The study is suffused with reverence and restraint. Whether or not it helped to sell issues, it was a choice that still seems perfect. *Ironwood 9* (Spring 1977) was the first issue since 1974 to include the date as well as the volume number on the spine. With the long delays in issues 2 through 6, we had lost too much time but had now made up all but one year. After #7/8, no issue was ever delayed more than five weeks so that our reliability gradually established itself.

*   *   *

One Saturday, about a week before we got issue #9 back from the printers, I decided to go for a drive. As usual, I had Joe Monsanto lift me so I could walk the ten yards to the door while he held my right arm. After he helped me through the side door, we turned to face the car—my good old Checker Marathon. I realized then that I had failed to have the car moved from the side of the house so there would be room for the two of us to get by. One of us would have to go down first, I told Joe. I meant to say more. The words were never spoken. Unaccountably, I found myself stepping off the three-inch stoop. It was the left knee that landed full force. I felt, heard no crack. But for the powerful ache in my knee, I was almost comfortable. A spring breeze heavy with orange blossoms. The terrible sad odor of mock oranges crushed in asphalt. How free it felt, falling through the air. I didn't think I had "broken my knee" or even sprained it. I was hoping it was a strained ankle, whatever that was. Mary heard the noise and came up with a neighbor who happened to be visiting. Before I let anyone carry me inside, I needed to get my bearings and plan ahead. Then, Mary summoned another neighbor, and together, the three women and Joe Monsanto carefully lifted me through the side door, past the dining and living rooms, down the hall to our room and the rocking bed. As I started rocking, the pain seemed to grow. Whether owing to an increased flow of blood to the injured area or simply the effect of time and excitement wearing off as the blood cooled, there was no way of telling. I telephoned an orthopedic doctor who had treated me for a slight knee ailment, made an appointment to have the limb x-rayed and set Monday, and phoned my regular doctor to check with him. An old friend came by at seven o'clock Monday morning, and got me dressed. Then he drove over to the Tucson Clinic and "borrowed" one of their auxiliary wheelchairs with telescoping adjustable footrests. With Mary's help, Dennis shifted me to the chair with my leg extended. Then Dennis and I "walked" the seven blocks to the clinic for the x-rays. Two hours later, we were back and I was lifted into bed. That afternoon I went to the orthopedic doctor. He examined me, checked the x-rays and fitted me with a 20-inch cast to immobilize the left knee cap or patella, which was broken.

For the next six weeks, all I had to do was take something for pain and wait for the healing to take place. Finally, it was time to see the doctor. He removed the cast, had me get a frontal x-ray of the patella and told me to return in a week if I couldn't bend the knee more than 10 or 15 degrees. In a week, I was back and the doctor made an appointment for me with a physical therapist whose office was a few doors away. Soon I was on a schedule of three one-hour sessions a week. As the weeks wore on and the bent knee gave way grudgingly, the forced bending became increasingly painful. I increased the sessions to five a week. To go there and back, I had to use Handicar, a service which employed a group of large vans with hydraulic lifts. Roomy as it was, my own Checker Marathon was too painfully tight for my leg and required my riding on the floor while stretched across the back. Getting lifted from there was close to impossible. After three weeks or so, unable to get an appointment with the orthopedic doctor, I asked the therapist if he could speak to him. I wanted to know whether my using the pool at Tucson Medical Center would help loosen the knee. He did talk to him but the doctor preferred to continue on course.

By now, we were well into May. Soon, we would leave Tucson for our third summer in Corte Madera. Mary got Mark Elder, the son of her old friend and learning disabilities supervisor, to come out and help me for the summer. With such an uncertain prognosis, it seemed too arduous to try and break in somebody local. The flight to San Francisco was extremely taxing even in the right front aisle seat with my left leg sticking out into the aisle. We were not allowed to rest it on anything during takeoff or landing, which usually meant that the person on my right had to lean forward and left to hold it with his own seat belt fastened. Mary had improvised a makeshift leg support from her huge straw bag by stuffing it with pillows, blankets, etc . . . But each flight was a separate battle, struggling to get the one seat and use what we could of our own remedies. Several times, total strangers offered to help us and saved the day.

Before we went to California, we made arrangements through my doctor there to continue physical therapy at a clinic four miles from the house. I got in touch with a poet friend whose husband, an orthopedic man, agreed to be my doctor. The next six weeks saw definite progress in getting the knee to bend more. By the fifth week the excruciating pain which would persist through most of a therapy session, was starting to crop up between sessions. I had begun to walk with assistance and was covering good stretches by now. The clinic had enormously long halls, wide enough, too, to accommodate three people side by side and still leave room for others.

It was when I walked at home that the pain began to interfere. Even if I dropped therapy, there was no guarantee that the pain would not visit me each time I walked. I called the doctor, having already told the therapist. He suggested a shot of cortisone in the knee cap and arranged to consult my therapist, who agreed completely. When I went to see him, every one of the 20-odd doctor's offices in the building bore the sign: I AM NOT RESPONSIBLE FOR THE PATIENTS OF ANY OTHER DOCTOR IN THIS BUILDING. After perfunctory greetings, the doctor asked what the trouble was and I recited the same history I had given him over the phone. Before I was finished, he broke in with a characteristic Marin County remark: "All I hear you talk about is pain." He didn't remember having promised me a cortisone shot, nor anything else. After wrestling with this for five minutes, he suggested almost as an afterthought x-rays of the knee, particularly from the left and right sides. I had the x-rays taken across the hall. Within ten minutes, the doctor had dropped the moralizing and talked with a mixture of aston- ishment and contrition. The x-rays had shown a good amount of dam- aged cartilage, which meant that the therapy was only making things worse and should be stopped. And yes, it would be best to give me a shot of cortisone, which might cure everything but might just as easily cure nothing. In the event, it had good results for a week or so, but cured nothing. By the time we tried to get in touch with him, the doctor was off on a three-week vacation with none of his associates willing to see us. Through Dr. Margolin, our doctor from pneumonia days, we saw another orthopedic man, a veteran army doctor who, it turned out, did not believe in forced bending. He wanted to try some kind of water therapy, but in the crisp East Marin climate, I didn't feel like risking opening the pores so regularly and then having to drive back and forth to the house. Still, the pain subsided gradually and what was then a one-in-three chance of surgery slowly receded. I learned to walk easily with two people and with some difficulty with a single person provided their strength and coordination were up to the task. Getting on the high rocking bed now required a second, intermediate footstool and a second person. Getting on and off the john required a second person. In practice, this usually meant Mary, or someone hired for that single purpose. Either way, it made our lives that much more constricting, expensive.

*   *   *

When I began writing, cummings, Williams and haiku were the first things I read. In Dick Shelton's workshop, reading became more systematic. Before long, my favorites were W. S. Merwin, James Wright and George Oppen, together with first books by Robert Bly, Bill Knott and Charles Simic. When the time came to plan a second special issue, I thought first of Merwin. With *The Lice* and *The Moving Target*, written in the late Sixties, he had broken new ground syntactically and in his exploration of consciousness. Stripped of punctuation, his lines floated on the page. The psychic data possessed the same immediacy, the same freedom from overbearing control. Merwin's assumption of a wolf persona in "Lemuel's Blessing" is one of several vivid portraits of the visionary at odds with his fellow men. Perhaps this poet's position is best indicated by the opening lines from "Noah's Raven": "Why should I have returned?/My knowledge would not fit into theirs." In spite of the simplicity that had marked much of his recent work, Merwin was an enormously sophisticated man, steeped in the European tradition but familiar with contemporary anthropologists, theologians, mystics and historians, as well as many of the third world cultures. He seemed at home everywhere but had a way, for all his friendliness, of keeping people at a distance.

Where Merwin came across as the lone seer whose ascent gradually removes him from sight, James Wright seemed more like one of us, stumbling under his own cross. More, he stopped to notice others, to share their degradation. As Robert Hass was to remark, "the suffering of other people, particularly the lost and the derelict, is actually a part of his own emotional life. It is what he writes from, not what he writes about." Although Wright eschewed the language of belief, there was a Christian aspect to his taking on this suffering. I had asked Merwin for poems a year before, but by the time he sent some, they left me unconvinced. Obviously, if I didn't feel I could print any, how was I to do a whole issue?

Therefore I wrote to James Wright in early Fall, 1976, outlining what

I had in mind. He answered after a week or two, pleased in a shy sort of way. He enclosed a brief essay by an undergraduate about the sentence in Wright's poems. The piece was intelligent and to the point but I was reluctant to take it up, especially this early in planning for the issue. I was a bit uncomfortable but ended by returning the piece. At that point, Wright expressed a hope that I would include Dave Smith and Peter Stitt. I got in touch with both men before very long and they agreed to contribute. Smith was an enormous help in assembling a comprehensive bibliography. He was to write on Wright's *Two Citizens*, a book Robert Bly had dismissed somewhat cavalierly. Steve Orlen agreed to focus on Wright's first collection, *The Green Wall* and Madeline DeFrees on its successor, *St. Judas*. A few months later, at the suggestion of John Logan or Tony Petrosky I wrote to Robert Hass. When he answered, it was to say he would do his best to write something on *The Branch Will Not Break*. As it developed, the Hass essay also included *Shall We Gather At The River* and other works. Dave Smith concentrated on *Two Citizens* but took care to include the final poems in Wright's *Collected*, those not included in *Shall We Gather*. John Logan wrote briefly on the prose poems of *Moments of an Italian Summer*. While Shirley Clay Scott concentrated on the central period of Wright's career, Peter Stitt and William Heyen wrote in a more general way, Stitt concentrating on the critical response to Wright's work. Robert Bly and David Ignatow, Phyllis Hoge Thompson and Leonard Nathan, contributed shorter pieces. Carol Bly sent a touching memoir and Jane Robinett wrote from Spain asking if I would be open to something from her.

What she wound up sending treated the relationship of James Dickey to James Wright. Dickey had been extremely critical of the original version of "At the Executed Murderer's Grave", which had appeared in an early edition of *New Poets of England and America*. Stung, Wright retaliated with a number of criticisms of his own. The two men began a heated correspondence which was scheduled to be published in a forthcoming *Sewanee Review* but was cancelled when Wright's style of writing changed abruptly. Within eight months of the original version of "At The Executed Murderer's Grave", a startlingly different version appeared in *St. Judas*, dedicated to J. L. D. [Dickey]. At the urging of Jane Robinett, I tried to secure permission to print some of this Wright-

Dickey correspondence, but the library needed someone there in person. When I sought Dickey's approval, it was not forthcoming.

Sometime in July, Robert Hass phoned and asked if he could bring over his Wright paper. He lived in Berkeley, a 40-minute drive from our house. When he came a day later, with his friend Phil Dow, he seemed a mixture of shyness and enormous personal confidence. He had, it turned out, bought many copies of our Oppen issue and given them to friends. He seemed to have a genuine concern for the whole spectrum of American poetry, not simply his own work or that of his friends. We had an enjoyable lunch and, after they had left, I settled to reading his essay. For all the negative stance of the first sentence, what stood out was Hass's love of Wright's poetry. Even if he hadn't wound up saying so in so many words, it would have become clear through the care and attention he gave to Wright's poems, individually and as a whole. Even more, one felt his response to poetry at large. His main criticism of Wright and, by implication a number of others, was that he had abdicated both will and reason, leaving the outer world in the hands of utilitarians, content to dwell in darkness while making of it a realm of pure sensibility, what Allen Ginsberg has called "the whole boatload of sensitive bullshit." This aestheticism, or decadence, flourished when the life of the spirit retreated or was driven from public life, where it ought, naturally, to manifest itself. Hass went on to show how, in "Autumn Begins in Martin's Ferry, Ohio", Wright succeeds in bringing the subject to light, seeing and feeling with both clarity and affectionate compassion. In its several parts the essay makes other points but it would require a short essay to deal adequately with all of them.

Dave Smith's essay, one of the first to arrive, concentrated on Wright's language in the last two or three books. He felt that readers and critics were misunderstanding if they took "this language's blunt and garrulous simplicity as a lapse in poetic control or richness." Wright's was an identifiable voice speaking urgently of urgent matters. This statement from a review Wright wrote of Robert Penn Warren's *Promises* aptly voices his own goal in the last books: ". . . to shatter his words and try again to recreate them, to fight through and beyond his own craftsmanship in order to revitalize his language at the sources of tenderness and horror." The following excerpt from the same review sums up Wright's own achievement:

. . . one can hear in the poem two movements of language: a strong formal regularity, which can be identified with a little struggle, but which is driven so fiercely by the poet that one starts to hear beyond it the approach of an unpredictable and hence discomforting second movement, which can be identified as something chaotic, something very powerful but unorganized. It is the halting, stammering movement of an ordinarily articulate man who has been shocked. The order and chaos move side by side; and, as the poem proceeds, I get the feeling that each movement becomes a little stronger, and together they help to produce an echoing violence in the syntax. . . . It is the exaggerated formality with which a man faces and acknowledges the concrete and inescapable existence of an utterly innocent (and therefore utterly ruthless) reality which is quite capable not only of cursing him, but also of letting him linger contemplatively over the sound of his own bones breaking.

Robert Penn Warren, one of the first I wrote, sent a brief poem for Wright. He was very humble about it and I was moved by the poem's searing honesty. Richard Hugo, William Heyen and John Unterecker also sent poems, all relating to Wright.

It was winter, 1977, when James Wright first sent me poems for the issue, the first one entitled "In Memory of Mayor Richard J. Daley". It was only four or five lines, and as I remember, was in the form of a prose poem. It read like a good ending to a poem but too much of a stub otherwise. Not wanting to convey any sense of rejection, I made a point of not returning the Daley poem, just letting it sit. There were several others which I took, and later, Wright sent more. I made it clear that I preferred poems that dealt, at least in part, with the United States. Although I think he wanted to send me more Italian poems, he sent what he could. One beautiful poem was "One Last Look at the Adige: Verona in the Rain," which I took immediately. And there were five others. About six or seven months later, toward the end of summer, the Mayor Daley poem was resubmitted, this time in regular lines, close to 50. The diction was clotted with grit, stinkweed, some on-again-off-again marriage of refuse, weeds, and human artifacts, of the ugly and the beautiful. By the time the poem ended, it was hard to tell whether "This is what you're up against." referred to death, Daley, or perhaps death-

in-life. Knowing Wright's capacity for mercy as demonstrated in his two
poems for President Harding, I imagine it was all three, unless it was
simply the first.

The last three lines in the second stanza went like this:

Ironweeds hunch up and live a long time, a strange forever.
They don't fall on the gravestones even in spring.
They don't fall in winter.
They go on living like the romantic
Mystery of cancer.

When I read the last two lines, I flinched and thought long and long.
I didn't want to alienate Wright or seem to be "improving" his poem.
So I concentrated on the fact that so many people I knew had friends or
relatives who had died of cancer or been afflicted with it. Regardless of
the accuracy of *romantic,* I could imagine some of those people shaking
their heads as they read the line. I wrote James Wright to that effect,
and was grateful when he agreed to drop the adjective.

Dave Smith reached Tucson a day before the rest of the Tennis Group
(an *ad hoc* group of poets, including Galway Kinnell and Bill Matthews,
who toured a number of university campuses that fall, giving readings
and playing tennis intermittently) and got in touch with us. Since Smith
was an avid reader and habitué of used bookstores, Friday morning Mary
Cuddihy drove him to a number of local bookstores where she had to
drop off copies of the James Wright issue. Later, she put together a
picnic lunch and we drove down to the river bed. In the last year, someone had leased much of the land immediately north of the river and was
boarding horses in an old, dilapidated stable made of corrugated metal.
The horses had consumed the ground cover and, except for the huge
cottonwoods, their felled trunks, and an occasional dark mesquite, the
ground was bare, closer to sand than earth. After lunch, a group of horses
approached us from the east. They divided at my chair and proceeded
to station themselves around it. Mary had gone off to the river to be by
herself and Dave and I were talking quietly while the young man helping me tidied up. Pretty soon, I was completely surrounded, two horses
in front of me sweeping their heads in and out of my lap. With my left
arm I did my best to stroke them. I could feel their hot breath on my

arms while another two tried to get at my neck from behind. I was grateful for the metal brace keeping their teeth at least half an inch away. They certainly meant well but I'm not sure what the results would have been. I alternated between deep joy at such a circumstance and a growing fear that one of them could let go with a hoof if something caused him to shy. The thing to do was keep still. After about 15 minutes in which Dave offered his help two or three times, I had my helper seat himself quietly on the ground to my right, and after several minutes, slowly pivot to his right until we were at right angles. Then he rose very slowly and walked south ten or fifteen yards toward the river. The horses obediently followed. I then had him slip back to me and bring the chair quickly to our station wagon. Dave was elated. This had happened to me once before but I hadn't expected it all over again.

It was then that Dave confided that he had just been told he had diabetes. I could imagine the kind of pressure that academic life, along with such a condition, could lay on such a talented, ambitious man with an overwhelming need to experience life and write from that experience.

Ironwood 10, the James Wright issue, came out the first week of November, just in time for the touring doubles group which included Coleman Barks, Galway Kinnell, Marvin Bell, Dave Smith, Stephen Dunn and Bill Matthews. Watching poets and others browse and purchase copies, one could feel the excitement mounting. Within the hour, news of the issue and especially the Hass essay was spreading. Inside a few weeks, the same thing would occur on both coasts. Orders and reorders. Among many enthusiastic responses, Bill Heyen's went furthest: "Your James Wright issue is the best thing of its kind since Allen Tate's *Sewanee Review* issue on Eliot. It may even be the greatest thing of its kind, period." Soon all kinds of poets, some of obvious distinction, prominent as Kinnell, wanted Hass to criticize their work in print. With the James Wright issue, *Ironwood* was back in the main stream.

To have remained there would have been easy, too easy. Still, if I was going to introduce our readers to more adventurous or difficult poetry, I had to be sure of enough readers, enough impact. I was coming to see *Ironwood* as a forum for various kinds of poems and opposing views of poetry. As classrooms began to order the issue, the conviction grew on me that this was an educational enterprise. In a time with no giants like

Stevens and Williams or Pound, perhaps it was important to focus the attention of poets, especially the young, on certain rare spirits whose lives and work represented the kind of dedication that took precedence over career. None of the poets I greatly admired were leaders of a particular group. Nor did they spend half of their time reading their poems on the college circuit. It would be all to the good, I felt, if some of these attitudes were to rub off on more people. The young need heroes, even if some of them turn out to have feet of clay. Within six months of the Wright issue, I resolved that we would increase the ratio of special to regular issues though I could not gauge how far this process would go.

Within a year of the issue, Robert Bly, in an essay for *The Nation*, had singled out *Ironwood* as one of only four magazines regularly printing worthwhile criticism. And Hayden Curruth ended a column in *Harper's* by recommending the James Wright issue. That mention alone brought in close to 75 orders. I had been sending Carruth issues I thought might interest him and he had gradually warmed to the magazine. Several times he recommended poets to me, first and foremost Hilda Morley. As an editor at *Hudson Review*, he had printed an impressively large and well-chosen sampling of her work. I valued him for his independence, his integrity, his plain, old-fashioned character. Half the time he answered my letters by return mail, rarely taking more than a week. For all their modesty, his letters, like his reviews, were warm and generous. They spoke with the kind of feeling I had seen in George Oppen, even though I had never met Carruth. He was to contribute relatively brief but significant essays to our special issues on Hilda Morley, Robert Duncan and Emily Dickinson.

In spring, 1982, Dave Smith published a collection of essays on the poetry of James Wright entitled *The Pure Clear Word*. The book was dedicated to me and to James Wright and included Hass's essay, Smith's own essay and a version of the one by Leonard Nathan. The book had less of a celebratory function, more of a critical one. It included earlier essays by Bly, William Matthews, Edward Butscher, Miller Williams and others, including Auden's foreword to *The Green Wall*, Wright's Yale Younger Poet volume.

For the summer of '78, a transplanted Easterner who lived in Point Reyes Station found us a house in Mill Valley. My left leg's having to be permanently extended required a gas guzzler with enough room for both legs. With its scores of curves and sharp turns, driving the narrow road up Mount Tamalpais was terrifying, especially when many curves were narrowed further by cars parked on our side. The house itself was enormous, the rooms huge, the ceilings high, at least four patios commanding radically different prospects near and far. Except for our having to pay an extra month, the rent was cheap.

Our first day Mary came down with a severe case of flu. I succumbed next morning. She was trying to help me bring up secretions when the phone rang. It was Tucson, a message from Gail Orlen. Mary got in touch with her, only to learn something had happened to Frank Stanford. We called the number she gave us and were soon talking to Ginny Stanford. Frank had shot himself the night before, three times through the heart, the day after returning from a trip to New Orleans where he had made a will. Not quite 30, he had been heard to say more than once that he had his doubts about living past that age. After hanging up, I looked from the rocking bed and spotted a deer on the dirt road, a utility road leading to the top of Mount Tamalpais. It was as if Frank had reappeared in another form. But poets and ex-Catholics are hungry for such realities, such symbols, and that too may have crossed my mind. The deer stood there nearly five minutes before moving up and off into the brush.

I remember my last phone conversation with him. It had taken place five weeks previously. His call lasted nearly an hour. By the time we hung up, he had finished his fifth beer. I kept trying to convince him that *Crib Death* would be his last small press book. I had in mind a University press such as Wesleyan or Pittsburgh. Unimpressed, he named several Pittsburgh poets he had little desire to be associated with. He sounded very high that day, very happy—no complaints. But who is to say at a distance of so many miles? Frank was one of those whose motto could have been, "Never let your banners droop." It was such a blow to have had Frank there, and then suddenly not. No one has replaced him or ever will. Strange that the poems he had sent a couple of years before that formed the basis of *Crib Death* had made me instantly apprehensive. Only an event of this magnitude could match that premonition.

In 1977, Ironwood Press brought out *Breaking Free* by Del Marie Rogers and *The Hacksaw Brightness* by Lynn Strongin. Both were printed in Tucson by Shandling Lithographing. As far back as the late '60's and early '70's, I had read poems of Rogers in magazines like *Café Solo*, *Choice, Kayak, Lillabulero* and *The Salt Creek Reader*. She was decidedly a poet of the deep image. At her best, the writing was economical, reaching peaks of intensity in the final lines. When the poems don't work, it is because the poet has been almost too careful. Reading over the contents of this book years later, I was surprised by how much they surpassed my expectations. As much as anything, the rhythms are what draw the reader, particularly in the final poems. If there is anything that could put off a reader, it would be that so many of Rogers's images are involved with decay, paralysis, dessication and death. Rooted as they are in a near desert landscape, these poems have earned the right to make visible its metaphoric implications. The cover was designed by Laurie Cook, using a photograph of a footprint in sand by Boyd Nicholl.

The voice in Lynn Strongin's *The Hacksaw Brightness* is unmistakable. If there is any resemblance, it is to the poetry of Hopkins, with its frequently inverted word order, heightened language and strong syllables that emphasize the weight of each individual sound, the unpredictable shifts in tempo. Even if, unlike Hopkins, it is the atmosphere of devotion rather than its object that draws our poet's admiration, the melody and rhythm are paramount. She is in love with innocence and a number of poems take the form of elegies for innocent girls or hospital roommates who have died. But she is attached to the living, alive to the dynamics of light, the earth quickened by the sun. Her ability to communicate the force of life in its crude form is manifest in these last lines of "Van Gogh": "To come home to a lamp's murkish yellow;/ to bend like crude animals, yet gods, over a plate of potatoes." Repeated front and back, the cover photograph was an imaginative rendering of a small German city built over the water which reflected the buildings while the sky, divided by long, slender branches, seemed made of ice, so densely gray was it. The Rogers book sold for two dollars, the somewhat longer Strongin volume for two-fifty. The two were the ninth and tenth in our chapbook series.

The *Ironwood* issues for 1978 (11 and 12) were not particularly distinguished, though each had its merits. #11 had several memorable poems by Stefanie Marlis, a pair of good lyrics by John Skoyles and another pair by Dave Smith. Reg Saner sent his magnificent "Bonfires" and Hilda Morley several quietly evocative poems. There were two long essays, the first on John Logan, the other John Taggart's 24 page-analysis of William Bronk. Both essays bore a vaguely similar relationship to what might have been a special issue. In Logan's case, I had allowed myself to request an essay as a result of pressure from James Wright for a Logan issue. At the time, with the Wright issue possibly hanging in the balance, I was afraid of rocking the boat. In April, I had asked John Taggart to write a 10 to 12-page essay on Bronk, going so far as to pay him the entire sum months in advance at his request. After all, I had heard Taggart praise Bronk and, given George Oppen's fondness for the latter, it was difficult to believe John didn't share that enthusiasm. More, his postcard that spring had used the word "admirer" to describer his relation to Bronk. As the months passed, Bronk's friends and admirers, some of them first-rate critics, kept wanting to send me essays as if we were already doing a special issue. The thing was, while I was open to a Bronk issue, it was much too soon, coming as it would immediately after James Wright. In August, I got in touch with Bronk, outlining my predicament and assuring him that Taggart's piece would certainly do him justice. For most of those who had written me, he had specific explanations such as "Whenever John writes on somebody, So-and-so usually likes to have his say as well." In closing, however, he stressed that John's views were not always consonant with his.

When Taggart's essay reached me, the most I could do was get him to cut maybe ⅔ of a page, leaving twice what I had asked for. As strongly as I disagreed with its tone and several of its leading conclusions, as an editor I had no choice other than to print it. Bronk was terribly upset, feeling that the hand that had reached out to shake his had blood on it.

Taggart's essay sees Bronk as having assumed Wallace Stevens's voice. Still, he adds, the "circle attendant to the voice must be included. We should not be surprised that not all of the circle's elements are taken up." The most noticeable element not taken up by Bronk is Stevens's symbolism, by means of which he unified imagination with reality. Without the vocabulary provided by the symbols, the metaphysic and theory of knowledge cannot be resolved or clarified, leading Bronk to frustration and despair, *a* world that is not *the* world. For Bronk, in other words, the world suggested by music and poetry, while more real than the supposedly real world, isn't real. We cannot live there. He sees Bronk's most perfect expression of this in *The World, The Worldless* (New Directions, 1964), a book he considers without parallel in American poetry for this century. This achievement is repeated here and there in isolated poems from later books but never with the equilibrium and consistent resonant variousness that marks this one. What goes unmentioned is that this book was edited by Bronk's friend and Taggart's mentor, George Oppen. We would have to know whether the poems in this book were pulled from other manuscripts or whether it represents a finished collection which Oppen merely cut and/or ordered. In the end, Taggart maintains, Bronk's work is a dark progress, his almost satanic pride consuming everything outside itself. I intended to invite letters from both camps.

When I asked George Oppen, he remarked that Bronk had many friends and if I were to mention that in my invitation, it might help to smooth things over. For balance, I printed within Taggart's contributor note his statement that if those in the small press world did not take this poet seriously, we could hardly expect the more popular or commercial publishers to do so.

The letters appeared in *Ironwood 12*, which came out on schedule that Fall. For the cover, I had Frank Stanford's "The Light The Dead See" reversed in white against a brownish-maroon ground. Although I had tried to avoid the color of the James Wright issue, this was exactly the same and the type too small to make an impact. The poem, which involves the poet seeing and speaking from beyond death, created an eerie sensation but, as presented, the cover remains *Ironwood's* worst. (*Ironwood 11*, on the other hand, reproduced a marvelously intricate plant drawing by Margaret Doogan).

Our 12th issue carried an interview with Ai, conducted by Lawrence Kearney and myself. In addition to a strong group by Frank Stanford, there were good poems from Jorie Graham, Lawrence Russ, Justin Caldwell, Gustav Sobin and Karen Fish, a brilliant high school senior. The two poems by David Katz stood out for the way they combined exploration with a sense of ongoing mystery. George Oppen urged me to devote an issue to my own poems, something I could not take seriously. Yet it led me to print three of my own poems, a decision I came to regret. For one thing, I found too many fellow poets and friends of the magazine telling me that mine were the best poems in the issue, which was simply not true. It was time for another special issue and I wanted a single poet. If everything worked out, the subject would be the Swedish poet, Tomas Tranströmer.

When I wrote to Tranströmer in November 1977, he responded with obvious relish while making clear he would not carry stones to his own pyramid. Since he had referred me to his translators the last time I solicited poems, I asked him for the addresses of Robin Fulton and Samuel Charters, already having Bly's. Tomas's reply mentioned a number of others, including Keith Harrison, editor of *Carleton Miscellany* and Kjell Espmark, a Swedish critic engaged in writing a book on TT, as many of us came to call him. When I telephoned Robert Hass, he agreed to write something if he could make it grow out of a lecture at Goddard College, where he would be teaching next fall. Hass also recommended his friend, the Swedish critic and polymath Göran Printz-Pahlson, then teaching at Cambridge, England. A few months later, he suggested I contact Joanna Bankier, an editor and critic who had grown up in Sweden and lived for a decade in France before coming to the States. Since I had heard that Helen Vendler was an admirer of Tranströmer's, I telephoned her as well, but she had just been given a position at the *New Yorker* and was also writing regularly for the *New York Review of Books*. She begged off on the basis of prior commitments and recommended Yvonne Sandstroem. A specialist in contemporary Swedish literature at the University of Rhode Island, Sandstroem was eager to take part and suggested writing on Gogol and Tranströmer.

When I wrote to Keith Harrison, he proposed an essay comparing TT's translators. In addition to their other translations, Fulton, Charters and Bly all sent me versions of "A Part of the Forest". I wound up printing them with the Swedish original on two facing pages. Anxious to take part, Lief Sjöberg offered to translate Kjell Espmark's "An Artist in the North," a chapter from the Swedish critic's book on Tranströmer. Here, Espmark concentrates on the Norwegian composer Edvard Grieg and the way Tranströmer identifies with the composer's difficulty in refreshing the sources of his own creativity. It is the urgency of their shared problem that makes Tranströmer's portrait of Grieg so convincing. Since Hass and Sjöberg had both warned me about Printz-Pahlson's tendency to procrastinate, I set his deadline a month early.

Dealing with this many translators, I secured a good number of poems for the issue. Even if one translator had published a version there were equally good ones on hand. "The Gallery," a four-page work from Tranströmer's latest collection, speaks to a generation nearing middle-age where men and women identify themselves with their social roles, a predicament that makes it even harder for each of us to really see or be seen. A number of prose poems ("Funchal" "The Clearing" "To Mats and Laila," etc.) demonstrate Tranströmer's success with the form, the way they shift subject matter and accommodate more than one tone. Robert Bly contributed several fine translations, including "From The Winter of 1947" and "Along The Lines," where Tranströmer succeeds in suggesting the extremes of cold or hot war alongside the purest sense of existing in the *now*. Samuel Charters contributed a translation of "Elegy," an untranslated early poem where the influence of Eliot is palpable. Altogether, the fifteen Tranströmer poems gave the issue a solid foundation.

We printed six letters Tranströmer sent to Robert Bly, rich in their detailed evocation of various Swedish landscapes. There he discussed certain crucial points in the poems of his that Bly was translating. The letters dealt as well with his career as a psychologist, his travels and the problems Swedish writers had with taxes. Included among them was a brilliantly funny cartoon worthy of the *New Yorker*. What the letters did was fill in some gaps, giving us a better sense of the man, the writer.

I was happy when Printz-Pahlson turned out to be a couple of weeks early with "Tranströmer And Tradition." In spite of its high-flown, often awkward diction and syntax, his essay dug deeply into rarely explored aspects of Tranströmer. From such a prestigious critic, it was doubly welcome. PP examined Tranströmer's earliest books, concentrating on precisely those poems which had not yet been translated into English, with frequent references to Wordsworth and the Eliot of "Tradition and the Individual Talent." PP viewed Tranströmer as essentially a poet of History, concluding "that his confrontation with History is also the driving power behind his nature poetry and his poetry of expression." *Baltics* was Tranströmer's most important contribution to his poetry of History. Nor should the fact that his burning imagination "provides us with a vivid disjointed vision of History . . . be taken as evidence of a placid or conservative bias on his part, as his detractors would have us believe."

Mark Rudman and Robert Hass made good use of their restless minds exploring Tranströmer; each took a good look at the soil in his shovel instead of simply classifying it according to its properties. Of Tranströmer, Rudman wrote that "his poems can be terrifying because the threat of self-dissolution is so intense." The fragility of identity and the impinging loss of selfhood provoke the poem 'out of the nest.' . . . Tranströmer creates tension through an uncanny sense of where the drama lies embedded in a given life situation which only the imagination can resolve . . . "His landscapes are not archetypal; there are archetypes embedded in the landscapes. He has apprenticed himself to *signs*." Finally, Rudman underlined the connection Tranströmer drew between his own dreams and the historical moment as he so often received it via the news.

Robert Hass began his essay with some notes on metaphor. For him, the "lyric imitates insight or being, or consciousness without object" while the discursive forms of poetry imitate life in time. They move and accumulate, ripening. He described Tranströmer's poetry as the work of a deeply-rooted man: "poetry that always wakes stunned from the rooted and local into a place where the self throbs with itself and the world seems elsewhere." Writing of *Baltics,* Hass compared it to a "slowly turning mobile" of mind and island where discourse takes place because the parts tug at one another and everything feels related to everything else by way of metaphor. *Baltics* ends, he noted, because the poem arrives in the sixth section at a figure for itself. While he didn't think the conclusion entirely achieved, that is, accomplished rather than wished into being, he couldn't remember many places in literature where it was.

Together with John Haines's essay, "On Our Way to the Address," these pieces helped rescue Tranströmer's work from too simple an apprehension of it as an extension of what Bly and Wright were doing in America. A number of important poets thanked me for having "rescued" Tranströmer from too tight an embrace by Bly and his disciples. While this was hardly the point, I had hoped with these issues to elicit as wide a spectrum as possible of favorable responses. The rest was incidental but seemed a healthy development.

Joanna Bankier finally sent us a balanced yet incisive survey of changing tides in the Swedish response to Tranströmer, from the late '50's on into the late'70's. This piece gave readers a sense of the sweep provided by time and the fresh perspective each generation brings to the original text. Mary Sears Mattfield contributed a study on recurrent images in the poetry of TT. Because it drew heavily on the Swenson/Sjöberg translations, the quoted material supplied a welcome corrective to the more widely-quoted versions of Bly and Fulton. With considerable regret, I decided not to go ahead with Yvonne Sandstroem's essay on Tranströmer and Gogol. It was a bit too academic, and while there might have been room for one such piece, I was determined not to print two or three. Still, I liked Sandstroem's translation of the Gogol poem very much, and was glad I succeeded in persuading her to let me use it.

Though Keith Harrison's review of TT's translators was relatively superficial, he had some interesting things to say about Transtömer himself and the difficulties facing a poet from as small a country as Sweden. In the single paragraph each wrote on the subject, Rudman and Hass had more interesting things to say about Swedish and translation.

Transtömer had written to me that there was every chance the Swedish government would pay for up to 200 copies of an issue devoted wholly to Swedish poetry, which they would receive free. I wrote the agency he named but heard nothing for about a year. When I wrote again, they wound up ordering a mere 25 copies. By the time their diplomats in Washington became interested enough to order a copy or two, a couple of years had elapsed and the now rare issues were selling for $9, which was more than they were willing to pay. The original list price was $2.50, for the 136-page issue. After a sharp increase in fourth-class postal rates and jumps in printing costs, we had raised our prices fifty cents.

The issue proved an enormous success. One result: the Sierra Club wanted to publish Transtömer's next book, "The Truth Barriers," in Robert Bly's translation. Although Bly was instrumental in bringing this about, the Sierra Club people wanted my advice before making a final decision. I remarked how Transtömer's spare, often stark poetry conveyed a sense of nature's innate strength and the dangers posed by human ignorance and willfulness. When I mentioned Leslie Ullman, a recent Yale Younger Poet who loved Transtömer's work and our special issue, my questioner was ecstatic. Ullman was an old college classmate she had lost track of. From there on, everything went smoothly.

The first page of *Ironwood 12* carried a eulogy of Frank Stanford and announced the Stanford Memorial Prizes. The principal one, $400, was for the best group of four or more poems submitted between Thanksgiving 1978, and July 1979; another $250 was added for the best single poem. By eliminating those with commercial or university press books from the competition, I was probably handicapping our contest. Though opening the floodgates to some terribly weak poetry, the contest drew some genuinely populist talents. I wanted these prizes to generate a richer flow of manuscripts from relative unknowns. After all, Frank Stanford was a relative unknown when *Ironwood* began printing him.

*   *   *

We had the Oppens out for lunch at our newly rented house in Woodacre, in June, '79. At some point, talking of women poets, Mary Oppen referred to the two young women whose work impressed them: Sharon Olds and Linda Gregg. We had printed Sharon Olds already but at the name Linda Gregg, something clicked. She was the poet Michael Burkard had mentioned more than a year ago. When printing poems by Debora Greger and Linda Gregerson, I had wondered if either could be Linda Gregg. Since Mary Oppen had mentioned having Gregg's manuscript, I asked if she could mail it to us. Next morning, when I phoned the Oppens to remind her, she had already mailed it. The following morning, it was at our little post office. Mary Cuddihy opened the envelope at our dining room table and we started reading. We stayed with the poems, page after page, for at least two hours, oh-ing and aah-ing. It was hard to find a poem we didn't feel like printing. Here was a poet without even a chapbook, just the kind of person our contest needed. Most of the poems were situated in Greece, many written in a high style. Still, the myths and gods and Greek landscape were not used simply as decoration or cultural affectation. These were passionate poems and the poet was living in this landscape as intensely as any I have come across.

It is hard now to remember what combination of letter and telephone got us in touch with Linda; we found out soon enough which poems were eligible and selected nine. The prize for the best manuscript of four or more poems went to Linda Gregg; Richard Terrill, the only other poet with at least four poems, shared the prize for the best poem with Michael Burkard. Later I became convinced that Terrill's "The Women" was a better poem than his "Abraham Lincoln." Other poems that spoke quietly were three each by Ann Guido, Mary Karr and Frank Stewart. Robert Winner, a New York businessman with serious health problems, contributed two perfect lyrics. There was a fine long poem by Coleman Barks and excellent work by Christopher Buckley, Paul Auster, Stan Rice, Jorie Graham and Stephen Dobyns. Furthermore, there was a touching interview with Tess Gallagher. Our reviews included a careful reading of Robert Hass's *Praise* by Steve Orlen and a brief, sympathetic look at Mary Oppen's autobiography, *Meaning A Life*. Other reviews examined books by Michael Burkard and Carolyn Maisel.

When we returned in September, it was energizing to have Tess Gallagher only a mile away. She had been living with Ray Carver for over a year when they moved to Tucson where she joined the University's Creative Writing faculty. Within a fortnight, we had Tess and Ray over for supper when Robert Hass came for a reading. She returned our hospitality with at least one wonderful meal, and she and Ray came for supper several times more, most notably when my best friend, Mary's brother George, came for a visit. A few weeks later, Tess gave her own reading, climaxing it with a beautiful Irish song she had learned in Ireland. The audience demanded and was given an encore. She taught Mary how to sing a couple of her Irish songs and gave us a lovely recording of them. I loved her attractive, open face, the way the eyes looked right at you. Tess's mind never stopped working and the feelings, too, were nearly always engaged. It was amazing how close she got to so many of her students, that rare teacher who can change people's lives. While Tess drew energy from fresh faces and people, she was able to put all of that to one side whenever her work demanded it. Here, her habit of fasting must have helped to strengthen her resolve. Though she had a fund of good stories, her sense of humor was not compulsive. Another attractive thing about Tess was her laugh, the infectious quality of it. From time to time, Tess would drop by and talk poetry with me out on the patio while with Mary she was more likely to enjoy drinking a cup of tea or checking out the Buffalo Exchange or Value Village, two of the best second-hand stores in town. On their last excursion Tess bought Mary a shirt.

Although I saw less of Ray, I liked him immensely. A chainsmoker, he made a point of stepping outside whenever he smoked, aware of my breathing difficulties. I remember his looking me in the eye, a cup of coffee in his hands. For much of that year, Tess showed us versions of Ray's stories as they were finished. The stories were impressive but the endings were often the best part. When Knopf decided to take Ray's most recent collection, *What We Talk About When We Talk About Love*, their editor, Gordon Lish, going through the stories with him, persuaded Ray to drop most of these endings for shorter, more Hemingway-like ones. While they remained taut and gripping, the resulting stories lost a discernible amount of the energy and fullness which had made them even more engaging. Donald Hall, who had been sent the originals, agreed.

When I considered adding fiction that spring, I pictured Ray as our fiction editor. To add fiction could mean a sharp increase in circulation. Without so much pressure to fill space by a certain deadline, I could be even tougher on poems. There would be fewer obviously, but more attention given to those we printed. We would have the benefit of Ray's connections, particularly on the academic side, without his getting entangled with the selection of poets or poems. When I broached the subject, Ray answered that he would be delighted to serve as our fiction editor were he to remain in Arizona but that he would in fact be leaving in June. What could I say? There went my dream of stories by Garcia Marquez and Toby Wolff.

*   *   *

In October 1979, Deborah Stavro of station WGBH in Boston came to interview me as part of a series of documentaries on small press publishers. They had chosen a dozen, including Black Sparrow Press, Daniel Halpern's *Antaeus*, Hitchcock's *Kayak*, Alice James Books, *Ploughshares*, and several others, some of which were minority-run. The Watershed Foundation had made funds available for the project. To make it easier for Stavro, I had put her in touch with Linda Gregg and Steve Orlen, both spending the year in or near Boston. She had already interviewed them and taped them reading from their poems. While it took awhile to adjust the microphone to my relatively faint voice, we worked things out and the interview went well. After having supper with us, Stavro and her assistant stayed for the night and were off next morning for Guatemala and Mexico. As for the documentary, the series ran into the budgetary cutbacks of the Reagan years and was never aired. I imagine those tapes in some auditory Limbo, too dated by now to be worth resurrecting.

*   *   *

The interview with Tess Gallagher featured prominently in *Ironwood 14*. It made clear how much her strength derived from essentially working-class roots, something she shared with Ai, interviewed in #12. This one fact distinguished the two women from most contemporary American poets. Seeing Linda Gregg's work in print only sharpened my appetite for it though public response was not what I had hoped. We might have to create a taste for this poetry. There was no ready-made audience for Linda's work, as there was for Oppen's or Wright's. Perhaps if several recognized poets explored the merits of her work at some length and we put together an even stronger selection, people would read it with more attention. Tess had become friends with Linda Gregg while teaching in upper New York State, and was wholly responsive to the extraordinary quality of her poetry. When I asked her if she could write something, our deadline was little more than two months off. Those I had already asked were doing shorter pieces. Tess gave a provisional yes, the proviso being that I help her in the revision process. This was the kind of thing I enjoyed but was rarely asked to do. As I remember, Tess began over the Thanksgiving holidays, wrote more on weekends, but began in earnest over Christmas vacation. I would go to her house or send someone and she would have four or five typewritten pages waiting for me, which I proceeded to revise. Much of the revision involved getting rid of various forms of repetition, along with certain tics that writers, particularly those in a hurry, tend to overlook. When Tess finished her final draft and I went over it, she had close to 15 pages of magazine space, easily the longest essay. Gerald Stern's "Poetry Itself" ran eight pages. Frederick Turner's piece, little more than a page, was brilliant, tightly argued. Turner's argument was based on those poems he had printed as editor of *Kenyon Review*. Although his point about

Gregg's giving renewed energy to the great abstractions was well taken, ("Gnostics On Trial", "Different Not Less"), it ignored what she was doing in other, often equally significant poems ("Copperhead", "The Defeated", "The Poet Goes About Her Business"). To avoid having what began to look like a manifesto distort the overall view of Gregg, I entered the lists myself, writing four pages. To do otherwise seemed to me like an abdication of editorial responsibility. Still, I did not argue with Turner or criticize anything he had written, preferring merely to stress those aspects of her work that he had overlooked. My piece stressed the role of "negative capability" in Linda Gregg's poems; her ability, in other words, to identify with nature, to experience, as though from within, the bodies of animals: deer, birds, snakes and others, while almost always respecting the otherness of the creature. Along with the four essays and notes we printed six published poems: two each from *Ardis Anthology* and *Kenyon Review*, and one from *Iowa Review* and *The New Yorker*. Without even a chapbook to her name, there was no other way to show our readers some of her best work, and a sense of the caliber of magazines where she had published. Here is one of six others we printed for the first time:

BLAKE

The sun is on the roof,
the laundry is drying in the light.
Air moves around me and I prepare.
Make a gift of myself. Make my feet soft,
and think of Blake riding
near the tops of the trees
past our house.

The bread is in the oven and we die.
The day is spread and we delay.
Blake already is in the sky.
What is joy in this dark room?
What is light to this?
All night the ghosts of disperse,
of chaos, flee through my dreaming.

I would not repent. Though the world
separated into all its parts

and could not go back.
Get out! Get out! Get out! I shouted,
until I could not tell if anything was left
to talk to that had ears. Still refused.
Then the sun smiled, and Christ smiled,
and my laundry grew soft in the warm wind.
There. See there. The world is good to me.
I am finished with knife and window.
My bed will be underground soon enough.
I will persist in this permanence
that flesh holds. The body smooth,
the voices speaking within.

Blake comes down, calling me.
Says this is the time.
The sea is hitting the rocks.
The light is crushed and flies up,
back to the sun.
Rejoice in the breaking of the light.
Rejoice when you are two and one.
In the leaving and the coming home.
Rejoice in the room that awaits you,
empty except for the empty glass.

I fly up. Disappear inside of him.
It is grand. I see the simple cow,
a red-tailed hawk and a lamb.
The creek with the small fish in it,
and sounds of the sea at the edge of a field.
The sound of it lightly under the trees.
Birds whistling. Wind and leaves mixing
in the slightly swollen heat.
The sound of the sea in his mind.

The glass is spilling.
They both shine in that room,
water and spilling light.

One person who wanted very much to write on Linda Gregg was Jack
Gilbert. Both he and Linda regarded their nine or ten years together as
a marriage. I had avoided asking Jack to write for fear readers would

discount his testimony. As long as I was free not to print it, I told him to go ahead. The result was a well-written but curious essay, some eight pages in all. In spite of suggesting that the special "magic" of a poet such as Linda could not, in the last analysis, be explained, he ended up doing just that in terms of left and right brain. It was too much, this kind of reductionism, coming as it did from such a passionate man. I remember phoning him and giving him hell.

The remainder of *Ironwood 15* was devoted to H. R. Hays's translations of César Vallejo, which I had read at the time of our first issue. Somehow, I was under the impression that all or most of the poems were from Vallejo's *Los Heraldos Negros*. Since only this book of Vallejo's had never been wholly translated into English, it was something of a coup for us to print it. Alas, I was mistaken, the victim of wishful thinking. Hays' versions were a *Selected* Vallejo. I agreed to pay him ten dollars a page, but for some reason he would not send me his originals. Perhaps the Spanish texts came from smaller, limited editions as they were first published. Some of my favorite Vallejo poems were James Wright's translations from *Los Heraldos*. When I realized so few were from the first book, I offered Hays twice what I was paying for the others. He mailed me six more. Not only were there several egregious mistakes, Hays failed to charge his language with emotion and meaning. I returned most of these. When I raised the question of what I called Vallejo's Catholic poems, Hays admitted to being an unbeliever from the age of twelve and remarked that he had never seen much in this first book, the very book Robert Bly had called "the greatest single collection of poems I have ever read."

When I began getting various Spanish texts of Vallejo from the university library, I saw after awhile that a number did not have the initial inverted question mark conventional in Spanish for lines that ended in a question mark. The same went for lines ending in an exclamation mark. After going through a number of these texts, it seemed to me that the final book or two certainly included the conventional punctuation. I wound up checking a number of bilingual texts and stayed pretty close to them. I also noticed several poems with three- or four-line sections of the English missing and got Hays to restore or complete these. He seemed to regard these experiences matter-of-factly. I was glad I had gone to such trouble checking these matters. I was glad, too, that James Wright's two-page letter saying he could not write on Hays had all the immediacy and most of the affirmative content we could have hoped for in a brief essay. By now, Hays was in his late seventies and there was a good chance he would not live more than another year or two. Because he had written that Vallejo's was not a happy marriage, the widowed Juliette Vallejo had not allowed him to publish a book of his translations. If she was not already dead by now, Hays might be, I reasoned, by the time anybody got around to telling her. Within a year of our issue, a small press on Long Island printed Hays's translations as a book. His death followed soon after.

Delighted by the special section devoted to her, Linda Gregg was even more pleased to be in the company of Vallejo. Indeed, the depth of her gratitude was nearly equal to George Oppen's. From the beginning, she had a special feeling for the way we placed her poems on the page, a sense that each poem had been cared for. One reason Linda was grateful was that the issue led to a book with Greywolf Press and a second with Random House.

She was afraid certain technical innovations she had introduced would become the property of better-known writers without being recognized as hers. According to one friend, this had already occurred in at least one case. He seemed to think, however, that some of these departures had originated with Jack Gilbert even if they were picked up from Linda's work. Most likely they were the property of both poets, developed in common. One such device was the sentence fragment, usually lacking a subject or verb. There could be two or three in a single line of poetry. One function of this device was to enable the poet to slow or speed up her lines. Another was that it helped lower the tone by establishing a kind of intimacy within poems written in a high style. Linda's writing was often done at night. It was easier for her to concentrate then. At this time, she rarely revised poems, at least in a conventional manner, preferring to start the poem all over again from the beginning.

That spring, Linda come to Tucson and stayed in Tess Gallahger's house, mainly while Tess and Ray were away. In fact, she taught a couple of Tess's classes during that period, impressing the students with her abilities. Linda was striking in every way. Slender and graceful, she had a head of thick, luxuriant hair which she brushed with the kind of comb used on horses. One friend later described her hair as red and white gold. Although at times Linda seemed like the perfect ingenue, within a minute or two of entering our living room, she was directing a series of incisive questions to Mary and me. Much of the time she spent sitting cross-legged on the floor, often letting her head hang downward so her long hair fell in front of her, a thick curtain she would part now and then to look up at us, like a serious child playing peekaboo.

Linda lived quite inexpensively, taking the bus on her way to and from Tucson, eating little, working here and there at odd jobs. So conscious of price was she that she felt we were overcharging, selling the special issue for $2.50. For several years, she had lived with Jack Gilbert on Greek islands where you could rent a house with a well for $10 a month. This kind of stripped-down living had certainly sharpened her perceptions.

One day, Linda and I drove 70 miles south of Tucson to the Canelo Hills Sanctuary. It was one of the last natural swamps or *cienegas* in the state, with abundant plant and animal life in its tall grasses, trickling stream and stands of cottonwood, a place for the eye and ear. Your hearing grew sharper. You noticed things in their separateness. And we remained silent, together in our separateness. The cottonwoods seemed to ingest the stone directly under them by way of their roots. Certainly, much of the lower bark had the hardened edges of granite; the color, too, not the softer corklike tan characteristic of these trees.

On our way home, when we had left the area of cattle ranches and mountains, I remember asking Linda which poets she liked. She mentioned Shakespeare. "I was referring to contemporary poets," I told her. "Jack Gilbert". When I pressed her further, mentioning George Oppen, she said she belonged to the world of Shakespeare—not the world of George Oppen. Here I should point out that Linda often expressed deep reverence and affection for George Oppen, and for Mary Oppen, as role models.

In April, Bob Nevins, an architect who had recently moved to Tucson, invited us to a birthday party for Robert Penn Warren who was to give the final reading of the university's poetry series. It was Warren's 75th birthday. Nevins had designed a summer home for the Warrens in Vermont and it was Warren, writing me in connection with our James Wright issue, who suggested we look him up. The party was only a few blocks away so we were able to walk there without much trouble. For all his age, Warren was vigorous. He had been steadily writing poems for several years now, poems that continued to draw a favorable response. A MacArthur award had enabled him to discontinue writing novels and concentrate on poetry. We talked about James Wright, who was ill with cancer. It was clear, there was a good deal of respect and admiration for him on Warren's part. Mary and I each had a chance to talk to Warren's wife, Eleanor Clark, a renowned writer with at least one National Book Award to her name. She was immensely attractive, gentle and sensitive. She had suffered for some years from a rare form of macular degeneration that distorted her seeing by affecting her peripheral vision. After an hour or so, our host called us to order and announced that there would be a reading of ten poems, written by as many poets to honor Warren on this birthday. The poems were almost all by contemporaries or near-contemporaries. At this juncture, I can only recall some of the names: Richard Wilbur, Richard Eberhart, Howard Nemerov and William Meredith. A short while later, when we had eaten our way through most of a buffet supper, there was a noise and I saw Mrs. Warren falling to the floor. The moment was immediately charged with danger. Making her way rapidly to the spot, Mary suggested that Nancy Murphy, a nurse friend of ours who lived nearby, be called. Quickly agreed to, it was just as quickly done. Nancy must have arrived within five minutes and a doctor not too long after. Given Mrs. Warren's age, there was no telling from my distance how things would turn out but she recovered completely within a day or two.

That summer, we returned to the house in Woodacre, a habit we hoped never to break as long as *Ironwood* lasted. One of the first things I did was head for Berkeley to see if I could find *Views Of Jeopardy*, Jack Gilbert's Yale Younger Poet volume. The book was 17 years old and the only copy was autographed and cost $7.50. When Peter Howard, owner of Serendipity Books, brought the book and gave the charges, I told him I'd take it. I heard him say, "Nobody could ever get *me* to pay seven-fifty for Jack Gilbert's autograph!" Within ten minutes, waiting in the street for Mary to bring the car, another voice exclaimed: "Ah! Another Jack Gilbert fan!" It was Julia Vinograd, a famous Berkeley street poet. She wanted Gilbert's address, which I didn't have. He had only just returned from Europe. Mary soon got in contact with Linda's mother, Frances Gregg, who kept in touch with Jack. She lived in Forest Knolls, four miles up the road and wasted no time inviting us for lunch. Linda's father had been an architect and the spacious house he designed for the family sat modestly on a wooded hillside. Deer abounded. Later, Linda's father had started an integrated summer camp where the four Gregg girls began as campers and eventually helped run things. The counselors included a number of left-wing activists and assorted free spirits.

Frances talked a good deal about Jack Gilbert and promised we would get to meet him soon. The Jack Gilbert we met seemed a whole lot older than the boyishly fierce young man who looks out from the back cover of *Views Of Jeopardy*. After my berating him over his Linda Gregg piece, Jack had expected me to be much fiercer and was relieved. He saw himself as middle-aged and felt that not enough attention had been paid to the poetry of middle age. Age had mellowed him and I found myself liking the result. Occasionally, though, he seemed intent on getting the moral drop. Yet he could disarm you, reminiscing about his mother, for example, who came from the northern tier of border states.

Sometime that summer, Jack took a bus from the city for the day with two full manuscripts. He read my chapbook, *Celebrations*, while I slowly leafed the manuscripts he had brought. Before I was finished, I had chosen six of his poems for our next issue. Though Jack seemed to like my book, knowing his high standards, I had to allow for politeness. He had two criticisms. One small one took me a year or two to remedy; the other, more general, was that I sometimes used images mainly for decoration. I was grateful to him for pointing this out. One question that obsessed Jack was which poets were putting pressure on the others. Pressure was a central concept for him, a method for getting the best out of everyone. Living as he had, in relative poverty and solitude, he obviously shared some of Bly's convictions about the importance of solitude to a writer. He believed in rigorous standards; even the best poets needed prodding now and then. During his tenure as poetry editor of *Genesis West,* Jack had turned down submissions from most of the better-known poets he had solicited work from. Having done something like this myself, I knew the feeling. Possibly the manner of his rejection notes may have earned him more than his share of enemies. I can't say for sure. The *Genesis* fiction editor, Gordon Lish, later became *Esquire's* fiction editor. In the early seventies, he twice featured large groups of Jack's poems in a special section of *Esquire* , even referring to Gilbert as the greatest poet to write in English since T. S. Eliot. True or not, this was enough to multiply any poet's enemies.

* * *

When it came time to print several new books, Mary and I had some unresolved difficulties with our printer, Stan Fabe, so we got in touch with Lanny Rosenbaum, his former assistant, who agreed readily to help us. For Frank Stanford's *Crib Death*, Lanny suggested Arizona Lithographers. Rather than the usual 500, we had 750 printed (the book is about sold out). Though the cost was 15% lower, printing and binding left something to be desired. For Tom Crawford's *I want to say Listen*, I turned to Isbell Printing. They had a reputation for being good and expensive but with the chapbook half as long and page-size smaller, the cost was bearable. For Burkard's *None, River,* I was on the verge of closing a deal with Isbell when Shandling phoned in a lower bid, significantly lower. I accepted promptly and did not regret my decision. The Stanford and Burkard books ran over 50 pages, Crawford's a mere 26 with the print run on Burkard and Crawford the usual 500. Well before he died, Frank had chosen *Crib Death* as his title. The other titles were similarly chosen. A Hazel Archer photograph of a Carolina cemetery was used for the cover of Stanford's book; a close friend of Michael Burkard designed and pasted up his three-color cover. A photograph of a flatbed semi with a huge redwood log and a man standing inside with his arms spread formed the basis of Crawford's cover.

Aside from each one's singular gift, their differences were what made me include Frank Stanford, Michael Burkard and Tom Crawford in our series. What they had in common was a distinct voice and character, together with a high level of craftsmanship. Michael Burkard had had at least one collection from L'Epervier and was expecting another. We had already printed him several times: poems filled with a dark, brooding intensity. Certain words appear in the poems, are turned over and begin to reveal unexpected properties, in themselves and in reality. Soon, the page is alive with subtle but real relationships, between word and word, word and line, line and. . . . Ashbery and Creeley had both influenced Burkard, and eventually came to praise his work in public. Duncan was another influence. About this time APR became interested. Given the number of poems Michael wrote, he was able to fill those large sections that magazine made available to at least one poet every issue. At some point, a significant number of the poems in Michael's vast backlog would reveal their merits or be revised and so become available.

Of the poems in Stanford's *Crib Death* many had achieved a new intensity. Here love and death circled each other, with death the ultimate victor. In some of the most wrenching, the real world of the poet would literally shove aside the metaphors in the last stanza and declare itself. No wonder I was afraid that someone had died when I first read the poems that became the foundation of this book! Here is one:

A MILK TRUCK RUNNING INTO A CRAZY MAID
AT THE CORNER OF GETWELL AND PARK

They pull a coat over an old woman's eyes.
They ask one another who the old woman was.
No one knows but she worked everyday
And was carrying a sack
Of newspapers and a carton of eggs.
So they say what happened
And someone says she got up
Off the bench and shouted,
When a cow drinks water we get milk
When a snake drinks water we get bit.
She lifted her white dress
And waded out into the intersection
Like it was a river.
They lick their thumbs, write down what is told.
The other maids are getting off work
Standing around wondering what got into her.
The cats from Memphis State are sitting on the bench
Talking about the new Ornette Coleman album
Waiting for the bus,
And the servants of the people are pulling out of parking lots
And into their driveways,
A beer in their lap
Smoke from a dead cigar in their eyes

And desire and desire and desire
Like a long way to go in a bad war,
So they eat a big supper tell everyone what to do
Send the children to bed early have words with their wife.
They set the clock and lie back in the sheets.
They think of toes being slit
And blood that can be heard like a bad tap.
They draw their coats over an old woman's eyes
And think about standing in a warm pool
A white sheet wrapped around them
An old woman holding them
Taking them down into water.

Though not one of my favorite poets, Tom Crawford was an authentic voice, a craftsman whose work needed honoring. He stood in direct relation to the Williams tradition of finding the music in ordinary American speech. I valued his poems for their wholehearted celebration of life and the natural world. I had printed Tom enough to feel a connection, so I went ahead with an earlier commitment to print his first collection.

Apart from the climate, one thing that made us happy to be in Marin again was the chance to see George and Mary Oppen. They would come for lunch and bring along Chinese potstickers, a warm, out-sized hors-d'oeuvre which was often delicious. Other times, they would bring some fancy chocolate dessert along with fruit, or a salad. Mary Oppen would disappear into the kitchen with Mary Cuddihy while George and I took the easy way out and gazed at the fruit trees from a corner of the deck. Often, George would tell a favorite story, one I was likely to have heard before. His Alzheimer's was already creeping up on him but the story would probably have been retold anyway. These stories had a fairly central meaning for George. One such story occurred during the Oppens' exile in Mexico City. A group of their friends had gathered for a quiet celebration in one of the wealthier homes. As George described it, the guests were almost all Jewish, old leftists for the most part, some even survivors of the death camps. All were comfortably off or well-to-do. George remembers mentioning the camps and such things to someone, an older lady, who responded: "Oh, but we were so happy!" Although I never asked him, I suspect the happiness referred to had to do with being unmistakably and unequivocally on the right side and suffering for it. But this is only a guess.

In the last year, the Oppens had bought a VW Rabbit. Twice that summer, they invited us to a picnic at Ft. Funston, a former Army base a few miles south of San Francisco. On both occasions, the Rakosis were present. Carl Rakosi was tall and genial, a kind of beaming presence who dressed with quiet elegance. At least four or five years older than George, he looked that much younger, with a great sense of humor. Rakosi had worked most of his life as a professional psychologist and social worker but had taught a number of years at the University of Minnesota. Leah Rakosi was heavyset, jovial, with a sense of humor that rivaled Carl's. They had one or two children, grown and gone. With Zukofsky and Reznikoff now deceased, they were the last of the original Objectivists.

The Oppens had mentioned our watching the hang gliders afterward. We were beginning to sample the salad and pass around sandwiches and a delicious paté Leah had brought when an unfamiliar voice asked those at the table if he could have some. There was a winged man 25 feet above us, casually treading air. We joked about it but it had really given Mary Cuddihy and me quite a jolt to see him up there, after hearing the voice. After the picnic, we strolled over to the long ramp of spaced and treated lumber which led up to the observation platform. The platform had been donated by the hang-gliding fraternity to accommodate those who wished to watch. As we mounted the wooden ramp, rungs vibrating under my chair, we could see four or five young men and women suiting up alongside their aluminum and plastic. Above, it was much colder and I was grateful for my extra scarves and sweaters with the wind ripping about us. Looking out toward the ocean, I could see two or three men in hang gliders going past, more or less parallel to the beach with occasional sorties seaward. The fliers lay with torsos in light-weight slings, hands on the control bar which they could easily manipulate to move left or right, up or down. All important was the air itself. Without sufficient, relatively stable wind currents, hang gliding becomes problematic at best. Too strong a current or set of currents can be equally dangerous.

The previous winter, Mary Oppen had sent me a color photograph of a surfer torn from a magazine which she had carefully pasted on a piece of writing paper. Knowing all the changes I had been forced to make, I believe she meant the picture as a statement on how one needs to live: that the only thing that does not change is change itself and that one survives by paying attention to such changes and making the necessary adjustments. Reading the *Seascape* poems and most of George Oppen's later work, you get a sense of this endless change. Even the new thoughts and sentences beginning in the middle of lines are an indication of this. In a new era, the old ways will not always do.

*   *   *

In the Fall of 1979, I had been one of three judges for the Arizona State Poetry and Prose Fellowships; the poetry fellowship went to Daniel Webb, whose candidacy I had pushed. Alberto Ríos, winner of last year's fellowship, was a close runner-up. Reading his poems for the contest allowed me to get to know his work. With the contest over, I got in touch with Ríos and soon learned that some of my favorite poems from the contest were unencumbered. He sent me those, along with others. I lost no time in taking four for *#16*, including "Madre Sofia", which wound up in two or three anthologies, including the Norton Anthology of American Literature. The others were almost as good. With Alberto only a couple of hours distant from Tucson, it was to become a close friendship.

Other people I sought work from were Joseph Stroud, Laura Jensen and Denis Johnson, each of whom came through with memorable poems. When you add Shirley Kaufman, William Bronk, Stephanie Hallgren, Kate Daniels, C. D. Wright, Gregory Orr, Robert Bly, Linda Gregg and Jorie Graham, (not to mention Jack Gilbert's six poems), the issue becomes our strongest since *Ironwood 9*. Our review section included a long, thoughtful review of Kinnell's *Mortal Acts, Mortal Words* by Hank Lazer. Also, Michael Burkard's impressions of Denis Johnson's *Inner Weather* and Lawrence Kearney's cautionary review of Tom Lux's *Sundays*. Joanna Bankier wrote a review/comparison of the Merwin and Matthews/Feeney translations of Jean Follain. Five years earlier, I had tried to have these same books reviewed. Finally, there was a brief appraisal of the Swedish poet Edith Sodergran whose pioneering lyrics ended with her death from tuberculosis at the age of 31.

* * *

Not long after returning to Woodacre, Mary and I drove to the city for some kind of international poetry celebration being held at the Palace of Fine Arts, a Bernard Maybeck building designed for a World's Fair early in the century. In San Francisco such festivals are often far less than advertised. We brought along some issues and a number of books and chapbooks, but our main reason for being there was to hear the poets. Isaac Bashevis Singer was there and there were rumors that Czeslaw Milosz might take part. I had read *Bells In Winter*, issued by Ecco Press during the last year, and been stunned by the immensely moving "From the Rising of the Sun." With portions in at least three languages, it was a poem that spanned continents and centuries, its 36 pages part of an even longer work. Other poems in the collection were remarkable for their sense of history, their deeply religious character and frank use of reason. Here was a poet rarely met with in our century. Philip Levine had mentioned Milosz to me back in 1973, recommending *Post-War Polish Poetry,* an anthology he had edited and translated. I made a point of securing the book and lost no time reading it. It was an almost uniformly impressive collection. Milosz's poems did not stand out as they might have with a larger, less modest selection. Zbigniew Herbert was another outstanding poet included in that anthology. It was hard for me to believe that this Milosz was the same man I had read in the 50's. His best-selling *The Captive Mind* was a relentless analysis of what it is like for a non-Communist intellectual to live under Communism. Severe in its critique of intellectual life under a Communist regime, the book remained free of most of the cold war cant in vogue at the time.

I poked my head in at the auditorium door a few times until I saw Robert Hass reading poems. Between poems I slipped inside and made myself inconspicuous. Good as he already was, it was amazing how far Hass had come. There was a sense of profundity here. I noticed an older man with enormous, beetling eyebrows. Smiling tentatively at Hass, he nodded, then stood and advanced to the podium. He read a poem in what turned out to be Polish, then read the same poem in translation. This continued for some time, with Hass taking the microphone every so often and reading what I now realized were the poems of Czeslaw Milosz. So powerful was the impact his words made that had I been standing, I would have staggered. Later on, as we drove home, I couldn't get the reading out of my head, words and images repeating themselves as our headlights probed the dark roads. I had brought *Bells In Winter* with me from Tucson and fell to reading and rereading it as the summer wore on.

By the first week in August, we had to ready a grant proposal for the National Endowment for the Arts. This usually involved at least an outline of the issues we were planning. This time, I wanted our second issue of the grant period to be a special issue. With no assurance either poet would consent, my first idea was a joint issue, Milosz and Zbigniew Herbert. Herbert was popular in America where he had taught at more than one university. His poems, intellectual in a way different from Milosz's, were probably richer in imagery and therefore more accessible to Americans. When we had finished with our grant application, I decided the time was overdue to approach Milosz. I reached him at home and made an appointment for a few days later at his office in the Slavic Languages Department at Berkeley. When I arrived, his desk was something of a shambles. A sign announced A NEAT DESK IS THE SIGN OF AN INSANE MIND. Past 70, a stocky powerful figure, he wore a grey tweed sport coat. Deep-set eyes riveted you to his face. His forehead flexed, his eyebrows went on their own expeditions. I told him of our wanting to do a special issue. He wasn't sure, he answered, whether he was primarily a poet, having written at least two novels and several books of essays, including a long history of Polish literature. Right now, he was busy translating much of the Bible directly from Hebrew and Greek into Polish. I sensed that this last meant more to him than any of the others, though he spoke warmly of having translated Simone Weil into Polish. He gave me an issue of *World Literature Today* devoted to his work. Knowing Milosz had translated the French philosopher's pamphlet on the duty of resisting the Nazis, I mentioned having translated Jacques Maritain's *The Peasant of the Garonne*. At this, he seemed to relax a little. We talked for a time about the Catholic Church, and its various changes. He was not very fond, to say the least, of Hans Küng, the no longer young German theologian who had taken on the Pope on the Trinity, Papal Infallibility, and a host of other doctrines and prac-

tices long part of traditional Catholicism. He considered Küng a dema-
gogue and also something of a prima donna. When I left him, I felt that
I had his permission to go ahead. So far, the only other poet I had
mentioned the project to was Bob Hass, who favored it.

*   *   *

By Spring, 1979, it was time for *Ironwood* to do something substantial
to honor Frank Stanford, to preserve and extend his reputation as a
poet. No other magazine seemed about to make the effort, and our experience with Linda Gregg had shown that a reasonable amount of space,
say 40 to 50 pages, devoted to such an end could bear fruit. Here, I
adopted a modest approach: A number of one or two-page pieces, each
dealing with a single poem. That way, it would be easier to secure contributors, including those new to critical writing. Such an approach would
not tempt writers to exceed their capacity or make unjustified claims. It
was the course *Field* had employed when dealing with recognized "greats"
such as Wallace Stevens or William Carlos Williams and seemed tailor-
made for Frank Stanford. Several of the Stanford contributors such as
Bruce Weigl, Franz Wright and C. D. Wright, had been published in
Field, and David Young was the editor-in-chief. Faye Kicknosway, and
of course Linda Gregg, were *Ironwood* veterans by now, though each
had published widely.

Joan Williams, who as a young woman had been Faulkner's mistress,
contributed a memoir of living in the Stanford house with her young
sons during Frank's fourteenth summer. Having known Frank's mother
for sometime, she had sought out this opportunity in order to prepare
herself for writing her second novel. Frank had been a kind and consid-
erate older brother to her eldest son, taking him boating and fishing.
There are some interesting glimpses of Frank's adoptive father, much
older than his mother. By the time Joan Williams stayed with the family, the father was dead after a long illness suffered when Frank was still
on the verge of adolescence. For all its sparseness of detail, I found this
memoir extremely moving. Details such as her surprising the boys in a
pillow fight where Frank allows the younger, smaller one to go on swatting him. Or the tenderness with which Joan recalls Dorothy Stanford's
devotion to her son and to the dying man. One tantalizing detail, per-

haps unsolvable, is Frank's mother's statement that he seemed to have changed early in high school when he came home one afternoon and asked Dorothy Stanford whether he was adopted. She told him yes but told Joan that all along she had referred to him as a "chosen child." One wonders whether this euphemism, designed to soften the fact of orphanhood, may have actually concealed it or whether the adolescent had simply forgotten those long-ago exchanges.

While I was still involved with the Stanford feature, I had a long letter from Greg Orr, whom we had printed in #16. He wrote at length of little magazines, how each one had a natural life span. He singled out several prominent ones that had outlived their usefulness. *Ironwood*, he was convinced, had managed to stay fresh, keeping on top of what was happening in the world of poets and little magazines. Near the end, he mentioned a symposium on Chinese poetry and the American imagination which had taken place recently in New York City, sponsored by the Academy of American Poets. The symposium included Gary Snyder, Kenneth Rexroth, Robert Bly, Jonathan Chaves, Stanley Kunitz, Yip Wai-lim, David Lattimore, James Wright, W. S. Merwin, and Hans Frankel. He was almost finished transcribing the panel's exchanges and asked if I would like to print the results in *Ironwood*. I was interested certainly, but wanted to have a look first. He was not long in sending the text, along with some preliminary written statements, submitted by certain participants, some of whom could not take part in the symposium. After a week I let Orr know I wanted to do the symposium. Then I phoned Jonathan Chaves to sound him out on translations. One of the first Americans to make a life's work of translating Ming Dynasty poetry, Chaves had already been nominated for a National Book Award for *Pilgrim in the Clouds*, a book of Ming translations. He sent me generous selections of three Ming poets: Hsu Wei, Li K'ai-hsien and Chu Yun'ming. The value of the symposium was that it did away with certain stereotyped views of Chinese poetry, showing how, while many had adhered to reading and translating Tang poetry alone, there were actually a number of different concepts of the poet's role that were useful to different individuals and generations of American translator-poets. In addition to the poet as hermit or the poet as Confucian sage, there was Ezra Pound's notion of the poet as something like a philosopher-king. Perhaps this last emanated from the more exalted spheres of what was

116

still a Confucian bureaucracy. The discussion also centered around certain aspects of Chinese poetry which various participants found valuable, such as the apparent space around words which enabled many to enter the poem, the intimate tone which made it easier for the poem to convince and move the reader and the modesty which disarmed many. David Lattimore contributed a translation of a Tu Fu poem of 100 lines, a poem dealing with a bridge swept away in a storm. Among other things, the poem was an allegory of the state in a period of turmoil. As his footnote pointed out, this was the kind of unwelcome warning that got Tu Fu exiled.

Apart from this feature and the Stanford section, at least 26 poets had poems in the issue. Outstanding were five by Robert Hass, four of them prose poems, which began the issue, something of a departure for him. For more than three years, I had pleaded with Hass for poems and was delighted when they turned up a few weeks before our deadline. Finally, there was an extraordinary poem by Bill Knott, "The Closet", an orphan's poem to a mother never known. Here is a small part of what Mary Carr wrote concerning it:

. . . Knott begins by writing a line a child would speak. He then lets the diction shift to carry us to the cruelty of adult knowledge. In these opening lines, he never leaves the confines of the closet. The world's sheer size overwhelms the child as the evil trinity of coathangers begin the transfigurations that characterize the poem. These rapid changes continue to foil the poem's speaker, to overpower him. So the response to death is gradually spoon fed, slowly learned. Despite the ugly lesson, the child continues to watch wide-eyed for a long time. It's this vigilance in the face of danger that gives the poem its poignancy.

Not long enough after the hospital happened
I find her closet lying empty and stop my play
And go in and crane up at three blackwire hangers
Which quiver, airy, released. They appear to enjoy

Their new distance, cognizance born of the absence
Of everything else. The closet has been cleaned out

Full-flush as surgeries where the hangers could be
Amiable scalpels though they just as well would be

Themselves, in basements, glovelessly scraping uteri
But, here, pure, transfigured heavenward, they're
Birds, whose wingspans expand by excluding me. Their
Range is enlarged by loss. They'd leave buzzards

Breathless——and the hatshelf is even higher!——
As the sky over a prairie, an undotted desert where
Nothing can swoop sudden, occur in secret. I've fled
At ambush, tag, age: 6, must I face this, can

I have my hide-and-seek hole back now please, the
Clothes, the thicket of shoes, where is it? Only
The hangers are at home here. Come heir to this
Rare element, fluent, their skeletal grace sings

Of the ease with which they let go the dress, slip,
Housecoat or blouse, so absolving. Free, they fly
Forte, angular augurs leapt ahead from some geometric
God who soars stripped(of flesh, it is said): catnip

To a brat placated with model-airplane-kits kids
My size lack hand-skill for so the glue spills, smears
Become second fingernails where——as in frost-glass
Door——a nose must peer. But the closet has no window

Accessible as that. I have to shut my eyes, shrink
Within to grasp its view. Falling asleep I'll dream
Mother spilled and cold, unpillowed, the operating-
Table cracked to goad delivery: its stirrups slack,

The forceps closed: I'll watch a team of obstetrical
Personnel kneel proud, congratulatory, cooing
And oohing and hold the dead infant up to the dead
Woman's face as if for approval, the prompted

Beholding, tears, a zoomshotkiss. White-masked
Doctors and nurses patting each other on the back,
Which is how in the Old West a hangman, if
He was good, could gauge the heft of his intended . . .

Awake, the hangers are sharper, knife-and-slice, I jump
Gropelessly to catch them to twist them clear,
Mis-shape them whole, sail them across the small air
Space of the closet. I shall find room enough here

By excluding myself: by excluding myself, I'll grow.

"The Closet" was one of twelve poems chosen for the first edition of
the *Random Review* and later awarded a Pushcart Prize. Altogether,
Ironwood 17 may have been our most attractive, even our best all-around
issue.

*   *   *

During the summer of '80, we saw the Oppens several times. George
was beginning to suffer the effects of Alzheimer's, though his stoic manner made it difficult to notice. Although he remained skeptical of political poetry, George made clear that there were times one simply had to
write this kind of poem, whether or not it achieved any lasting effect.
Discussing poetry by prisoners and conscious feminists, he pointed out
the importance of our "getting the news" from these hitherto silent or
marginal groups. Since George was such a severe and exacting judge of
standards anyway, his caveat regarding political poetry isn't as extreme
as it sounds. For example, when Mary and he were rereading the poetry
of Yeats, she recalled how they had found only three poems they felt
still deserved to be considered great. If George really liked a poet, it
could mean that he liked one poem with all his heart and soul; often, it
would be two or three lines that really captivated him. Here, Blake was
the exception. Blake and Rilke. George read every translation of Rilke
that came to his attention with avidity and interest, but never found one
that did complete justice to the original.

Celebrations, my first chapbook, had just been published when Jim
Hartz asked me to read at Intersection with C. D. Wright and another
poet. When we reached the small auditorium, George and Mary were
already there, although there was half an hour before the reading. To
shorten the anxiety of waiting, I elected to go first. George accompanied
me to the area behind the curtain that separated reader from audience.
Even though I had more than a few friends in the audience, his quiet
presence was reassuring. At the conclusion, George and Mary waited in

line to buy my book before I had a chance to give it to them. The evening turned out easier and more gratifying than I had reason to expect. For one thing, Jim Hartz likened my poetry to Oppen's; for another, he singled out *Ironwood*'s freshness and versatility for favorable comment. His remarks encouraged me to persist in what had become a conscious goal.

The issue of *World Literature Today* devoted to Milosz proved absorbing. Almost all who contributed were Polish speakers, some former students of Milosz. The magazine had moved from the University of Minnesota when Ivar Ivask, the editor, moved to the University of Oklahoma. Then Oklahoma established the Neustadt Prize for literature, a $10,000 award which Milosz won in 1978. Previous winners had included René Char, Gabriel Garcia Marquez and Odyseas Elytis. Zbigniew Herbert had previously nominated Milosz for the same award but his statement had never been printed. I wrote to Ivask and secured Herbert's address along with *WLT*'s permission to print the statement. Their reply hinted that Milosz might win that year's Nobel Prize for Literature. Sure enough, a week later, he was awarded the Nobel prize for 1980.

One of those I had first asked to write on Milosz was Mark Rudman, a poet who had written brilliantly on Tranströmer and was deeply interested in the fate of Eastern Europe and its literature. At Milosz's suggestion, I got in touch with Lillian Vallee at the University of Wisconsin, seeking her help in translating a couple of essays from the Polish, plus guidance in selecting passages from *The Land of Ulro*, Milosz's philosophical chef d'oeuvre. She generously offered to outline each of *Ulro*'s many chapters. Doing my best to digest her outline, I got in touch with Louis Iribarne, who had translated *The Issa Valley* and was about to begin *Ulro*. A high school classmate of Robert Hass, Iribarne taught at the University of Toronto and was involved in several translation projects. Although I would have to nudge him periodically, he proved easy to work with, and a first-class translator. A successful poet and editor, Patricia Hampl had recently published an imaginative autobiography, *A Romantic Education*. Given her closeness to an East European heritage, and her experience writing a different kind of autobiography, Hampl was a natural choice to write on Milosz's *Native Realm*. Concentrating chiefly on the long "From the Rising of the Sun", John Peck offered to write on the eschatological aspects of Milosz's poetry and thought. There were other writers, such as Hank Lazer, who wished to take part, but the most I could do was read what they had written without any promises. I wanted a full issue but it could be useful to have further essays in reserve in case others dropped out. As it later happened, those who did drop out were all writers who had been asked or had offered to write after Milosz was awarded the Nobel Prize.

The Polish writer Milosz most wanted me to include was Stanislaw Baranczak. Originally, I had rejected Baranczak's essay on *The Land of Ulro* because of its melodramatic, cold war opening. Had the book been *The Captive Mind*, such a beginning might have been appropriate. During the summer, Robert Hass and Robert Pinsky pressed me to reconsider. I agreed, provided Baranczak lower the tone of his opening. When the essay was resubmitted, full of the younger poet's energy and convictions but minus the earlier beginning, I agreed to print it. Jean Valentine proposed a series of notes on Milosz, stressing those qualities that survive translation. For all its modesty, her own writing proved superb in its subtly-restrained evocations. A number of the other essays made clear how aware the authors were of the real and potential limitations imposed by the transition to English. Long ago, Robert Hass had agreed to write something for the issue but, more importantly, was already working with his friend Robert Pinsky on translations from Milosz. When I reached California, they were totally absorbed in the project. Their task was complicated by Milosz's deep-seated need to retain certain idiosyncracies of Polish syntax, even when these threatened to diminish the dignity and force of the English translation. For him, not to do so must have seemed like the worst kind of betrayal, ample warranty for the age-old proverb, *translation is treason*. Another complication was the presence of Lillian Vallee, the co-translator with Milosz of *Bells In Winter*. One of Milosz's best graduate students, Vallee was intelligent, hard working and passionately devoted to Milosz's work. Moreover, her knowledge of Polish far exceeded that of Hass or Pinsky. New to Berkeley, Robert Pinsky had been asked to read at Cody's sometime in June. At some point that night, he dedicated his reading to two or three of the "great translators", including at least one who had translated Milosz and was in the audience. He had no way of knowing that Lillian Vallee, whom he had not included, was there in the room, having just returned to Berkeley. When word reached Milosz, he is said to have been furious.

Sometime in July, I got to look at several of the longer poems Hass and Pinsky were translating. Renata Gorczynski had worked carefully with them on the literal Polish, not merely the words, but the location of stresses and rhymed syllables. With "The World", for example, she would read the Polish over and over, enabling her auditors to hear the musical effects. There were recurrent struggles with Milosz over "The World", a sequence of twenty short poems written in 1943, that many critics consider his masterpiece. He was afraid his two brilliant translators were being too sophisticated in their versions. When Hass finally gave me a tentative version of the poem, we showed it to a ten-year-old, Michaela Sloan, daughter of two of our closest friends. Enchanted, she would ask each week if it was going to be printed. Familiar with the traditional forms, Hass and Pinsky were fearful of slipping into doggerel. Even the original Polish did not follow a simple a b a b or a b b a, but varied often from one poem to another, with the rhyme falling sometimes on the penultimate syllable. The translators settled, finally, on splitting up the poems in the sequence, Hass taking the simpler, more literal options and Pinsky the ones that permitted more liberties. Those that remained were translated by both men together. It should be noted, finally, that Lillian Vallee made her own literal translation of "The World" available to the two translators.

Another question that absorbed us as we approached our deadline was Milosz's relationship to Eros. Robert Hass considered the erotic an important component of Milosz's sensibility as a poet and this view got considerable support from a section we were printing from *The Land Of Ulro*. When I asked Lillian Vallee to translate Aleksander Fiut's essay on Eros in Milosz, she insisted that Eros played only a minor role in Milosz's work. Furthermore, she considered the Polish language ill-equipped to deal with the erotic. This, along with her need to finish her dissertation, made it obvious: I had to get someone else. Joanna Bankier, a contributor to our Tranströmer issue who knew Polish in addition to her Swedish and French, was my choice but by the time I reached her, Milosz seemed uninterested. Time was getting short so I wound up taking an already-translated essay by Marek Zaleski on the critical response to Milosz in Poland. This gave us a third Polish contributor in addition to Milosz himself. Bankier agreed to translate an Aleksander Fiut interview with Milosz which had taken place the previous year in Paris but this could not be ready until our next issue.

By now, Milosz had come back from Poland where, unbelievably, he had returned to a hero's welcome. With his wife in extremely poor health, he had gone with his two sons, already in their twenties or thirties. In the wake of his Nobel Prize and Solidarity's rise to power, the State Publishing House had finally printed a book of his poems. The twenty thousand copies sold within 24 hours, many waiting in line overnight to obtain their own copies. Another printing of two hundred thousand was ordered. Not long after his return, Milosz and his wife agreed to come for lunch in Woodacre. It turned out to be a hot day, hotter as the hours went by. When they arrived, Milosz was radiant, his wife winsome and friendly. Mary had thoughtfully prepared a mostly cold lunch with cups of minestrone for openers. At some point during lunch, Milosz brought up the death camps. For a man with his share of survivor guilt, the visit to Poland may have acutely revived this part of his past, for all the surface euphoria that marked his visit and its aftermath. He devoured the meal with great relish, imbibing freely of the wine. Mrs. Milosz was relatively quiet, though she responded readily to those who addressed her. After lunch, Milosz unwrapped large folders bulging with black and white photographs of the trip to Poland, many of them enormous, the shapes wider than we are used to in the States. It was an exciting occasion for Mary's son Bradley who, at 21, was visiting from the East and had taken up photography as a serious hobby. Milosz was especially kind to him and Bradley himself moved by the man and the photographs. There were several of Milosz with Lech Walesa, holding their clasped hands aloft in salute as thousands of workers cheered; several, too, of the dockyards in Gdansk with the broad hull of a large ship close behind. Later, when I brought up the subject of covers, Milosz wanted us to use one of these whereas I feared it would overpoliticize our issue. Besides, the photograph was nearly square and would have had to be reduced to where it lost most of its intimidating bulk. Other pictures showed Milosz standing with dozens of individual writers, political figures and other celebrities. In one, he is talking to the head of Poland's Communist Party. When I asked him if the man had treated him with civility, he looked confused so I repeated the question. This time he

answered: "I gave him a copy of *The Captive Mind.*" There was a lovely
picture of Milosz with his two grown sons standing at the grave of his
mother, their beautiful umbrellas opened into the rain. Milosz would
not hear of my using this in any form whatever. One great wide photograph had Milosz with his back to the Bug River and beyond, where
Poland's lost territories lay. Cropping much of the right half to avoid
ending up with a small square, I decided to use this photograph for our
cover. Inside, we would reproduce the complete photograph on two
facing pages.

A week before, Robert Hass, free now, had phoned, asking what I
wanted him to write on. What I had in mind, I told him, was something
that could tie together Milosz's life and writings without neglecting the
evolution of his ideas: an essay at once explanatory, biographical and, in
some degree, critical. Hass agreed to go ahead. Indeed, he may have
had such a piece in mind all along, one which would enable him to
include books first published in Poland or Paris, along with later collections in English.

With August drawing to a close, Mary was beseeching me to stay an
extra week. So far, I had held out. One day, I had the young man helping me drive the two of us westward onto the Point Reyes peninsula.
From there, the road winds and rises through a number of large dairy
farms. In the summer, the grasses turn lion-colored. Often the peninsula is covered with fog, but this day there was sun everywhere. We
followed the road, determined to go as far as it led and at length found
ourselves at Drake's Beach, the spot where Sir Francis Drake is said to
have landed in the late sixteenth century. The ocean was calm, the beach
nearly deserted, gulls and other shore birds arriving and departing. I
found the whole scene with its simple, intense colors and fullness of sea
air, intoxicating. It felt so good just to be alive. All this work and study.
To live in the present, wasn't that what poetry was about? We stayed a
couple of hours before returning to the house, convinced it was not only
all right but important that we stay at least a week longer. Mary was
overwhelmed. In spite of our work load not disappearing, we made it
back to Drake's Beach during that same week. Bradley, still with us,
helped drag my wheelchair through the dunes and over the damper,
hard-packed sand to water's edge. The winds were freezing there but
exhilarating. I was glad we had brought along all kinds of scarves and

sweaters. The same week, we made another trip north to Bodega Bay and beyond. Here, we could look down sand cliffs to the enormous rocks where waves broke and shore birds perched. You could see north and south for miles. Surely, it was the right way to end the summer. The time had come for a final conference with Czeslaw Milosz. I made the appointment and drove over to Berkeley. The sign was gone now that had read: THIS SPACE RESERVED FOR CZESLAW MILOSZ. It had been one way for the University to honor its first professor of humanities to win a Nobel Prize. I had intended for a friend to photograph it and use it for the cover of our special issue. When I broached the subject as we began looking at photographs during his visit, Milosz had pronounced the sign obscene and declared that he had just had it removed from the premises. Now there was a more modest, indeed ambiguous sign: RESERVED FOR SLAVIC LANGUAGES. After we had chatted for a few minutes, Milosz brought up "The World." A week before, Robert Pinsky had let me know that Hass had talked Milosz into letting it be printed. His exact words: "You know Bob. He could talk the bark off a tree." Yet I suddenly found myself having to defend our (?) decision to print "The World." I rehearsed several reasons, among them the idea that, with the poem in print, poets as skilled with traditional forms as Richard Wilbur would want to try their hand at translating it, so that this translation need not be regarded as definitive. When I had finished, Milosz's only response was to accuse me of bias. Though I wanted to answer him in kind, it was hardly my place. The silence was excruciating. Finally, it dawned on me that he was not going to prevent me if he couldn't convince me. Exhausted, relieved, I left his office looking ahead.

While Bob Hass had yet to mail his essay, he had sent me two of the *Separate Notebook* poems, "The Mirrored Gallery" and "The Wormwood Star", one running near a dozen pages, the other ending on a seventh page. As for "The World," it would take anywhere from ten to twenty pages, depending whether each of its twenty short poems was given a page to itself. Although the translators, particularly Hass, had offered me all three, to print them all might invite some last-minute switch.

The *Separate Notebook* poems resembled great broad rivers which flow at different rates depending on tides, climate, other factors. A single long poem could vary from one-line stanzas to couplets to page-long sections of prose to stanzas of free verse, ending with a short rhymed lyric. While often distinguished, the prose in them need not be poetic, it could be as indigestible as a dead cow, the roof of a house, an old Ford chassis. Most were carried along at their different speeds by the river, making it more humanly interesting, freer, unpredictable. The poems, too, were obviously more inclusive than most of Milosz's, generous, with the tone changing from one section to another. Yet the tyric impulse survived and moved the whole.

Using only one of the *Separate Notebook* poems, I was in a much stronger position when I saw Milosz to claim the privilege of printing "The World". It was hard for me to believe that Daniel Halperin, editor of *Antaeus*, who had published the books of Hass and Milosz, could resist the chance to print at least one of these poems. As far as I know, none of the three appeared in *Antaeus*, difficult as that is to credit. I took "The Wormwood Star." As for "The Mirrored Gallery," I settled for a single poignant lyric from that long sequence and used it on our back cover:

from A SEPARATE NOTEBOOK: The Mirrored Gallery

You talked, but after your talking all the rest remains.
After your talking—poets, philosophers, contrivers of romances—
Everything else, all the rest deduced inside the flesh
Which lives and knows, not just what is permitted.

I am a woman held fast now in the great silence.
Not all creatures have your need for words.
Birds you killed, fish you tossed into your boat:
In what words will they find rest and in what Heaven?

You received gifts from me: they were accepted.
But you don't understand how to think about the dead.
The smell of winter apples, of hoarfrost, and of linen.
There are nothing but gifts on this poor, poor Earth.

translated by Robert Hass and Renata Gorczynski

Here, through the voice of a dead mistress, Milosz gives expression to the age-old complaint of traditional women, particularly those who live with writers and thinkers. More than that, the brief poem is a perfect example of his gift for elegy, probably the dominant mode in his work. When Robert Hass first suggested to me that Milosz was basically an elegist, it was too early; my own acquaintance with his poetry had not had time enough to deepen. Now I can perceive how deeply right Hass was. In the last six lines, the poet voices his own extraordinary need to preserve and immortalize those he has known here on earth along with the things he has experienced with them. This is preeminently true of the poor, servants, the tortured and betrayed. One is reminded of Rilke's description of what he is attempting in the *Elegies*: ". . . our task is to stamp this provisional, perishing earth into ourselves so deeply, so painfully and passionately, that its being rises again 'invisibly' in us." When the woman in the poem says "you don't understand how to think about the dead", and then goes on to speak of objects smelled, touched or felt on the skin, she is echoing Rilke, who asked us to keep "life open towards death." Rather than death as extinction he had in mind death imagined "as an altogether surpassing intensity." Like the woman, he wanted us to open ourselves to the world, to give over to the thing seen. For Milosz, a fortunate survivor troubled with guilt for what he may consider his undeserved luck, doesn't want an immortality that leaves anyone behind, or unjustly punished. In spite of his refusal of the "Catholic poet" title, he remains a good shepherd, one who goes to any length to rescue the one who has strayed furthest.

A few days remained of our stay in Marin. Though Hass had still not mailed or brought over his essay, he had given me a brief introduction to "The World," noting the difficulties, spelling out which poems had been translated by one poet or the other and which represented a collaboration. In it, he absolved Milosz of all responsibility should the translation fail and thanked Lillian Vallee for her advice and for providing a literal translation of "The World". All this and an explanation of the circumstances that gave birth to the poem. But when would the essay arrive? Each day he would promise to bring it on his way to or from the Napa Valley Poetry Conference, an event held at the end of summer. We were sitting around the dinner table, not wanting to believe it was our last evening. At 10 o'clock the phone rang: Bob asking

Mary if I was still up. He was just leaving Napa and could be there in an hour. Yes, I told Mary. Close to 11:00 P.M. he arrived with Alan Soldofsky. Grinning sheepishly, he withdrew the essay from his brief-case: 42 typewritten pages. We got out some wine and talked for awhile about Milosz, Phil Dow, poetry, Linda Gregg, one thing and another. At length, I withdrew to my rocking bed, rocking and reading, my left arm with its burden of pages trying desperately to remain flexed against gravity while I scanned the pages, one after one. It was, like most of Hass's major essays, a tour-de-force, managing to do everything I hoped it would. What set it apart from the others was an introductory section of about four pages. Here, the scene is a Dow Chemical peace demon-stration, and Hass himself part of "the raging army of an aroused middle class." It is a graphic portrayal of the mixture of despair and hope, res-olution and confusion, that marked the late Sixties in America. From there, he comes to his first reading of *The Captive Mind* and certain much-anthologized poems of Milosz, chiefly his war poems. Then he follows Milosz in his career and intellectual development, from his early association with the Catastrophists, always careful to include inserts with titles and dates between horizontal lines whenever called for in the text. Among other things, the essay discusses his break with the Communist-led government and the influence of Simone Weil.

According to Hass, Weil appears to have been the principal influence on the later Milosz. Rather than "buy the unity of opposites too cheaply" this student of Marx taught him that in thinking dialectically, one should make the contradictions as acute as possible. She gave Milosz permis-sion to dwell in contradiction, thus releasing, Hass is convinced, "Eros—in the form of dream, memory, landscape . . ." One effect: unlike American poets, Milosz is often unwilling to end his long poems by identifying poetry with nature or with consciousness. If his ending could be said to lack resolution, so does the world. That such poems brought one back to the world at a point of tension spoke well for their (post) modernity. Milosz was not persuaded that nature or consciousness or even poetry itself was good. He would prefer to suffer multiplicity.

Trying to capture some of the naiveté of the poem itself, Lillian Val-lee's essay on "The World" took the form initially of simple questions and answers. Leonard Nathan wrote on "Ars Poetica", a poem from *Bells In Winter* which had fascinated me since first reading it, dealing as it does with the demonic. Marisha Chamberlain's essay was a workmanlike analysis of the six poems written at the end of the war regarding the Holocaust, the Warsaw Uprising and related matters. Linda Gregg, who had taken a class on Gnosticism from Milosz, wrote briefly from the standpoint of a student. Mark Rudman's essay concentrated on "From the Rising of the Sun", probably the most admired Milosz poem in English at the time of his writing. His essay underlined Milosz's role as an exile and explored his stance as a poet of historical irony. Unlike Hass, Rudman played down the importance of the erotic as a component of Milosz's poetry, preferring to see Milosz as cerebral rather than intellectual like Mandelstam. Were he writing today, I suspect he would change his evaluation. He paid tribute to Milosz as a prose writer but felt his brand of rational or intellectual poetry tended to lose some of its quality as poetry in translation even if we could still get a sense of the quality of his mind, the range of his imagination, and the depth of his concerns, which came through best in the longer poems.

During the summer, there was talk of Eva Hoffman's writing a piece on Milosz for the *Sunday Times Magazine*, which would include all or part of at least one long sequence we were doing. With all the glamour surrounding major media, I was leery of this arrangement, afraid their using our material before we did could rob our issue of its freshness and surprise. Hass sent her a note enclosing six of the 20 short poems that made up "The World" and another six from two other *Separate Notebook* poems. He made it clear that she should clear any discussions with me before going ahead. I never heard from her. The piece appeared with none of the poems we were printing; what was used came from an earlier collection. Perhaps their length made our poems poor candidates for reprint, perhaps the *Times* was as loath to share double billing as we were. Someone broached the idea of having Herb Caen, a prominent San Francisco columnist, mention the issue. Once again, nothing seems to have come of it. Although I did not dismiss the idea, to tell the truth, neither I nor anyone else had much of an appetite for public relations. One development that came as a total surprise was the Cal-Berkeley Library's extension division ordering 50 copies at the retail price to be sent to libraries in Poland. Payment was immediate. For this special issue, we had printed 1500 copies, a procedure we decided to adopt from here on, with regular issues remaining at 1150 to 1200 copies. Unlike the vast majority of little magazines, our special issues drew shifting audiences, some of whom became and remained subscribers while others dropped away. I decided to have every other issue be a special issue, appearing if possible in November. From the start, the Milosz issue sold rapidly. One store in Cambridge, Massachusetts, Grolier's, actually sold one hundred copies. The day their issues reached them, our Midwest distributors, Bookslinger, doubled their order, and later went beyond that.

At least four poets who had agreed to write on Milosz withdrew or failed to submit their pieces. All had come aboard after he had been awarded the Nobel Prize. Whatever band-wagon psychology usually operates in such cases seems to have gone into reverse. I would have to plan for these special issues with two teams in mind: A first team of significant poets and/or specialists and a reserve group of possible substitutes with enough motivation to write without guarantee of publication. The maddening thing was how many "contributors" who failed to write had gotten in touch only after the deadline, or not at all, as if their contributions were strictly a private matter. From here on, I would write or telephone them at least once in the month before summer, and again, about a fortnight before our deadline. This way, I was prepared to switch contributors before things were irrevocably set. There were obviously the solid dependables who did everything right. Thank goodness for them.

*   *   *

Although *Ironwood 19* was our tenth anniversary issue, not much fuss or celebration was made over it, before or after. Anyone else would have used *#20* for the anniversary, it sounded so round and inviting. But we did not have time to reschedule our special issue for April, '82. Because we had lost a year somewhere during our first five issues, neither the issue nor the date came even close. For *#19*, I requested and was sent several poems each from Denis Johnson, Honor Johnson, Alberto Ríos, Joe Stroud, Susan North and Rolly Kent. Also, three superb poems came unsolicited from Jorie Graham and the same from Sharon Olds. Fine poems were no surprise from Cleopatra Mathis, Bill Mayer, Jean Val-

130

entine, John Peck, Elizabeth Libbey, Raymond Carver or Hugh Seidman. But Mark Rudman did surprise me with ten pages of "By Contraries."

Born in good measure from Mark's involvement as writer and reader with Milosz and the Milosz issue, "By Contraries" represented a departure for him. It did borrow certain formal and structural elements from Milosz's *Separate Notebook* poems—I remember his suggesting another Milosz issue at the time. Some of the prose passages in the long sequence evoked the New York of my childhood—huge holes at construction sites, an iron ball swinging to pulverize ancient brick walls. As a new poem, it invited both praise and criticism and, to me, the urge to make suggestions and work with Mark. He seemed open to this. For one thing, I hadn't taken the poem yet; for another, he was free to reject or refuse those suggestions. In fact, he accepted a number and probably rejected as many. In some cases, he wound up reworking and improving the passages in question. Difficult as I was to please, I had come to realize that I was often rooting for the poem, like a judge rooting for the defendant. To reach for the old cliché, I saw many poems the way the optimist is said to view the glass of milk: half full rather than half empty. It is hard to say whether, at bottom, this represented a need for control, or simply two facets of my own character struggling with one another over the fate of the poem. Certainly, the primary energy came from the poet. If I was any help at all, it would most likely be by helping him separate the precious metal from the slag which had obscured it. Even here, such improvements might rob the poem of a certain rude strength akin to Michelangelo's *Slaves*, where the bodies have not wholly emerged from the parent marble. Besides, poems are often happier when not divorced from their contexts. Several years later, when I saw Rudman's poem in its book version, it had undergone even more revision. Which struck me as about right.

There were other excellent long poems. Gustaf Sobin's "Irises", Karen Propp's "Talking", and Will Inman's polyphonic "Requiem". Two poems by Michael Palmer closed out the poetry. The issue included an interview with Milosz and Jonathan Chaves's essay responding to certain members of the Chinese Poetry panel quoted in *Ironwood 17*. The essay's real subject was the cultural colonialism of Western writers and intellectuals, including at least two panel members. The issue ended with timely reviews of Michael Palmer's *Notes On Echo Lake*, Alberto Ríos's *Whispering To Fool The Wind*, and Charles Wright's *The Southern Cross*. We had printed poetry by so many men and women. It is amazing how often a story is involved in these transactions: how many phone calls, letters, revisions, recommendations or long searches.

I have not mentioned David Fisher, whom Mary and I had gotten to know the previous summer. David had won a William Carlos Williams award for his second book of poems, *The Book of Madness*, poems of great power dealing with his insanity and time spent in mental institutions. A few years earlier, he had escaped from such an institution in Sonoma without being forced to return. The first time we saw David was when he came over to our house in Woodacre one Saturday afternoon. We offered him a beer, though he may have been carrying his own. Every ten or fifteen minutes, he would pop a couple of aspirin. He seemed quite agitated until the pills began to work. Perhaps it was simply the unfamiliarity wearing off which caused him to relax more. He had lots to say, much of it describing his present life, the children, the woman he was living with, with detours into his correspondence with poetry friends such as Hayden Carruth and Bill Meredith. He had quite a ribald sense of humor and would occasionally enjoy putting you on the hot seat only to smother you with apologies immediately after. My overall impression was one of great goodness and innocence along with high manic energy and much suffering. I think we fed him some kind of lunch. I was afraid the succession of beer and aspirin might plow him under but the reverse was true. He grew calmer. His interest in my poems became more intense after he had read my small chapbook. There was one experimental poem that he read aloud with genuine feeling and gusto. He was a first-class reader. When I asked him if he would be willing to read that at my own reading, scheduled some three weeks later at Cody's, he readily agreed. The night of the reading, I had him go last, afraid such an old pro might otherwise upstage me. Within a day or two of his visit, he was sending us letters, often several a week, decorated with funny drawings and large red hearts inscribed like lockets. Our problem was that we lacked the time and energy to devote to this one correspondent. He never complained, though the humor often had a bite to it, a way maybe of unloading both good and bad energy. We saw him a couple of times more that summer. Once, driving through

Golden Gate Park, I saw him grimly jogging along a cinder path. I felt like an eavesdropper. David had so much intelligence, wit and affection, but I would not want to carry his burdens, even with those gifts. We chose two of his poems for the Anniversary Issue.

It was time, we decided, to reproduce a painting for our cover, using the four-color process. In spite of the old adage, poets were starting to judge magazines by their covers. For several years now, I had become increasingly familiar with Jim Waid's paintings. A Waid drawing had graced the cover of *Ironwood 14* but acrylics and oils were a lot tougher to reproduce. One morning in December, I dropped in at Jim's studio. As always, the walls were thick with paintings, with dozens more stacked below. Jim's paintings were noticeably wider than they were tall. This was certainly true of those with a good deal of bright red or vermilion, the kind I hoped to use. I was hoping to find a canvas taller than it was wide, so the reproduction could occupy more of the cover. An abstract painter, Jim was quick to concede that certain details of his canvases occasionally suggested the real contours of plants or leaves. For years now, he had been using acrylics. Going from one wall to another of his tall, roomy studio as he replaced the canvases behind us, I found myself face to face suddenly with a crowded desert landscape. It was filled with representations of prickly pear, the upper half divided by the spiny verticals of ocotillo while a brownish sky glowed, pulsing. What came off the canvas was light, energy, compression. This was what I wanted. It was fine with Jim. He had not set out to do a figurative painting, it just happened. The thing was to make sure we had a slide. That day or the next, a friend of Jim's with experience in these things made transparencies, including the one we needed. When he phoned it was to tell us the film had turned out badly. Jim agreed to let Ray Manley whom our printer used for these jobs, do it, provided it was at Jim's house. And so it was, and was done properly. In a few days we had our slide and Jim's paintings were off to a show. Rather than use the white or ivory background favored by the art magazines, I tried for something faintly pinkish-yellow like the desert floor. It turned out perfectly. The cover was a success. Robert Hass even phoned to ask if the painting was for sale, but the price was beyond what he was then able to pay. Today, most of Jim's work has more than doubled in value since the Metropolitan Museum of Art purchased three of his earlier pieces.

Two poems from the issue, Cleopatra Mathis's "Fort Wall at Myti-
lene: Greece, 1923" and Jorie Graham's "Remembering Titian's Martyr-
dom of St. Lawrence" were awarded Pushcart Prizes for that year. Still,
I remained fond of a number of others as well, among them Susan North's
"Blue Horses":

BLUE HORSES

Already it's not going
by the book. The mare's
in trouble and I remember
more of your hands than today.
She's been waxed up since Monday,
the foal diving in her belly
like a hooked fish. I wish
I were just animal. I'd let you
slowly undress me and not worry
for order in the universe.
She's wearing a circle
in the field, pawing, sweating.
The great white and brown body's
a mountain. Labor
takes her down in its fist.
If she were less strong,
she could die more easily.
I won't think about your wife
or how long before you come again.
I would never color
inside the lines
or use the green
the nuns named grass.
My sky was yellowpurple,
unrepentant as a bruise.
Those blue horses kept me after school.
Even now it is the same. We take
the consequence of what we see,
owe the colors everything.
By evening the mare will be buried or nursing.
If you drive in, I will be feeding chickens

or stretching fence in the last light.
When we go to the kitchen,
I will turn to the sink,
the cold well water running
clear and hard across both arms.
You will come up behind me,
placing your right hand
on the counter, your left on my hip.
Whatever I pay for this is too little.

"Blue Horses" doesn't need analyzing, or any help from me. Still, it has many of the ingredients I like to find in poems we print. For one thing, it is a love poem and good love poems are rare in this half of the century. For another, instead of the lover being frontally addressed to the exclusion of everything else, the poet is doing her own work caring for an expectant mare "waxed up since Monday," and trying to ease a foal into the world. As her preposition so deftly announces, the poet is trying not to worry "for order in the universe." Her childhood, the lover's wife, feeding chickens or "stretching fence in the last light", all these help situate and ground her. How many of us let our real worlds carry our emotions into the poem? Not many. The bluntness of the last line proves it the poem of an adult, one who has paid the price and is willing to go on from there.

* * *

Early in September, 1981, Will Inman, Clint Colby, John Hudak and Jim Fitzgerald were at the Bisbee Festival when one of them broached the idea of a similar festival for Tucson. By November 8, they had called a meeting of the Tucson Poetry Festival Committee. Those they asked to join included Margaret Bret-Harte, Mary Blake and myself. We set about trying to prepare a poetry festival for at least a year ahead, trying to keep it clear of the university, among other groups, while making room for a diversity of ethnic talent, local poets in particular. Those first meetings we spent getting to know each other, with a good deal of idle speculation. By early February, we were organized, beginning to click. At this point, my job involved writing poets we wanted. While there was much wrangling, most of the time the list of those invited reflected my own leanings. Our first choice, Wendell Berry, could not be on hand because of ewes giving birth at his farm. To give ourselves enough time, we settled on the week-end of Friday March 25 1983. Gary Snyder agreed to come in Berry's place. Other readers were Alberto Ríos, Tess Gallagher, Diane Wakoski, David Ignatow, Leslie Silko, Susan North, Tony Hoagland, Rolly Kent and William Pitt Root. There was also a Papago dance group with Ofelia Cepeda. One task I was given was to meet Gary Snyder's plane and take him to the hotel where the poets were staying. It was a pleasure to see him again. Years ago, he had come to my house with Drum Hadley, a poet who lived a few blocks away and had since taken up ranching. I remember our discussing the bullfight, which Snyder saw as a metaphor for Spanish Catholicism and its hatred of the body. He had also some interesting things to say about Dom Aelred Graham, author of *Zen Catholicism*. Graham, a Benedictine monk who became prior and headmaster of my old boarding school, Portsmouth Priory, a year after I left, was touring Japan, trying to gain more first-hand experience of Japanese Buddhism, and monasticism. When Snyder first saw my hand-carved black walnut table, he had exclaimed: "There's only one man who can cut wood like that." Before he could name him, I had interjected: "Jim Sloan" (the maker). The man's name was Dave Lynn, a close friend and neighbor of Jim's in Canyon, a tiny community of free spirits in a small Redwood forest not 20 miles from Berkeley. For Snyder, Dave was a prototype of the scavenger, a builder who incorporates used materials in his projects such as part of the old Oakland pier, marble from a former courthouse, even a used 2600 gallon wine barrel which he converted into a bedroom for himself, thatching the outer walls with shingles. Snyder felt this was ecologically sound and beneficial. As we got into my ancient Caprice station wagon, I asked Snyder what he thought of gas guzzlers, explaining that my bad leg required this extra room. He seemed to feel that this old car made all kinds of sense for me.

*　　*　　*

Li-Young Lee

Bruce Andrews

William Bronk

Albert Ríos (Hal Martin Fogel)

Beverly Dahlen

Lucy Perillo

F. Howe (Ben E. Watkins)

Tess Gallagher (Pat Ellis)

Hilda Morley

Bruce Weigl (Dan Brod)

Michael Burkhard (Joe Mucha)

Tucson Poetry Festival, April, 1987, Carol Thigjen, Czeslaw Milosz, Michael Cuddihy, Mary Cuddihy, Bradley (Mary's son)

After working on the Milosz issue, I realized how easily *Ironwood* could get trapped into being identified with traditional rhyme, meter and other seemingly outmoded devices. What better corrective than for us to yield some magazine space and attention to the growing movement known as 'language' writing. After all, we had printed members of this group as far back as our second issue when we carried two poems of Bruce Andrews and, soon after, Lyn Hejinian. A year later, it was Leslie Scalapino, separate but related. If you spent summers in the Bay Area as Mary and I did, it was hard to escape the doings of the 'language' poets, or the controversy surrounding them, especially if you spent time with writers. In New York, where most of the movement's Eastern wing were gathered, their activities were not as prominently featured. I asked Ron Silliman, considered by many the leader of the Bay Area group, to put together a selection from a spectrum of 'language' poets. As I wrote in a brief prefatory note: "They see the language and language habits poets inherit as hindrances to perception and feeling, but even more, to the precise expression of these. However esoteric or difficult much of their work may seem to some people, their concern with form and the investigation of the structure of the self through the medium of language aims at the liberation of the larger society. If there is an avant-garde in poetry today, it will most likely be found among them."

Right off, the problem was who to have comment on this new movement. I wrote to Frederic Jameson and Peter Scheldahl, who were considered sympathetic without being partisan, but one was in China for the year, another busy with other projects. I asked Robert Pinsky, but he was busy with teaching and his own poetry. Having called on him three times for essays, I did not want to bother Robert Hass. After trying three or four others without success I settled for Silliman himself and Kathleen Fraser, who had ties with many mainstream poets, including Iowa poets and the New York School.

In order to sell enough copies and make sure the issue was read by mainstream poets and readers, I needed another feature which spoke to a different audience. At about the same time, Stanley Kunitz sent me Hilda Morley's "The Shutter Clangs: After Donne's 'Goodfriday, 1613, Ryding Westward' ", a ten-page elegy for Stefan Wolpe, Morley's late husband. He was convinced of the poem's sustained achievement and seemed to be suggesting that I do some kind of feature on Hilda. I had already printed Theodore Enslin's review of her only book when I first printed four of her poems. There seemed little point in printing so long a poem unless you were going to do a feature. Our printing the long poem made it even more necessary that we add at least half a dozen shorter ones. As with Linda Gregg, *Ironwood* broke its own tradition of not reprinting poems, while making sure the original publisher received credit on the same or a facing page. Not only was it important that readers see Morley's best work, they must see who published it. This would help marshal support. Hilda and I began what became, for her at least, a voluminous correspondence. She must have sent at least a dozen envelopes filled with poems, some with 60 or more—she had been writing since before puberty. Several fine poems were written at 13 in Palestine where her parents, early Zionists, took her in the '30's. They remind one a great deal of H.D., whom she came to know a few years later in London. When it came to finding people to write on Morley, the choices were obvious: Levertov, Kunitz, Carruth, Josephine Jacobsen—all were friends and admirers of her poetry. Now I had only to add Ralph Mills and Carolyn Kizer. True, the group was made up mostly of poets in their sixties or older, but that seemed as it should be, given Morley's age and the role several had played in helping her get published. What amazes me is how the Black Mountain poets, with the exception of Robert Creeley, seemed to regard her mainly as a hausfrau or academic, with little attention given to the poet writing. It was Creeley who took some Morley poems for the *Black Mountain Review* where Denise Levertov saw them and was impressed enough to get in touch with the poet even though she herself had never visited the college. As depressing as this story would otherwise be, it shows there are still people out there waiting to be discovered.

In designing a cover for this issue, the problem was how to create a unity from division, those very real differences separating Morley from the 'Language' poets. For one thing, Morley made extensive use of the white space of the page, more so than Charles Olson, who had urged poets to consider the entire page as the field of the poem. A master of nuance, her poems show precise diction, a supple syntax and a sense of measure, the way her rhythms are built and sustained over a sequence of lines. Consider only this quotation:

> Till the late cold strikes
> they spin in obstinacy
>   (light
> of the mountain on the brown leaf
>   swung

I did not want a straight line or static border, nor even a simple, beautiful curve. Something between a map and a battlefield might work. Then it struck me that a jigsaw puzzle with its jagged baroque contours would provide us with the edges we needed. Within days of returning to Tucson in September, we were invited to supper by an artist friend with several grandchildren. Did she have any large picture puzzles? "Why yes, what on earth would you want with one?" I explained what I was up to, and she let me take it home for an indefinite period. We set it on the large dining-room table, where it sat week after week. It was huge, and tough to get started.

Within a month, a small section had spread until nearly a quarter of the puzzle was done. We didn't need the entire thing, simply a continuous edge that ran at least nine inches. Two more weeks and we had it. I had someone trace it with a ballpoint pen on newsprint paper. For colors, I decided on a shade of fuchsia for Morley and a light, flat green for the 'language' section. Even the typeface was to conflict: Baskerville for Morley, a sans serif Optima for the others. Like many borders in wartime, the division between the two areas suggested a link between them and the latest news from the front. The way the two sections touched was enough to make one ask "Who's invading who?", enough to satisfy everyone's paranoia. When we took the issue to the printer, I brought along a large Skira volume, *Modern Painting*, wanting to show Stan Fabe a specific Matisse painting with the two colors I had in mind. When he saw it he was ecstatic: "That was my favorite Matisse when I was in art school!" Stan and Mary were both on hand when the covers came off the press. The press men had accidently left the slightest separation between the two sides, resulting in an op-art effect where first one color, then the other came forward. Mary loved it and it stayed.

For the two months between starting rough pasteup and taking the issue to the printer, we had an intern helping us, a recent Oberlin graduate. Before, on the few occasions such an opportunity presented itself,

I had always shied away, since room and board was all we could offer. This young man knew this and came anyway but, once there, decided he wanted to work for me part-time to earn some money. I had expected John to know the ropes better—he was an intelligent young man and had written a few interesting poems. After showing him various things as I did them, I would try and get him to do them himself while I watched. We were proofreading the issue one day when he demanded: "When are you going to let me take some responsibility?" That night, after we got back from supper, I suggested to John that he try pasting up part of the issue, starting with Ron Silliman's introduction to "Realism", his name for the mini-anthology he was editing for us. Then I went into my room to work on something else. Every once in a while, John would come in and ask about something. He seemed so happy, I was inwardly congratulating myself on being a good teacher. While he was supposed to proofread everything before he pasted it up, I noticed that he had not found any typos, though I had already picked up one or two looking over his copy. He wanted to rewrite the text at several points, but it seemed well done to me. When I told him it was actually a long quote from William Carlos Williams, one of America's foremost prose stylists, the information caused hardly a stir. The thing was, he had found only one typo in two days of proofreading. When the issue appeared, I got an interesting response from Ron Silliman. He was pleased, polite, but firm about one thing: his introduction would have to be done over again. What had happened was that two proofs, each of which usually contains some two and a half pages of material, were pasted up out of sequence. It's the sort of thing Craig Martin, who had done our paste-up so creditably since the James Wright issue, would normally catch in final paste-up, but didn't, probably overawed by all those pasted-up pages. I promised him a front-page apology and let him know I would reprint the entire introduction in our next issue, which we did.

Silliman titled his small anthology "Realism." The poets, he emphasized, were concerned with the real world and wanted language to reflect that, to disrupt or undermine many of the linguistic conventions which masked that reality by creating a false consciousness. The anthology ran some fifty pages, with twenty-five contributors, seven of them women. For me, Barrett Watten's "Introduction to the Letter T" was easily the most imaginative and gripping of the selections, combining as it did history, sociology, imagination, economics, the history of technology with the demonstration of the steps by which, on a display terminal, one changes the letter X to the letter T. Each step is visually reproduced with a short but mysteriously suggestive statement below. Other selections that stood out for me were Rae Armantrout's "Single Most", Ron Silliman's selection from "Albany" and Hannah Weiner's selection from "Spoke." While, like many readers I found Kathleen Fraser's "Partial Local Coherence" more various and quirkily interesting than Ron Silliman's introduction, I was made jubilant by her poem, **"Medusa's hair was snakes. Was thoughts, split inward."** I liked Bob Perelman's "Housing Starts" but it didn't seem like a 'language' poem or anything James Tate could not have written. Perhaps the Iowa influence was surfacing.

The issue sold well enough in the Bay Area; what copies were not sold within the first six months went soon after or were used for classes. Within a couple of years, it had become another rare, out-of-print issue.

* * *

After *Ironwood*'s second issue, we asked Laurie Cook to replace Frances Curtis on final paste-up. An artist and draftsman with a genuine love of poetry, Laurie lived at the Rancho Linda Vista commune thirty miles north of Tucson. She knew her job and was able to work on paste-up sooner and more often than her predecessor. The problem was, she found it more convenient to do things at the ranch, which meant that, at the time I needed them, changes would be harder to make. Furthermore, in the rugged ranch environment it was harder to keep proofs clean. With issues 4 and 5, we switched to Bob Winters, who worked for a Tucson newspaper. I remember bringing the final proofs and a dummy of the issue out to his trailer. Winters was fast and did an extremely good job. For him too, it was difficult to work at our house, six or seven miles from his and even further from his newspaper job. At the end of the Oppen issue, I remember inviting him over for supper so we could finish up on the table afterwards. When he moved to Florida after that, we turned again to Laurie Cook, who pasted up #7–8 and #9 for us.

With the James Wright issue, we obtained the services of Craig Martin, another newspaperman. Craig was tall, genial, a man who exuded an aura of stillness and concentration. Once the final proofs had arrived, I could relax. As long as Craig was cutting and pasting, things would move from chaos toward clarity. Day after day, the pile of smooth pasteboards with their neat, shiny rectangles mounted. Normally, Craig would arrive at 10 AM, working steadily until nearly 1:30, when he broke for a quick lunch before heading for his newspaper job. Though rarely asked to read proof, Craig frequently spotted typographical errors or misspellings and called them to our attention. When it came to replacing small errors in the text, Craig could often do this cheaper and more quickly than the typesetters. Delving into my hoard of old type, he would fashion one word from the wreckage of three older ones. After pasting up one issue, it was Craig who told us we could get our repro proofs waxed at the printers for next to nothing. When we tried it, we soon discovered how much time it saved us, how much more flexibility it gave in moving proofs. It was easier to make it stick than glue or tape; easier to lift it and shift positions. The whole process proved a lot cleaner. Before I began saving my completed paste-ups for the rare book department of our University of Arizona library, we would use the bare reverse sides for the next paste-up, including even some of our chapbooks.

The only exception to Craig's reliability was the prospect of his being summoned by the paper to go in a couple of hours early. In practice, this usually meant canceling paste-up for the day or having him come an hour earlier in order to work at least two hours. When the time came to print poems of Susan Howe where one phrase or line of words should overlay another without blocking more than the lines that intersected, it was Craig who knew the proper technique—something he called a double burn. Here, the type was shot once by the camera with the superimposed type pasted on a layer of clear acetate before everything was reshot. Otherwise, the white of the surrounding paper would have blocked the type underneath. A third innovation was his getting the newspaper to print up sheets of pasteboard with a vertical centerline and horizontal lines indicating the horizontal and vertical dimensions of each page. This way, using a light table where the light shone from below the paper, Craig had very few measurements to make. The savings in time were enormous: what once took four hours now required

142

two and a half. Since our final eight or ten issues were much longer on average, the change was extremely helpful in preserving our sanity and meeting our deadlines.

* * *

Given the greater frequency of special issues, it should not have surprised us to discover a slight falling off in the number of poetry manuscripts. After all, one special issue a year meant a reduction of 100% in the number of poems we were printing. It could also mean a delay in having one's poems printed because of the greater interval between regular issues. The time had come, I decided, to offer again the Frank Stanford Memorial Prizes. In addition to the publicity and the incentive, this would insure a greater flow of manuscripts. The poems had to be submitted between May and November, 1982. It is not always easy to tell who is entering a contest. To me, anyone otherwise eligible who submitted poems during this period was *ipso facto* eligible. Invariably, those that spoke most of the contest, of eligibility, rules, etcetera, were the poorest poets. In this case, the two who sent the strongest work were Laura Mullen and James Baker Hall. Here is the second of four poems which won Laura Mullen the major Stanford Memorial Prize:

BROKEN PANTOUM FOR THREE VOICES
(Only one of which is love.)

The water is so blue, so blue . . .
The body would swear by its own heaviness.
This water is full of dogs. No. The sky
Swells, thrashes, there are clouds at the edges.

The rocks are dragged out in a net of foam.
The heavy
Hollow-throated barking you hear is the undertow,
the snarl.
You smile hard, your lips are white at the edges.
I don't believe you any more, I don't believe you.

I heard myself saying it too, (the undertow)
Leaving the light off I leaned on the cold mirror.

(He read a book. His face was shot. he said,
    I don't believe you.)
The calls of the northbound geese grind the darkness
    down.

The black mud of the bay slides under silver water.
This is the darkness of wings, the darkness of
    deep water.
The sound of the stones dragged back into the sea
    is the sound of the wearing away.
He says, *wake up.* In the morning my jaw aches.
    I don't know why.

What drags the geese north, in a net, through the
    dark?
I walk at the water's edge, for the wet stones.
I hold out my red hands and smile so my face hurts.
I say, these are for you, if you believe me.

I am going to fill my pockets with stones,
And walk into the blue of the water, the sky.
And the weight of the body? *Now I believe you.* Rapt
In the undertow, the snarling smiles of foam,
    the teeth of the sea

While the poem superficially resembles an exercise, its lines are so right in perceptions musically linked to one another by various kinds of partial rhyme that the effect is one of trance, the trance of the writer becoming the trance of the reader as he or she falls under its spell. Each of the Mullen poems is different but the same sense of music inhabits all four, along with the same freshness of seeing, the same unflinching seriousness. As for James Baker Hall, his "First Snow" shared the individual poem prize with John Taggart.

Looking back over *Ironwood 21*'s contents, two conclusions are obvious. Of 46 poets, only 10 have more than one poem and all but three of these are two poems. More importantly perhaps, I am struck by how good most of these poems are. Just to look at a title or a name summons up memories—handwriting, the color of ink, revisions made or attempted. At least a dozen of these must have been revised at my urging. The long columns of black print light up like stops on an elevator as my eye meets each name and it becomes, for that eternal instant, the only poet, the only poem. I remember placing Kip Zegers last because of his own immersion in the working life of New York City, the way he uses it to write about Walt Whitman and Whitman to add resonance to this city life. The old man who disappears into the subway takes us out of the issue and back into the streets.

Three things that enriched this issue were Michael Heller's essay on *cante hondo* or deep song in Garcia Lorca where Heller explores Lorca's understanding of the duende, David Ignatow's selections from his more recent notebooks, and Ernesto Cardenal's "With Walker in Nicaragua," a 13-page documentary poem which had won prizes in Europe. Cardenal was that rare phenomenon, a Latin poet of the left who wrote more like Pound and Williams than he did like Neruda. The Ignatow passages, while not equal to the best of his published notebooks, were provocative of thought and reflection, examples of the moral conscience of the artist working on the materials of everyday life. It is a role American Jews have filled to their credit, enriching all of us. Cardenal's poem had been sent by Jonathan Cohen the previous summer. Cardenal had been a Trappist monk and a student of Thomas Merton, the Catholic radical and poet who participated in dozens of social movements and anti-war petitions and publications. By the time I received the poem, he was Minister of Culture of the Sandinista government in Nicaragua. At first, I was somewhat taken aback, expecting more of Pound's piths and gists than I found in the General Walker poem. Instead, the text seemed fairly continuous, unbroken because it was taken from published narratives and reminiscences of Walker's lieutenants and comrades. The translator, told by the poet of the precise sources of the poem, went to the originals and copied narratives word for word in the original 19th century English, avoiding a poetry that would have been twice lost in translation. The poem gives a voluptuous portrait of a virgin Nicaragua in the 1850's, "that warm, sweet, green odor of Central America."

The fact that, prior to reading this poem, I myself had never heard of General Walker, is a sad commentary not only on my education but the way America educates its sons and daughters with regard to Central and South America. Within a year of the gold rush, in spite of having studied law and medicine in Europe, Walker had left his native Tennessee for California where he would spend several years as a journalist. He was not a General but what was called a filibusterer, at a time when the word meant freebooter, not someone who talked a proposed bill to death, thereby preventing a vote. As small a space as Walker receives in the average American History text, a plank endorsing his expedition to Nicaragua became part of the Republican and Democratic platforms in 1860, the year Lincoln ran for the presidency. I suspect Walker's instituting slavery in Nicaragua had something to do with this.

After I had taken the Walker poem, Jonathan Cohen sent us a rare daguerreotype print of General Walker taken in July, 1860, before he sailed from Mobile on his final expedition to Nicaragua. Though he wears no uniform, the "ice-blue" eyes Cardenal refers to are evident. For the cover, we were going to reproduce a poem by Mary Cuddihy's great-grandfather, Thomas Deaken, a sea captain, written in the late 1860's or early '70's. We had our printer center the rectangle with its hand-written poem but a blue line proof soured us on the idea. Since Jim Sloan was in town, I asked him for advice. The best thing, he thought, was to enlarge the handwriting so readers could concentrate on individual letters and words rather than content. He suggested sepia, which matched the original. Although we discussed using the Walker photo, we preferred Jim's idea. Before going ahead with the enlargement, I wondered aloud how the Walker image would work superimposed on the handwriting, using an oval shape to avoid boxiness and suggest a sense of the period. The idea took hold. Jim cut up some paper, leaving an oval-shaped blank to fit over the photograph. The picture looked terrific and we decided to go with it for issue #21.

As Bernard Devoto shows in *1846: Year of Decision*, the songs of Steven Foster, for all their innocence, are truly representative of an era that saw America take over a sizeable amount of Mexico, using all kinds of deceit and brute force in the service of imperial greed. Just so, poems like Deaken's with their dreamy idealism, their nostalgia, seem to fit this highly-educated man with his deaf-mute mistress. Deaken, too, died far from home, lost somewhere off Cape Hatteras.

*   *   *

If someone should ask me how I know when I come across a really good poem, I couldn't give them a single reason except that I don't stop reading. It feels so good, I go back and I suppose that's the spark, I want to read it, to be with it, like a woman you fall in love with. You want to be with her. Well, I want to be with that poem. Often, I have to go through all the usual routine, checking the diction, tone, rhythms, integrity of line, the voice, you name it. But it's like buying insurance on a house, it's not what makes you buy the house in the first place. It boils down to knowing something instead of knowing *about* it. As in the story of the young man who complained to the theologian: "Here I am looking for God and you talk to me of religion." Having said this, I should add that as with most activities, handling the mail and dealing with poems as they arrive, I operate nine-tenths of the time on a much lower level.

After several years, I settled into a routine. Each morning my assistant would pick up the mail from our post office box. It was hard for me to resist opening the mail immediately. I had become a "mail junkie" years before I even knew the term. My attention would be drawn by a beautifully hand-written envelope with an unconventional ink. As a rule, such envelopes held better than average poems. On the other hand, there were "poets" who needed enormous envelopes just to send a 12-line poem. If they had enclosed a group of poems they didn't want to retype, I could understand. But a single poem?

Most poets enclosed a stamped self-addressed envelope with a note informing me that poems were included. Without a return envelope, the poet wouldn't get his poems back, which is why magazines put notices to that effect on the title page. Many listed magazine credits along with book titles. Occasionally, some self-important faculty member would try to impress me with an eight-page resumé. Or a housewife might feel the need to tell me something about her husband or children. Worst were the poems which announced "26 lines" along with "First North American Serial Rights", as if it were the original Declaration Of Independence. Those who used these devices never seemed to write anything I wanted to publish.

As for listing publications or titles, if you recognize the quality of the magazine or book publisher, you may read such poems with an extra degree of seriousness, though I have often been disappointed in my expectations. First-class magazines manage to print rather terrible poems now and then, or they catch a poet on his one bright day. Ultimately, you are back to square one, alone with the poems.

Then there's that well-known poet. You ask him for work and he sends you his student. The message is clear: print my student and we'll see what we can do. Actually, the message is more likely ambiguous. As a rule, the student's poems leave something to be desired. So you send them back, mustering whatever kind words you can manage. If that's the last you hear from the teacher, you can be pretty sure the cynic in you was correct. But there are always students who, on their own initiative, take advantage of their connections. Occasionally, student poets deserve the recommendations they get. Wise recommendations are more likely to come from poetry's elder statesmen, people like Hayden Carruth, Stanley Kunitz, and Denise Levertov, or from another editor. In fact, one way to make a friend of a good poet whose work you can't use at the moment is to suggest an editor you respect. I have done this a number of times, though not often enough. Finally, if someone were to ask me the ideal number of poems to submit, my answer would be: "Six poems." And if they asked me what to say in the letter they sent with their submissions, my answer would be the same: "Six poems."

I had four categories for poems until I came up with a system as simple as it was complex. This involved initialing each envelope with its category. The inch-high initials were easy to read, identify. Envelopes went two places, the basket or the Chopping Block. Initials were C for Contenders, S for Stroke, RR for Reread, nothing for Chopping Block. Poems with no chance of being taken were sent to the Chopping Block, a wooden box replacing the steel drawer in my filing cabinet. Rereads were placed in the same baskets as all categories but the Chopping Block. A Reread required further readings to absorb what was going on in the poems and reflect on it. While not ready to be taken, a Stroke deserved a positive response, aimed at eliciting further submissions. Strokes could become Contenders, at least a couple an issue. As the word suggests, Contenders were finalists. Both this and the Stroke category had intensifiers, meaning that three C's would suggest even greater excellence in a Contender, three S's the need for me to write with more understanding to a Stroke. Five C's could mean that five poems were likely to be accepted.

Among Contenders, the majority were selected by a process that involved weighing one poem against another, one value against another. We were part of a fallen world where it was more accurate to speak of "better" or "less good" instead of simply seeing "the one thing." After I had reached a tentative decision for or against, I would often show these poems to Mary, though I was more likely to seek out her opinion when on the verge of taking a poem. Cautious, Mary would read a poem many times through before announcing any conclusion. She had what I liked to call a good "bullshit detector" though remaining open to experimental work. She was quick to spot when poets were imitating other poets or repeating outworn gestures. I valued her for our disagreements.

*   *   *

Without knowing it, Pamela Stewart started me on the special Robert Duncan issue. After hearing Duncan read in California, possibly San Diego, she wrote me full of enthusiasm. One long poem really impressed her. Six weeks later, we were in California for the summer. I set about trying to discover the name of that poem and whether it had been printed. I am fairly certain I phoned Duncan himself about "the long poem" but, given the vagueness of my description and the number of long poems he had written, Duncan had no idea what poem I could be talking about. To repair my relative unfamiliarity with Duncan and his poetry, I set about rereading the four books of Duncan's poetry I owned: *The Opening of the Field, Roots and Branches, Bending the Bow* and *Caesar's Gate*. Gradually, I bought or borrowed a handful of others. Meanwhile, I sought Michael Palmer's help. We talked it over one day and Michael set up a luncheon meeting for the last week of August in a restaurant close to Duncan's house. Duncan was friendly, talkative. When we reached the issue, it was soon clear that Duncan, unlike Tranströmer, wanted to select those who were going to write on him. We listed a number of names, putting checks on those Duncan wanted to have write on him. Foremost were Wendy MacIntyre, Michael Davidson and Bruce Boone. Duncan also mentioned Carl Rakosi, whom he had been seeing a great deal more of since George Oppen's memory had begun to deteriorate and Kathleen Raine, the English poet and Blake scholar with whom he had corresponded. It was her understanding of the significance of myth that made a contribution from her important to him. He chose Mark Johnson because he was writing a book on Duncan's "Passages," an ongoing sequence with much of the power of the *Cantos,* inclusive and formal in ways that were new. Others, including Thom Gunn, refused. And there was Hugh Kenner, a name raised by Duncan and myself. Kenner's essay, quickly agreed to by the critic, required four letters and endless telephone calls before it reached us seven weeks after our deadline. His piece, when it came, took the form of a computer printout, made up of endless folds. It took five or ten minutes to work out the sequence which he had titled, "1680 Words On Duncan's Words." So enraged was the young man helping me unfold it, impatient at what he termed "the conspiracy of inanimate objects," that he actually began swatting the Kenner missive with his fists.

Others I attempted to enlist included filmmaker Stan Brakhage, Robert Creeley, Gary Snyder, and Guy Davenport. Davenport, who lacked the time to acquaint himself with Duncan's work of the past decade, was rather put off by his recent practice of publishing work in small, rare editions. Some had quarreled with Duncan and saw no reason to make such an effort without overtures from him. Denise Levertov, I learned later, would have been happy to write but, when I raised the subject, Duncan would not let me ask her. An essay we didn't print was Michael Heller's, discussing the same subject, "Poem Beginning With a Line by Pindar", as Wendy MacIntyre's did. I bring up these failed approaches to suggest the scope of such an issue, how much had to be attempted in order to achieve what we did and how much more might have been achieved. Occasionally, a reader will ask why we didn't get such-and-such a person to write on James Wright, George Oppen or, as here, Robert Duncan. Often we tried to do just that. In Duncan's case, it meant trying John Ashbery, who turned out to be seriously ill and could not oblige.

One difference with this issue was the amount of time I spent hunting down printers who had worked with the poet. Even close friends and associates admitted Duncan was hell on editors and extremely demanding of printers. Still, some of the best considered this a challenge and rose to the occasion. What concerned me here was how Duncan's poems were set, not his prose or the essays written on his work. I managed to visit at least three who had worked with Duncan and spent hours trying to run down others, finally talking to some on the phone. The problem with printers was, they were expensive and had work scheduled months, even years, in advance. A major new collection, *Ground Work I*, scheduled by New Directions for Spring, '84, six months after our special issue, confirmed my decision to bring out a special Duncan issue at this time. Because Duncan was so fastidious when it came to the spacing in his poems, James Laughlin, his publisher, had cannily gotten him to type his own manuscript, giving him specially treated paper that the offset people could film later on. Part of the ongoing sequence known as "Passages", the four longer poems Duncan gave me, were all ones he himself typed. Only "The Dignities," which ran three double pages, was done on specially-treated paper. With our page size, there was no way, Duncan had thought, that we could possibly print these poems, particularly "The Dignities". I spent a couple of nights tossing and turning, trying to think up ways it could be done. Certainly, one couldn't simply turn the poem sideways and expect it to fit, the lines were still too long. I thought of ways to fold the paper but decided to check with the printer, the sooner the better. When he heard, Stan Fabe made it sound like a piece of cake, but said he would consult his production man first and get back to me. He phoned me from Tucson with the good news. The first two poems, "Whose" and "Close", would fit snugly on two facing pages. "At The Door" and "The Dignities" could fit on two facing fold-out pages, using front and back. In a letter dated September 16, Duncan praised my proofreading of these poems and the four others he had had Robert Bertholf send us. But because, when he answered the phone a few days before, I had interrupted his train of thought, he turned on me in a way that left me reeling. What Duncan called my editorial demands were almost all things he had promised me on his own or had agreed to for at least a year. Particularly galling was Duncan's announcement near the end of the letter that because of its Pound associations, he was giving "The Effort" to *Sagetrieb* for their special issue. I had spent two years trying to find this poem and had only recently managed to hear it on tape. There might not have been an issue without it. Since Duncan valued the process as highly as the product, I felt justified in printing his letter on the back cover. Having seen the issue, our readers would get a whiff of the process. Although they sympathized with my predicament, friends of Duncan discouraged the idea, raising the possibility of a lawsuit. Sick of it all, I dropped the idea. Owing to the long hours of work, the stress, conflict and other factors, I was having difficulties with my heart. For several years now, Mary and I had talked of giving up *Ironwood*. She had suggested stopping with issue 20 while I countered with 24. Finally, the doctor gave me Beta-blockers for rapid heartbeat, which seemed to help once the system got used to them.

To give readers a sense of the issue's contents, I need to summarize a few of the essays. Rereading Duncan's *Tribunals* for the first time in a decade, Hayden Carruth pointed out how the syntax creates a rising tension, how it "lunges forward on the beats, over the beats, a wave cresting and falling against the shore." In closing, he underlined "the way the poet's life has been lived on the page in remarkable candor and in even more remarkable poetic control, and distancing: perhaps our most consistent, most energetic conversion of experience into art."

For Michael Davidson, Duncan's relationship to the tradition was not expressed by originality but through his ability "to respond to the demands of immediacy." Duncan may appear irresponsible because unable "to synthesize a strong literary ethos or heritage into his work", but he demonstrates "the ability to respond" by being able to read the fluctuating pattern of reality as a meaningful text. Implicit in this idea is the notion of "repetition, or what Duncan prefers to call 'rime', by which original moments, events, ideas are interrelated in a dense weave." This radical "traditionalism" marked Duncan as "one of the most paradoxical of contemporary poets."

The Berkeley Renaissance group, Bruce Boone suggested, was the only serious gay poetry band since World War II. Duncan and Jack Spicer were the leaders and Ernst Kantorowicz, a Berkeley history professor, its guiding spirit. A member of the Stefan George group from his early days at Heidelberg, Kantorowicz even made a special trip to Switzerland at the time of George's death to keep vigil over the poet. While the group distrusted institutional authority, personal one-on-one authority was the glue that kept them together. Although there was no indication Duncan and Spicer were ever lovers, the Spicer years largely coincided with the years before Duncan's permanent liaison with the painter, Jess Collins. Duncan, not Ginsberg, was the first prominent homosexual poet to publicly acknowledge his preference in a pioneering

1944 essay. Surprisingly, the essay argued for gay behavior at the price of a gay identity. In his poems, Duncan evolved a strategy of sensuous abstraction that allowed him to present gay sexuality from a positive, loving, celebrational viewpoint but this breakthrough took place at the cost of a rupture with the existing gay community. For Boone, Duncan's brand of combining gay emphasis with universalist humanism deserves serious consideration if it can be done without rolling back advances for gays. According to Boone, Duncan initiated much of the group's ideology including ideas like Dictated Poetry, The Invisible World and even "serial poetry". In each case, Spicer carried them through, usually to extremes with which Duncan took issue.

Perhaps the most valuable portions of the issue were the 38 pages of Duncan letters to Robin Blaser and Jack Spicer and the chapter of his *H.D. Book*. The letters demonstrate Duncan's unflagging energy, the rigorous conscience of the writer forever on the alert. Along with his awareness of the important values at stake, the H.D. chapter reveals the wealth of Duncan's historical understanding and his sophistication when it comes to Christian iconography. Even if his preferences are gnostic, antinomian, theosophical, Duncan is clearly a man of the West.

The cover portrait of Duncan by his friend Jess showed him dreaming, meditative, the eyes going separate ways, the titles of *The Zohar* and other beloved mystical books clearly legible. What an unexpected piece of luck to encounter such a magisterial work and be allowed to reproduce it!

Ironwood 23 was noteworthy for eight long poems by writers as accomplished as Tess Gallagher, Jim Schley, Jordan Smith, Frank Stanford, Ai, Sharona Ben-Tov, Beverly Dahlen and Hilde Weisert. Weisert's "Coney Island Elegy" demonstrated a deep sense of rootedness in a place known for the transience of what normally happened there. No matter how far she had to go to come to grips with the subject, the poet never failed in her obligations to language. Jim Schley's poem, "Return by Water" was equally remarkable for the way it incorporated different levels of reality, different places as well. This was also the first time we printed Beverly Dahlen, a six-page section from *A Reading*, the name she gave her ongoing series of prose/poetry writings, including even criticism. I had read a selection of hers in Nathaniel Mackey's remarkable magazine *Hambone*. Leading off the issue was Rosemarie Waldrop's translation from Edmond Jabes's *El*, or *The Last Book*, a distillation of the Hebrew mysticism of the Cairo-born French poet who moved to Paris after Suez. The issue contained eight poems by Stefanie Marlis, a Marin County poet we were printing for the third time. The work possessed immediacy, her extraordinary lines brimming with fresh perceptions. True, there were places here and there where the influence of Linda Gregg or Jack Gilbert seemed all too powerful. Yet the poems are radically different from theirs. The number of images and the speed with which things happen and change distinguish her work from theirs as well as from others. Then there were the eight poems of Michael Burkard. In these extraordinary lyrics, the world was there, turning, its weight and beauty intact. Increasingly, love was there, and desire, along with fear and diffidence. Burkard was reclaiming a lost landscape, and making much of it emotionally available to the reader. Metaphor and story were not simply agents of perception or memory but equivalents for deeply buried aspects of the self. If Robert Duncan was right in insisting that we ask of a poem that it "not gratify but testify", then Burkard's poems were testimony that compelled respect.

Other poems I found myself reading over and over were written by Robert Gibb, William Bronk, Jordan Smith, Irene McKinney, Denis Johnson, Louis Jenkins, Alberto Ríos, Michael Waters, Phyllis Martinez and several others. In saying only this, I may have done these poems and their authors a terrible injustice. Mary Karr contributed an intelligent, closely-argued appreciation of Bill Knott. In addition, Frances Mayes had reviewed the latest books of C. D. Wright and Patricia Hampl along with Susan Mitchell's first collection. Although I have come increasingly to admire Susan Mitchell's work, I found Mayes's criticisms of Mitchell painfully on the mark. Hoping a timely review of two of our leading poets would give rise to some interesting comparisons, I had asked her to review Tess Gallagher's and Jorie Graham's latest. Mayes thought they had received enough attention and that we should give the space to relative newcomers. It was difficult to quarrel with that. Of the 50 poets in the issue, close to half had at least two poems each or longer poems running three to seven pages. Though I had toyed with printing the long poems in a single section, I was convinced this would only make it easier for the casual reader to avoid them altogether.

Several years before, I had seen Judith Harper's cover painting in a large show at the Tucson Museum of Art. It may even have won a prize. Although the painting bore some resemblance to the style of Bruce McGrew, one of her teachers, Harper concentrated on the lower, or desert part of the canvas, integrating it with the upper part by means of a curved ochre wand, resembling an ocotillo branch, the sort of device John Marin used to knit together many of his watercolors. The greyish-blue sky was hypnotic, palpable as aluminum. It was bright enough, this painting, to support, even cry out for, a black border with the issue name and number in red. This was one of the covers Mary and I continue to love best.

*   *   *

By the time Mary and I settled into our summer house, George Oppen had spent six months in nursing homes. Weeks ago, he had been moved from a Jewish nursing home in Oakland where they could no longer cope with the sometimes violent behavior that marks this late stage of Alzheimer's. When Mary and I saw him for the last time, he was in a small hospital in Walnut Creek, wearing the kind of white hospital gown I had worn years ago. He was sitting in a regular chair, arms and legs bound loosely to the corresponding parts of the chair. When we shook hands, I was struck by how powerful his grip was, more so than at any time in my experience. George had always spoken in a low, quiet voice but now you had to lean well forward to hear him, his speech was that thick. Mary and I could catch only a word or two at a time. It was hard to believe this was the man I had heard eight summers back read his poems at Intersection, keeping a packed house enthralled with no tricks at all, just his voice and what he had to say. For some reason, a recording device must have failed, since he was asked if he could do it over again. Without a hint of annoyance, he had repeated the entire reading. I think back now to the night George and Mary invited us to an Italian restaurant in North Beach to witness, later on, a small change in their will. Afterward, we drove to Fort Mason where Mary Oppen proudly showed us the patch the city had allotted them in the community garden where she grew huge heads of wonderful spinach. Thanks to the methods of French intensive farming, which all involved were using, the soil was black. Among the heads of spinach, enormous mushrooms had sprouted without any input from Mary or George. The soil, it transpired, had come from what had been a mushroom farm. The moon was full, the place inviting in an eerie kind of way. At some point, George gave me a tiny pearl heart with a metal backing, which he had picked up in the street and kept for some time. He suggested I keep it, then maybe pass it back to him at some point. I treasured this so much I forgot the injunction. Had I kept it on my person, now would have been my chance to return it.

George went on talking. Mary Cuddihy was able to lean way over, ear close to his mouth. She was better than I at interpreting his words. He was telling his own Mary that they weren't kids anymore, that things would be all right, that she must go on writing, that there was no time to lose. A few minutes of this was enough to break your heart. The nurse came in with a lunch tray. He didn't want to eat much but took a sip or two of his soup. After the nurse left, Mary would give him soup or jello every couple of minutes, but there had to be an interval between. Every once in a while, George would flex his arms and legs, trying to break his bonds. There was a good deal of strength left in those limbs. After an hour had elapsed, Mary and I said our goodbyes and slipped from the room. As we came out of the hospital into the noonday heat, I could feel it rising off the asphalt while the sun concentrated on my body. It was a long drive home.

A week later, Mark Linenthal called to tell us George had died in a nursing home in Palo Alto after a brief battle with pneumonia. Given the degree of suffering and deterioration that had taken place in the past few months, the family had requested of the doctors that no extraordinary measures or life-support equipment be used to save him. In a few days, there would be a service at Fort Mason. Although I hadn't expected George to be around much more than a year, this was a real shock. Next day, I drove north to Bodega Bay and beyond, spending several hours looking down on the ocean, huge rocks scattered here and there with the water surging around them. This was George's native atmosphere: the sea. I thought of him as one of those rocks, patiently suffering the extremities of weather and sea surge, open to whatever came his way. He had had for me a quality of being there, what the French call *disponabilité*. I left feeling better about things. When George's niece Andy Meyer phoned a day later to ask if I could say a few words at the service, I agreed. The other speakers were Mark Linenthal, Robert Hass, Carl Rakosi, Robert Duncan and Eve Haight, in that order.

When it was my turn to speak, I had a few notes. To steady myself, I fixed my eyes on Carl Rakosi and directed my words mainly to him, that genial, beaming presence sitting near the center. It helped calm me. Mostly I spoke from the perspective of the ocean and rocks, noting how rare my link to George had been, adding how open he and Mary had been to so many our age or younger, much younger even. Hass's speech concentrated on George and Mary as figures local to San Francisco. More disturbing, Carl Rakosi spoke of death and of helping take George to the Jewish Nursing home in Oakland—George's first tentative efforts to relate to a totally new environment. Then Robert Duncan read several of his favorite Oppen poems, poems he admitted not having read much while George was alive, surprised apparently by how much he liked them, his eyes filling several times with tears. Finally, George's great-niece, Eve Haight, read from a series of letters he had written to her, an aspiring poet, between her fourteenth and eighteenth years. To give the reader a taste, I quote the first:

Evie Dear
Lord help you, but there's no help for it really: you'll be a poet Don't forget to bring yourself along—your whole self. You know about that, of course, but don't forget. In which case all will be well. In which case "it'll be alright": 'it' and the poetry

With love George

After I heard Eve Haight read those letters, so marvelously funny and wise and touching, it got me thinking about another Oppen issue. The letters were the kind of thing that could provide the spark. They had all the accessibility that his detractors criticized Oppen for not having. If there were few poems left unpublished, there *were* letters beginning to accumulate in the Oppen archive at San Diego. With a decade elapsed since our first Oppen issue, it might be time to test the water.

The service closed with the andante of Bach's sonata for flute and basso continuo, an old favorite of George's. The flute was played by Alec Mourelatos, Linda Oppen's husband. Afterwards, as people began to stand and stretch and talk to one another, I found myself being addressed by all kinds of familiar faces, including some I couldn't recognize. Robert Hass asked whether I wouldn't agree that both Milosz and George Oppen believed there were certain things more important than poetry. I could only nod my agreement. Later, at the reception held by the family, Robert Duncan came over and said something nice about the issue, his first words to me since his letter. I mumbled a few words and did my best to move on. Coming through the high dormer windows, the sun made it extremely close in that crowded room. One glass of wine and I was sweating badly, anxious to get back to Woodacre and the rocking bed.

For several years, I had been trying to get Rachel Blau-DuPlessis's consent to our printing a series of letters George Oppen had sent her in the late '60's and early '70's. A decade earlier, when we were putting together the first Oppen issue, she had sent me copies. Why I hadn't asked to print them, I don't know. With George so vigorous, it may have seemed premature. Perhaps he would have refused. This time she sent them, a dozen in all, some running two or three pages. The subjects ranged from politics to race relations, sex and gender, anthropology, Williams, prosody, and more. For a brief while, we are permitted to share the mind of an extraordinary man. A few weeks later, Milosz mailed me a large number of "inscripts", mostly epigrams or finely chiseled paragraphs with reflections on poetry, life, ambition, fame, place, and other subjects. When Bob Hass had shown me the group, I had marked which ones I wanted. They had been translated mostly by Milosz himself and, during the next few months, I asked for a number of changes, about half of which he accepted. Milosz's remarks were polished, formal, yet amazingly frank for all of that, George's letters more responsive to the changing needs of his correspondent. Many of his dealt with her rather than himself, another mark of the man. I intended both contributions to form part of an issue on Poetics, an issue that would avoid focusing on a single poet, concentrating instead on questions of form, value and technique. I wanted our Poetics issue to find us near the mainstream, with strong contributions from traditionalists and revolutionaries of one stripe or another. I had written and was hearing from Kunitz, Donald Hall, Denise Levertov, Tess Gallagher, Donald Davie, Stafford, Simpson, Barbara Guest, Hayden Carruth, Allan Williamson and Charles Simic. Others remained to be heard from.

In planning the Poetics issue, I made it a point to include something on the Ann Arbor paperback series, Poets on Poetry, which had essays, interviews and notes by mainstream poets such as Donald Hall, Philip Levine, Maxine Kumin and Galway Kinnell, along with mavericks like Richard Kostelanetz, Robert Francis and Donald Davie. With only ten pages in which to deal with 21 books, Reginald Gibbons, our reviewer, could not always afford to be specific. Apart from Bly and Kinnell, whose interviews he believed deserve a separate volume, a single book could easily include the best of the interviews. He questions what they have to say as having 'only the casual blunt force of opinion, rather than the pondered and pent-up force of a statement to be made once and for all— or at least passionately.' Donald Hall he faults for offering readers of this series too many McBooks. To keep his essay free of the taint of person- ality, Gibbons puts much of what he has to say in the form of anonymous quotations from a rough dozen of his authors. He stresses the tendency, in recent years, for many young poets, understandably reluctant to question or criticize those on whom a teaching position may depend, to seek the community of the profession rather than an artistic community. Gibbons quotes "There seems to be little fire of necessity in the aes- thetic decisions of creative writing students" and then exclaims, "How would there be, when their artistic progress is ostensibly being made easier rather than hindered by institutional support. . . ."

With almost two-and-a-half dozen contributors, it is impossible now to deal coherently with the Poetics issue. While I had hoped that at least half the essays would concentrate on technique—questions like the line, sound, diction and so forth—only five, Levertov, Gilbert, Donald Hall, Charles O. Hartman and Alan Williamson, did so. Donald Hall's piece was the most thorough here. Three contributions that bear one way or another on sculpture are Donald Davie's, Michael Heller's and the inscripts of Czeslaw Milosz. Heller's piece probes deepest, exploring Pound and Rilke's ideas of form in relation to the sculptor each favors, Gaudier-Brezska and Rodin. As Gaudier wrote to Pound, "sculptural feeling is the appreciation of masses in relation. Sculptural ability is the

defining of these masses by a plane." If you translate gists or images for
masses and spatial planes for lines or spacing 'or image-constructs', you
begin to have a sense of the structure of the *Cantos*, the planes and
masses being, in Heller's words, "quotations from Jefferson and Adams,
politics, economics and so forth." With Rilke, the influence of sculpture
is even more profound. When he writes of "The Archaic Torso of Apollo,"
"there is no place/that does not see you. You must change your life," it
is the perfection of the statue, its rested totality, that calls us towards
our own wholeness. Davie brings in sculpture through the writing of
Walter Savage Landor, the 19th century romantic poet who suggests
that the lapidary or "chiseled" effect, rather than evidencing a lack of
feeling, is in fact "the aftermath and proof of very strong and tumultuous
feeling." Davie goes on to criticize our foreshortening of historical perspective "by which we make the unmanageable abundance of the inher-
ited past somehow manageable." For Landor, even the word "medio-
cre" meant not something run-of-the-mill or boring but rather "a standard
of accomplishment which, though relatively many attain it, many more
never do." Since epigram and epitaph are sculptural in nature, they
help us situate the prose or poetry of Milosz that leads off the issue.
Milosz's sentences and fragments have a durable, gemlike quality to them,
resembling Latin, as in the following:

> To find my home in one sentence, concise, as if hammered in
> metal, Not to enchant anybody. Not to gain a lasting name in
> posterity. An unnamed need for order, for rhythm, for form,
> which three words we oppose to chaos and nothingness.

Other essays include Tess Gallagher on the narrative impulse, Robert
Glück on allegory, Charles Simic on poetry and history, Kunitz and
Simpson on the roots and circumstances attending the birth of one of
their poems, Michael Palmer's selections from his notebooks, and Alberto Ríos on what it was like to grow up with Spanish forbidden in the
schools. Apart from Milosz, Gibbons, Davie and Heller, the three that
stood out for me were Fanny Howe on "The Ecstatic", Eva Heisler's
poem "Hiding Places", and Dick Barnes's "Matching Heaven With
Heaven". All three are relatively short yet have a great deal to say. In

160

her four pages, Howe penetrates the mind of Hopkins as well as anyone I have come across. She is equally at home with technical questions:

> Enlisting strong syllables to emphasize the individual weight of each sound, and therefore giving each word equal time, his lines make unpredictable shifts in tempo. This "sprung rhythm," together with inscaping, were intended to produce compositions of words, where the content was actually secondary to the musical and visual impression.

She is equally successful with the eighteenth-century Puritan poet Edward Taylor. Heisler's prose poem is marvelous in its evocation of the beginning poet trapped in the family while making her first secret discoveries, her "small cramped poems." The Barnes piece concerns breaking in horses, with the accent on paying attention to the horse rather than getting him to pay attention to you. The rider's task is to blend the life in his body with that in the horse's body. When you ask your horse to do something it should be his idea. Barnes is obviously describing a Taoist approach. Substitute writer for rider and you'll get the idea, though he himself never mentions writing.

Our Poetics issue we called *Bearings: Approaches to Poetry & the Poem*, having in mind the nuts and bolts of poetry, the navigational aspect, even the deep-seated attitudes poets take to their work. Given its richness and diversity, the issue enjoyed a modest success but might have reached more classrooms had more essays spoken to one another or to a more limited range. For our cover, I chose a watercolor by an old friend, Jim Sloan. Our first totally abstract painting, it was a choice that drew a good deal of favorable comment. Apart from the best of the art books, I have never seen a painting reproduced as well. The transparency and translucency were almost more obvious on our cover than in the original. Within the next year or those that followed, a number of poets and teachers used the issue, but not as many as I had hoped.

One thing that plagued us was our typesetter's decision to change to a new form of computer-run Baskerville some time during the issue. Reading the galleys, I had sensed a difference. During paste up, I realized that one typeface was smaller and, for my taste, more attractive. When one essay began opposite the final page of another with a different

Baskerville, the discrepancy was hard for us to miss. Whether readers picked up on it we'll never know. None mentioned it. Still, out of some thirty, only two or three essays ended opposite others with a different face. While we could have delayed the issue another several weeks, it hardly seemed worth it. Those essays where the face had been changed grew their own typos in abundance. The first two *Ironwoods* had used hot type where all errors you corrected stayed fixed, so you had only to check the entire line. Then, when our typesetters switched to more contemporary methods, you had to read the entire paragraph, sometimes several, to be certain no additional changes had been made, since the new technology made it both necessary and easier to add on other small adjustments. Whether this was purely determined by the process or was used to charge for avoidable corrections, I don't know. With the switch in typefaces, you pretty much had to read the entire essay word for word since more or fewer characters might fill the line using the new typeface. Then hyphenated words ending the line, for example, could show up in the middle of the next line, still wearing their hyphens. We talked to several other editors and found our experience repeated all across the country. On the front page of *Ironwood 25*, the first sentence reads: "In typesetting Alan Williamson's essay for our last issue, three quotations crucial to his argument were 'lost' by the computers after being correctly printed in the initial galleys." An apology followed, telling readers where they could read the correction. Our printers blamed our problems on electric surges caused by unexpected storms during the August monsoons. But there are devices to protect against this. The few knowledgeable people we checked with were convinced someone had pressed the wrong button.

* * *

We had Czeslaw Milosz for lunch that summer. For some reason, we had not seen him the previous one. It had been more than a year since he gave the Charles Eliot Norton lectures at Harvard, the first poet since T. S. Eliot to perform this office. He had also taught classes on Dostoyevsky there and later at Dartmouth. The mind-set of the students being what it was, he had been forced to introduce his particular Christian approach more gingerly than he might have otherwise. He thanked me for the copy of *Ironwood 16*, praising the issue and singling out what he called my *weltanschauung* or world view, which he felt held the poems together. Though I was flattered, I was even more embarrassed by such praise, having prided myself on what I considered the diversity of poems in *Ironwood*. If Milosz was correct, perhaps I had betrayed myself and my goals.

He talked at some length on Catholic teaching and practice regarding marriage and divorce, pointing out that, until roughly the year 1000, no attempt had been made to register marriages, in churches or any other place. What all this suggested to him was that those earlier centuries were a good deal more chaotic and confusing than the current authorities would like it to appear. One of us pointed out that the church wedding, complete with white bridal gown, only went back to the early 19th century. Milosz's remarks on the history of the institution of marriage within Catholicism, while not prefaced by any more general statement, seemed to suggest that the Church lacked a very clear-cut tradition in its first millenium and so might well find a way that was more open to change than the present rules and attitudes, provided there was a will to find that way.

Milosz was alone this time, since his wife had died sometime in the last year or so. His own English was good but he often had some difficulty catching the intent or meaning of a joke or funny story and would look at the speaker in a puzzled way or, just as often, with a slight, tentative smile on his face. If you repeated the story, he would make up for this the second time around with a rush of feeling.

With the Duncan issue, we ordered 2000 copies and got back 2300. In spite of previous assurances by a number of Duncan confederates, we sold roughly the same number, 1450, as we had with our other special issues. Mary McArthur had told us about her unsuccessful attempt to donate issues of her magazine to the University of North Carolina. So far, we had been reluctant to donate issues that cost so much to produce. With our surplus of Duncan issues, we decided to wait until two more issues had appeared and send the three, #22–#24, to at least forty elite colleges and universities, most of them in the Northeast, or mid-Atlantic states, explaining that they would receive two more issues as they appeared, ending with #26. This amounted to a five-issue subscription. At that point, we would invoice the libraries, hoping they would renew the subscriptions themselves. Given their endowments and traditions, these institutions would be more inclined to carry out serious study and research. They included colleges and universities with strong creative writing programs. As indicated by computer, the pattern of university subscriptions suggested that the more run-of-the-mill libraries would follow the lead of the best university libraries in their region or vicinity. We enclosed a brochure describing the contents of our first 20 issues and mailed these to all libraries on our list with a cover letter. First, though, we had sent away for a list of gummed labels with the addresses of all college and university libraries with an annual acquisitions budget of at least a million dollars. To help pay for these issues, we asked for and received from the Arizona Commission on the Arts a grant which was matched through CCLM by Mary's brother, George Cusick.

Initial subscriptions came from Princeton, Yale and Kenyon College, among others. Six months later, an additional 65 colleges and universities, most of them in the Midwest or Far West, were sent two-year subscriptions. Nearly half the total wound up subscribing to the magazine, and other university libraries followed suit. Of the remainder, a handful turned down the gift and a few were never heard from.

Ironwood 25 included work by about 50 poets, only 13 of whom had more than one poem or an extended sequence. Of the larger groups, Amy Bartlett's four poems and Michael Waters's two and Lucia Perillo's three were each excellent in their own way. Susan Howe's six poems and Fanny Howe's seven-page selection from *Franklin Park*, are, both of them, unlike anyone else's work. For those with a thirst for things mystical, Stephanie Strickland's 18-page selection from *The Simone Weil Book* should repay whatever effort they put into reading it. Finally, there are superb short poems by Robin Behn, Carolyn R. Miller, Linda Gregg, Wendell Berry, Ellen Bryant Voigt, Jon Silkin, Thomas Lux and Denis Johnson. A few months after #25 came back from the printer, Czeslaw Milosz remarked during lunch at our house how much he liked Berry's poem. I had liked it myself, feeling that a man who lived from and on the land as he did, had found a way to convince us that these time-honored forms were indeed suitable for his special occasions. What pleased me most was how deeply his honesty and self-scrutiny pervaded the poem without in the least marring its ceremonial aspect. The two Howes were sisters. Fanny, a novelist and poet, was a convert to Catholicism who also wrote brilliant, incisive essays. Many people considered her a worthy successor to the Objectivist, Lorine Niedecker. Susan Howe was something of an unorthodox Dickinson scholar, her restless intelligence trained on the American past. That her poetry was related to that of the 'language' poets did not prevent its being permeated by a profound sense of history. They were the daughters of Mark DeWolff Howe, a famous Harvard law professor who had tangled bitterly with Senator Joseph McCarthy. An Irish novelist and playwright,their mother had founded and run the Poet's Theater in Cambridge, Massachusetts during the 50's.

The issue contained a long interview with Denis Johnson, Kathleen Spivack's vivid memoir of Robert Lowell and, finally, Hilda Morley's 17 page review-essay of H.D.'s *Collected Poems 1912–1944*. After a half page concerning her own adolescent years as an apprentice poet in the Palestine of the 30's, nourished by a "living landscape of sea, fig trees, olive trees, close to the Greek landscapes of H.D.'s Imagist poems", Morley details their meetings in London; how, for example, when she asked H.D. about D. H. Lawrence, she smiled and would only say, "You make me feel so historical." Morley retains a high regard for *Sea-Garden* and several of the early H.D. collections. Though there are interesting poems issuing from H.D.'s relationship to Lawrence and Freud, Morley considers much of her middle period as marked by repetition. She examines H.D.'s preference for the hard over the soft, for ice, snow, the frozen and for what is averted, renounced, withheld. This she views as representative of withdrawal, "standing apart, making oneself different from others." It is in *The War Trilogy* that H.D. comes into full command of her powers. These changes are prefigured in "R.A.F." and "May 1943", written during the blitz, where H.D.'s true, everyday voice is heard, along with the voices of others. Much of this more casual speech carries over into *The War Trilogy* which Morley considers "a major achievement for the variety of material alone, as well as the resourcefulness of the language, all of this reflected "in a marvelous suppleness of meter, of line-break, of rhythmic speed and slowness—above all the poet's daring in making use of so many kinds of utterance and unifying them by means of a voice which . . . is usually in a state of exploration and discovery."

The issue ended with an exchange of letters between Michael Davidson and Jack Gilbert, concerning Gilbert's essay in our Poetics issue, *Ironwood 24*. As usual in such cases, half what each man has to say the other man misses. Still, it was the kind of exchange I wanted *Ironwood* to foster and stimulate. At bottom, attitudes toward Semiotics and the "Language" poets were involved.

Two poems in the issue won Pushcart Prizes, Robin Behn's "Over 102nd Street" and Lucia Perillo's "Jury Selection", reprinted here:

JURY SELECTION

If they only could have put that in the papers, how the winter
    light hangs thickly in those southern Massachusetts towns,
sucking orange at four p.m. from the last spasm of daylight, then
    glowing morbid and humming
with a sound barely audible—not human, more like some rasping
    harmonic twanged
from the animated hulk of machinery that somewhere keeps it
    all running: this town
where the fish have been abandoned for over a century, the old
    men left
with just the memory of fish swimming in their bones, telling stories
    about the Azores
from their perch on rusted forty-gallon drums that have come to
    rest on the riprap
that's been brought in to seal the village from the sea. And what
    it would feel like to be a man
walking around smothering inside the fester of all that—you can
    almost understand why they did it,
raped that woman on the pool table at Big Dan's, in the broad daylight
    of Bobby Darrin singing Volare for a quarter
then Mack the Knife on the replay,
        . . . *cause old mackie's back in town* . . .
           felt   and the mown green
smelling of wet wool and—yes, sweet jesus—even fish, their blood
    stirring with the sea.
You can almost understand why a woman might have needed it.

But before it gets too complicated, remember: we're supposed to
    work with only the available labels

to construct questions that will discern shades of meaning, measure
   culpability. Whether this woman
has a houseful of gray babies in dirty sleepers, which one's father
   has been named,
where it has happened before, who had drunk which kind of liquor
and how much. She says she only went into the tavern for a minute
to tug on the silver nozzles of the cigarette machine, but the
   thin curtains that line her bedroom windows
are clearly visible from the street. The whole town knows. Even
   some of these young men
carry the blue nickels of her thumbprints on the back of their thighs,
   from this time,
but also the times before. Who whimpered, which ones came in her
and how often, which ones merely watched without speaking from the
   threshold.
The men were of a darker race, refusing to speak our language and
   moving their dark arms
in the ancestral motions of urging we only dimly remember, which still
   arouse us even in our embarrassment, through the electric current
of testimony. Whether a crime has been committed (because the woman
   has
   her Chesterfields, her change coins clenched & sweaty in her palm)
or not, their long-boned faces make this offense more palpable—
   the slick skin
and elegant hard moustaches recalling to us the brown eyes of our own
   lives, when in darkness
the vestiges of something we do not claim to know rise out from our
   bodies
and we seize it and do violence.

We all do violence.

Because the woman was as dark as any of the others,
with no green card and a name you won't find in the phone book.
What is on trial here is a thousand years of women plodding on thick
   legs, arms draped with string baskets,
towards some market in another continent, where boats pull into the
   waiting lips of shore
to meet these women and laud the correctness of their sexless march
   with fruit and cod and men come home
with the musk of Ecuadorian whores still riding on their loins.

In the end, the real trial takes place in words exchanged
in pissed-up alleyways between tight stone buildings, in words
that are to us gutteral and pronounced with too much tongue.
In the end the jury forgives everything but the pool table.
And on the streets of town, in the late afternoon light,
mothers tear their dresses away from their stout provincial breasts,
     and carry placards, and weep,
and spit at no one in particular,
for the love of their sons,
not the love of their daughters.

    The poem starts with winter light "sucking orange at four p.m. from
the last spasm of daylight", the image reminiscent of Eliot's "patient
etherized upon a table", though more physical than Eliot and without
his latinate diction. The first stanza makes adroit, convincing use of sy-
nesthesia. Words like "morbid", "humming", "audible", "rasping",
"twanged" and "fester" speak to the mind through the senses. "With
only the memory of fish swimming in their bones," the old men perch
over riprap brought in to seal the village from the sea and tell stories of
the Azores. The jetty is emblematic of the town—sealed off from the
sea, the young men, with little working experience, already condemned
to share the fate of the old. The unnamed town is New Bedford, scene
of a gang rape on a pool table.
    Instead of simply expressing outrage, Perillo makes two statements
that are, to say the least, provocative: "you can/ almost understand why
they did it" and "You can almost understand why a woman might have
needed it." The word to keep in mind is "almost". Strictly speaking, to
almost understand is not to understand. And if, according to the French
proverb, "to understand everything is to forgive everything," forgive-
ness remains a divine attribute, implying a sin that must be atoned for.
Again, the second statement says "a woman", not "the woman" or "all
women. "So Perillo is hypothetically including herself but not the victim, attempting as she is to see things up close, from inside. The two
statements speak for a segment of public opinion, which has a way of
crystallizing in such statements. Much of what follows deals with evidence. In the very next sentence, she addresses her readers as we. We
are both public opinion and potential jurors, and have to weigh the evi-

dence for ourselves. A thousand years of history are involved in the years of thick-legged women plodding "towards some market in another continent where boats pull into the / waiting lips of shore . . ." The poet shows the controversy being fought out in words "in pissed up alleyways between tight stone buildings . . ."

That "We all do violence" is something of a liberal cliché until the author explains it in terms of how we project our own repressed or unconscious drives onto darker races. Even here, though, this is a likely rallying cry for liberal public opinion, something we should all consider without swallowing it whole. Nowhere in fact does Perillo render a verdict, though she does remark near the end that the jury "forgives everything but the pool table." Saddest of all and closest perhaps to the essential truth is the way "mothers tear their dresses away from their stout provincial breasts,"/ . . and weep,/ for the love of their sons,/ not the love of their daughters." If this is male dominance, it is the elder women of the tribe who sanction and enforce it, a theme Perillo returns to in other poems.

Despite my arguments in favor of the poem, Mary Cuddihy found the statements offensive in view of the atrocious nature of the crime, with the arguments used to deny the reality of a single rape advanced here to minimize a gang rape. At a small supper not long after, she invited two other women, one a distinguished novelist and poet, to read and comment on the poem. When the two women agreed with Mary, I summoned Alberto Ríos, also present, to give his opinion. After studying it carefully as a poem, he read it in terms of the women's objections. He considered the poem excellent and daring in its use of these statements.

Original writers rarely wrote what you expected or wanted them to. We were the jury, Alberto felt, and that was the point of the poem: to make us think for ourselves on a difficult, serious subject instead of merely nudging an existent response. I went ahead, sticking to my decision, and received no complaints from our readers. Perillo wound up with a Pushcart Prize.

*   *   *

By mid-July, I had gotten John Taggart's agreement to contribute something to a second George Oppen issue. He agreed as well to our reprinting an earlier piece on *Seascape*. Robert Hass gave me permission to transcribe the tape of his tribute to Oppen, delivered at a public celebration of his 75th birthday. Working from the tapes proved difficult but fascinating. Certain words tended to combine while others came apart in the middle. I thought back to the *shwa* so dear to linguists and grammarians. Often, this sound would drive the early and final letters of a word into the background so that the *shwa* sound linked up with the strongest nearby consonants. Ever scrupulous, Hass corrected the final text, modifying a few of his remarks.

Another thing that had prompted me toward an Oppen issue was the announcement, at the close of the memorial service, that the Archive for New Poetry at the University of California in San Diego was interested in acquiring, by sale or donation, all letters and papers from or having to do with George Oppen. This meant that these would become available to scholars within a year or two. It would be simpler, then, and less subject to bureaucratic delay if I got permission to use such letters before they were transferred.

Not long after the Oppen memorial service, I phoned Eve Haight to ask if I could use George's letters to her as part of our special Oppen issue. She made it clear she wanted them printed as a book. When I pointed out that neither action precluded the other, she agreed to send me the letters. Within a fortnight, Anita Barrows, a poet and friend of the Oppens, phoned to say that Andy Meyer, George Oppen's niece, who engaged in an extended correspondence with her uncle, was going through the letters. Rachel Blau-DuPlessis would be including some of them in the volume she was preparing for the publishers. Was I interested? With few unpublished poems lying around, I certainly was. Before long, Andy telephoned me and we set up an appointment to meet and discuss the letters. I don't recall exactly how many she brought but I went over them with her. Andy was tall, attractive and sympathetic, with an acute intelligence and a sense of the irrational that was close to the sources of poetry. Looking at early drafts of such *Seascape* poems as "West", it was obvious that her influence was more than marginal. Of course, poets use what comes to hand and transform or invent when it can take them no further. In this case, however, some material was simply brought over into a different context with powerful results. Both the letters to Andy Meyer and those to Eve Haight, her daughter, showed an emotional range wider and richer than normally available in the poems.

Equally important for the Oppen issue was to contact the people at

U.C.-San Diego in order to gain some kind of access to the Oppen letters and papers as soon as these became available. I set about getting in touch with Michael Davidson. The Oppen papers, it turned out, were scribbled or typed on every kind of paper imaginable, undated and mostly thrown together at random. As Davidson was to write: "More often than not, such gatherings were done by means of pipestem cleaners, pins or wires and other household items. Several manuscripts are held together by means of a nail driven through the pages into a plywood backing." When I let Davidson know my intentions, he promised to get back to me as soon as any kind of order and relationship was established within the collection. We had a year but, in such a setting, time can evaporate.

As I saw it, Burton Hatlen's huge special issue of *Sagetrieb*, *George Oppen: Man and Poet*, made my task that much more difficult. I didn't want to use these people, except maybe one or two. Most would already have said what they had to or wanted to. Keeping scholars to a minimum, I determined to put together an impressive collection of poets. One scholar I tried right off was Norman Finkelstein, who had two or three essays in the Hatlen issue. Wanting to make it the focus of our Oppen issue, I asked him to write on *Seascape* but what he sent me only touched on two or three of the *Seascape* poems. When I confronted him about this, he admitted to having reservations about *Seascape*. Sobered by the experience, I wound up returning his essay. Of the remaining scholars, the two that seemed most appropriate for the issue were Hugh Kenner and Marjorie Perloff. While Perloff expressed her intention of writing on Oppen's short lyrics, she mislaid the letter I had written with all of this spelled out and phoned me just before our deadline. Anxious to write something, Perloff was confident she could do it quickly. When I reminded her of her original topic, she suggested Oppen and the anthologies. She asked for time to think of a new topic when I pointed out that John Taggart had already chosen that one. She came up with "Of Being Numerous" and had something ready not long after our deadline. Though "Numerous" may well have been Oppen's most important poem, it had been covered extensively in the sixteen years since his Pulitzer Prize. Now, there were four people coming to grips with it: Perloff, Kenner, Burton Hatlen and the English poet Jeremy Hooker. As it turned out, Hooker and Hatlen had most to say. Influenced by the Russian formalist Bakhtin, Hatlen concentrates on the plurality of voices in *Of Being Numerous*, exploring the processes by which these voices emerge. Hatlen's five linguistic processes are interrogation, negation, repetition, interruption, and dialogue. Without ignoring continuities of meaning, he shows how the voices disclosed in the poem vastly enrich its meaning. Read Hatlen's way, the entire formal structure makes a good deal more sense.

In what he terms "a brief and highly contentious digression," Jeremy Hooker develops some ideas first put forward by George Steiner, who described Heidegger's "hard clarity" as a "characteristic bit of ontological-Nazi idiom". Pound's desire to produce "poetry that is hard and clear", he finds a disturbing echo of this. He is likewise disturbed that Gaudier-Brzeska's perception of mass in sculpture lies so close to his perception of human "masses" in the war, which he viewed as a great "remedy" for reducing them. The problem here is that such ideas are "both a taproot of much that is valuable in Modernism, and are capable of terrifying misapplication in the social and political sphere." As for Oppen, Hooker questions whether his seeing implies a distance between the seer and the thing seen, since seeing in this way makes possible the separation of self from will. Yet he is careful to point out that Oppen is remarkably free from male egotism and denies the primacy of the self as a knowing subject. It is hard to be certain that the great strain between the one and the many in "Of Being Numerous" is not built into the very method which seeks to define "the boundaries/Of our distances." To Oppen's courageous question whether one's distance from the people does not increase as the intensity of seeing does, Hooker points out that "it is not the same as asking whether the intensity of *his* way of seeing, rather than of all seeing, isolates the one from the many." Aside from this digression, Hooker's reading has many valuable things to say.

While relatively short for such a 'big' subject, Perloff's essay begins, like an Oppen letter, in full stride. For one thing, she immediately examines and cross-examines the title. Much of Perloff's method involves microscopic attention to sound, including the look of words. Here, Perloff seems totally fair to Oppen. This may be why she can end her essay referring to "this beautiful and difficult long poem." She sees the poem as the record of a survivor of a shipwreck himself in the modern city. Nowhere does she attempt to take seriously the questions Oppen asks himself in the poem, thereby implicitly accusing him of bad faith. Making no allowances for Oppen's philosophical bent, she repeatedly points to abstractions and faults him for using nouns instead of images. Even though the full name of each is given at the beginning of the book, people's names are treated as if he considers them abstractions. That the poem could be the honest poem of a shipwrecked survivor, whether of Communism, the '30's, exile or whatever—and still be about what Oppen says it is, does not seem to have crossed her mind. Having lived in New York from the early '30's up to the mid '50's, I can vouch for the changes that took place in those early '50's. Coming East from L.A. two or three decades ago, Perloff may have seen it quite differently. I know I would, had I come from L.A., so often referred to as 'seven suburbs in search of a city.' Apart from that, I see the shadow of William Carlos Williams lurking behind many of her critical remarks. A native of New Jersey, Robert Pinsky makes some of these same points but does so openly and less judgmentally. Hugh Kenner's brief for Oppen quietly focuses on one or two important points.

I had hoped that the issue would focus on the poems from *Seascape* onward. Apart from our reprint of Taggart's earlier *Seascape* essay, there was Michael Heller's piece on Oppen's "Going Down Middle Voice", which explored the influence of Simon Weil on the later poems. Here, Heller was correct in pointing out that Weil's influence on Oppen, like that of Heidegger and Maritain, took the form of the pressure a certain kind of intellectual and moral eminence exerted on him, holding up a standard of rigor and intensity. It is curious how Weil could be so instrumental a force for both Milosz and Oppen. Another point made by Heller was that the real test for Oppen was which poems he recited to himself as he lay wounded in that Alsatian foxhole. Blake, Reznikov, Wyatt were the names that came up. It is hard to think of a more extreme test.

In his tribute, Robert Hass shows how, in Oppen's poetry "you can actually watch, as the words are laid down on the page, the process from which the perception of the thing gets born into its numinous quality as a word, an abstraction out of the thing." At the level of prosody, the great discovery of the Objectivists was "not the image as a picture but the formation of the image as an x-ray." As soon as they had turned the imagist picture into an x-ray, it became clear that an image was not "a picture of a thing, but a picture of the mind perceiving a thing." From there, the morality of perception came to be an issue. So, moment by moment in Oppen's work, you have a sense of an "enormous ethical pressure brought to bear on the act of perception." Hass goes on to point to the sentence as an activity of perception and therefore of consciousness itself where the effect is great purity, as with bird flight or the running of children.

Of the remaining contributions, three took the form of memoir: Philip Booth on the Oppens in Maine, Marie Syrkin on George's meetings with Reznikoff, her late husband, and Sharon Olds's collage of incidents from her visits to the Oppens in San Francisco. Cid Corman's huge review-essay of *Primitive* also contains biographical elements. There are other worthwhile essays by poets as distinguished as Louise Glück, Hilda Morley, Charles Bernstein and Jack Marshall. The issue contains two pieces on the stages in the writing of "Disasters," in some ways the single most significant poem in George's final collection. There is another short piece showing three stages in the writing of 'West' from *Seascape: Needle's Eye*. Even more valuable are the letters to Georges's sister, June Oppen Degnan, showing George's state of mind as he starts writing poetry again, as well as his responses to current events, Jung and other matters. Finally, there are the illuminating selections from George's Daybooks. It was almost a year from the time I first contacted Michael Davidson that he sent me his selections. At my request, he also sent along xeroxes of the original pages from which they were culled. What he had chosen was breathtaking in the depth and scope of its particulars: epigrams, unpublished poems, earlier versions of published poems and germs of others, comments on various contemporary poets, imaginative flights, and deep philosophic self-questionings. After closely reading the pages from which these excerpts were taken, I found only a couple of things to drop and an equal number to add in their place.

Finally, I included four uncollected poems from the era of *Discrete Series*, the first three of which had appeared in *Poetry*. The chances are that today's average mainstream reader would prefer them to most poems in that book. Among these Daybook jottings, there were several poems the average poet would be happy to include in his latest collection. Finally, there was the cover. I had long ago fixed on Mary Oppen's collage portrait of George. It was done in a Cubist manner, the arms fashioned of newspaper pages with photos of oil derricks and other unlikely juxtapositions. George was wearing what looks like a bathrobe with a red figured lapel, the result of draping a tie around neck and shoulders, open-necked to reveal a white shirt. In the portrait, the hair looks like chunks of granite shooting out at odd angles the way curly hair does. The brow is knit, the eyes black, stormy. The upper left quadrant of the picture is painted a medium yellow. The sad, severe countenance with hands folded reminds me of an old matador in a greyish suit of lights waiting his turn to kill or be killed. Unable to buy it from Mary Oppen, I did the next best thing and used it as the cover. I leave our readers with these lines from our back cover:

> It is impossible the world should be either good or bad
> If its colors are beautiful or if they are not beautiful
> If parts of it taste good or if no parts of it taste good
> It is as remarkable in one case as the other.

The issue wound up over 100 pages longer than any previous, so we jumped the price to $4.00. For all its 320 pages, it came back from the printer a few days before our November 1 deadline. Not only had it been a labor of love, there had not been many problems along the way. It was fitting that Andy Meyer, George Oppen's niece, whose correspondence with her uncle had contributed so much to the issue's weight and substance, should be there to help us celebrate and mail out the issues.

*   *   *

At the time we brought out issue #20 featuring the 'language' poets, it had occurred to me that one function of *Ironwood* on the national level might be to represent aspects of Bay Area poetry to the country at large. The San Francisco scene was split into so many diverse, often mutually hostile groups, that there was no single magazine to deal with the range of these groups or individuals beyond the *Poetry Flash*, a monthly newsletter which performed its calendar functions well and strove heroically to cover all groups with brief essays, reviews and interviews. Moribund if not obsolete, the Beats continued to dominate local T.V.'s educational channels as if nothing much had happened since the 50's.

By the time we had featured Linda Gregg, Milosz and the 'language' poets, I realized that we had assumed a certain function, without my being aware of it. The Duncan issue carried this development further. Even as we put the second Oppen issue to bed, I was already beginning to think about an issue on Jack Spicer, whose importance had been eclipsed by the arrival of the Beats.

One group of poets whose critical perspectives and acumen I had called upon was the Stanford group, five poets who had studied with Yvor Winters and Donald Davie. The word neoclassical came to be associated with the five. For one thing, they were drawn to large themes and to civic concerns; for another, both their poetry and their criticism exhibited sanity, clarity, coherence and flexibility. They shared a fondness for the long poem and the extended sequence. While they might seem to look backwards in time, much of their work was exploratory, even experimental. I should add that their mutual differences were many, tending to widen over the years. Each of the group published at least one volume of criticism or scholarship along with poetry collections. The group included John Peck, Robert Hass, Robert Pinsky, James Mc-Michael and John Matthias. Peck wrote for us on Milosz, Matthias on Duncan, Pinsky on Oppen, Hass on Wright, Tranströmer, Milosz and Oppen. All but Matthias and McMichael had poems in the magazine.

If one emerging function of *Ironwood* was to highlight certain developments in the poetry of the western United States and, more particularly, the Bay Area, another was to present avant-garde poets and movements to a largely mainstream audience. In practice this meant combining mainstream poetry with more avant-garde work in the same issue, making sure you didn't push your mainstream audience too hard or too fast. Whatever the fate of "language" poetry as a movement, I was convinced some of their values and practices were bound to find fertile ground among our other contributors so that mainstream poetry would begin to change. I have already seen a number of mainstream poets like Karen Brennan where this is happening.

* * *

In thanking the National Endowment for the Arts for a grant in support of *Ironwood 18*, the time had come to make it clear that our accep-

176

tance should not be construed as implying agreement with the policies of the Reagan Administration, particularly its foreign policy in Central America. America was out of Vietnam by the time I first asked for a grant, and issue #18 the first one typeset and printed since the newly-elected Reagan had enunciated his foreign policy. I had no intention of using my front page to harangue readers and supporters on various political evils. If our grants were not intended to make us silent accomplices of policies like our Central American one, then there would be no problem. If on the other hand, we were left alone, that was one small proof of relative freedom. After two or three years, one prominent contributor complained that in publishing my disclaimer, I was speaking for all contributors, including him, and he supported the administration's position in Central America. In a political democracy, he felt, it should go without saying that government aid implied no uniformity of views. I pointed out that "democracy", like "freedom", was a word used by all kinds of governments, including dictatorships, and that it had to be constantly verified in practice, which is what I was trying to do. In introducing our final issue, when it came time to thank the National Endowment, I included my usual disclaimer, but made a point of adding: "Obviously, our views do not necessarily reflect the views of individual contributors."

*   *   *

Apart from poems by William Bronk, Barbara Guest, Alan Williamson and a special section exploring the work of Beverly Dahlen, *Ironwood 27* consisted entirely of unsolicited work. At the time I first wrote to her several years before, Guest was suffering from a writer's block. When I told her I had spent my first twenty summers in Water Mill, she mentioned having rented a house that used to belong to our family, the very house I grew up in. The poem she finally sent me, "An Emphasis Falls On Reality," ends in a way that suggests such a house:

    This house was drawn for them.
    It looks like a real house.
    Perhaps they will move in today,
    they will cross the transcendent

> lawn into ephemeral dusk and
> they will move right out of that
> into night, translucent,
> selective night with its trees that are
> the darkened copies of all trees.

Other poets whose work stood out for me were Phyllis Thompson, Bill Tremblay, Steve Orlen, Sharon Olds and Diane Glancy. Then there were two extraordinary longer poems by Yehuda Amichai, "The Elegy on the Lost Child" and "Jerusalem, 1967", both translated by Stephen Mitchell. In addition, we printed three shorter Amichai poems translated by Chana Bloch, moving in their simple humanness, their basic wisdom.

Among those who submitted essays on Dahlen's work were Mark Linenthal, Gayle Davis, Peter Holland and Rachel Blau-DuPlessis. Advised by the publisher Eileen Callahan that the pages of the unbound books had been damaged by insects and mildew, we reprinted Robert Duncan's "Afterword" to Dahlen's *Egyptian Poems*, along with the poems themselves. In contrast to most language-oriented West Coast poets, Dahlen, according to Mark Linenthal, was remarkable for her psychological concerns, "concerns which have feminist implications and mythic dimensions." "Language," says Dahlen, "takes the place of the body which deepens in silence around it." Still, she considered language too material, too much body, to serve as vehicle for thought. Quoting her to the effect that "The emptiness in which the poem appears . . . is a part of the poem's meaning as form," Linenthal concluded that "silence itself speaks" in *The Egyptian Poems*.

Rachel Blau-DuPlessis's essay explored the seemingly endless meanings of the word "reading" from Dahlen's lifelong sequence, *A Reading*. So dense in their multiplicity are her reflections that I can only indicate a few of them. The word "palimpsest" suggested "the desire to manifest, by some verbal or textual gesture, the sense of presence, simultaneity, multiple pressures of one moment, yet at the same time the disjunct, the absolutely parallel and different. . . ." DuPlessis considered *A Reading* "an articulation between lyric (the force moving) and documentary (record without judgement)." There were no marginal notes, no asides in *A Reading* because there was no distinction between text and space, text and comment. "All is margin, all is center." In addition, *A Reading* was

an interminable analysis, a point emphasized by the Freudian psychia-
trist Peter Holland in his essay. Robert Duncan's *Afterword* took Dahlen's achievement with utter seriousness, reverence even. Duncan pointed
out that he himself had asked to write this introduction which he saw fit
to place after, not before, the poems.

The issue reprinted all eight of *The Egyptian Poems* plus eight pages
representing three sections of *A Reading* as well as Dahlen's more discursive "Something/Nothing." Here is a section from book four of *A
Reading*:

> it goes on you can't look at it
> for fear of injury blindness
> trying to see it out of the corner of an eye
> a room, *cirrus can barely get under the door*
> he said and I laughed
> he knows so much we don't have a leg to stand on.
> what if knowing what if a kind of green
> serious older
> what if older
> getting the religion mixed up with the language
> I labored
> I had not been working here very long
> a short time ago
> when bottles
> sea green bottles
> and the smoke inside
> I said I thought it was trapped
> some small animal
> closer to animal
> and the smooth bodies of women
> women. women how they
> love it such an expansiveness of flesh
> such lovely breasts ridges
> no wonder the gorgeous bones *that thing*
> *which it is and no other thing*
> the filtered light
> I thought o god touch touch touch
> lover her in the palm of my hand
> in my very only body

that line that hill that was me
I can barely believe turning bodies into art
how they long for it skinny flaming
licked up in it sucking his cock seasalt
the hair
holes eyes all air and curling

*

San Francisco
February, 1979

Finally, the issue contained an essay by Norman Finkelstein, "Pressing For The End" which deals with those poems that seek "relentlessly to end themselves, poems which, almost mute, rise out of silence, sing suddenly and just as suddenly cease, falling silent." The essay discusses this in the work of the older Objectivists like Zukofsky and Oppen, before devoting three pages to Creeley and another three to Jack Spicer. It was here, in the discussion of Spicer, especially of his first poem in the sequence, *Language,* that I began to realize how much of Spicer I had failed to take into consideration. It is here that Spicer writes "No one listens to poetry". As soon as the poem admits this, "it achieves a state of 'aimlessness' like that of the ocean, its unattainable model—and promptly ceases to exist as utterance." Rising as it did out of properly theological concerns, the essay was able to plumb the depths of poems central to their authors and all important for an understanding of their overall achievement.

After four years, I opted for another Jim Wade painting for our cover. This one was wholly abstract, the nearer plane nearly all vermillion, the more distant one closer to earth colors.

Early in Spring of '85, I received a circular from Dawn Kolokithos in Oakland outlining a proposed conference on Jack Spicer scheduled for June '86 in San Francisco. It would include a symposium with dozens of participants, and other related meetings and lectures. While she was anxious to commit *Ironwood* to some kind of special issue, I was leery of printing all these people without some notion of who they were, and how much they could contribute. Attempting to sound her out, I telephoned but the connection was broken twice and my message apparently undelivered. When we reached Marin that summer, I learned, to my chagrin, that she was in Europe. I was thinking hard about special issues, with Emily Dickinson in mind as well as Spicer. Sometime in 1986, a Dickinson anniversary would occur and a Spicer one about the same time. The more I read each poet, the more I sensed a deep affinity—both poets had religious backgrounds and had retained a profound sense of the invisible in their poetry. Perhaps the connection lay here. Had I been able to reach Kolokithos that summer, the special issue might have been confined to Spicer, provided I was allowed some choice regarding whom we printed from the Spicer symposium.

There was, it developed, a series of poetics lectures scheduled at New College in the city for that fall, with three poets lecturing on Spicer: Susan Howe, Robert Creeley and Beverly Dahlen. I determined to get in touch with all three and convince them to let us print at least one lecture from each. I succeeded with Dahlen and, not long after, with Susan Howe. In both cases, what I wound up with was, I think, two lectures. In fact, I soon had a nearly finished version of Dahlen's, amazing for how well it combined conventional but imaginative scholarship with her own painful probing of the unexplored depths of her subject. I had heard respected poets who admired her work speak of her inability to write prose. Here was a living refutation. When I received it, the Howe essay included enlargements of Dickinson's handwriting, showing that she had often failed to end her lines on the expected end rhyme but in a manner more akin to our contemporary practice, especially that of the Black Mountain poets. At this point, there may be no way to prove conclusively that this was intentional—the lack of space in the small, handmade booklets in which she inscribed her poems may have been a factor. Still, I could see how, in a number of cases, she could have written them in the conventional manner but somehow chose not to. If it cannot be conclusively proven, it cannot be disproved either.

Creeley was harder to get hold of and pin down. Provided we worked from a tape and didn't bother him with questions about grammar, spelling and sources he agreed finally to let us print his lecture, which he titled "The Girl Next Door."

Were we to include Spicer in such an issue, Lew Ellingham had something valuable to contribute. For several years, he had been conducting a series of interviews with members of the Duncan-Spicer circle and had accumulated an impressive number of manuscripts and interviews that amplified and corrected one another. After hearing synopses of several, I asked to look at one he called "The Death of Jack Spicer," made up of full exchanges by ten friends of Spicer, including Harold Dull, Jim and Fran Herndon, Robert Duncan, Stan Persky, Robin Blaser and Ebbe Borregard, woven into a narrative sequence that gives a convincing picture of what happened. Since this is how many of the best historical accounts are arrived at, you actually get to see the process. It has the thickness proper to history, many strands of causation with a certain tentativeness that allows for mistakes, particularly minor ones, Ellingham recommended John Granger, making available several chapters from his Ph.D. dissertation on Spicer. I also sounded out Bruce Boone, who had shown a strong interest in Spicer when writing for the Duncan issue. Without being very specific, Boone gave me a tentative go-ahead. Still, what he said led me to expect something long and complex, since Spicer was his absolutely favorite poet. A number of Spicer-philes let me know that they loved Dickinson and were aware of all kinds of parallels.

While mainly preoccupied with finishing up the George Oppen issue by November, I found the time, on returning to Tucson, to contact Hayden Carruth and Paul Metcalf regarding Dickinson. Metcalf, with an abiding interest in the literature of the period when his ancestor Herman Melville lived and wrote, readily assented. Dickinson was the only major figure from that period whom he had failed to write on. Hayden Carruth agreed to write something provided it was on the short side. Again, Dickinson was almost the only major figure in American poetry he had not written about. Then I telephoned Gilbert Sorrentino and Ross Feld, each of whom had written importantly on Jack Spicer. A profilic novelist, Feld had contributed a number of brilliant essays to *Parnassus*, a tightly edited, deeply intellectual journal of reviews with a flair for controversy. I wanted these two because, though neither was a scholar, each one wrote well and knew his subject.

That fall, when Lynn Sukenick joined the University of Arizona Creative Writing faculty for a year, we saw quite a bit of each other. A few years earlier, at U.C.-Santa Cruz, I had interceded for her in a tenure dispute. Lynn was spending more time now on a novel and a series of short stories. When she heard that the following Fall's *Ironwood* would be a special issue dealing with Dickinson and Jack Spicer, she offered to take part, writing a piece on Dickinson. What she came up with was beautifully written, wonderfully accessible, full of the kind of paradox that Dickinson was famous for. In "Piecing Emily Dickinson", she borrows part of E.D.'s voice to write her 19 scrupulous paragraphs—a living quilt. The patch below shows more than any summary I could make:

> A line break is a pause that seeks its own extinction, that hungers forward. A dash is not as progressive; it merely separates one thing from another. Huge amounts of time can live on either side of a dash. Dickinson's use of the dash creates grammatical Possibility (is the word more attached to what is on its left or right, or to a line below or above) and its factotum, Choice. Dashes allow a word to stand alone as it would in a Lexicon, her favorite book, her version of a book of law. (Her grandfather, father, brother, all lawyers.) The word, standing alone, is filled with Definition. Then we must discern its attachments in order to make progress.

It was with great pleasure that I placed her series of notes at the head of the issue.

Paul Metcalf spent several months concentrating on Dickinson—the poems and letters primarily, but also Richard Sewall's *Life* and Jay Leyda's *The Years And Hours Of Emily Dickinson* as well as Susan Howe's recent *My Emily Dickinson*. More critical of his subject than other contributors, Metcalf considered her too demanding of her friends or potential lovers. The reason she was able to let go in her letters was that she knew it wouldn't happen in the flesh. For all their passion, the love letters are too "romantic and abstract." He criticizes her, and by extension Amherst itself, for her indifference to the Civil War. After all, it was her chief poetry correspondent and adviser Thomas Higginson who placed himself at the head of a troop of Black volunteers engaged in enemy territory. Austin, her brother, paid $500 to send a substitute, probably an Irishman. He recognizes a patronizing tendency in her letters, natural in such a "proud and arrogant clan". Metcalf thinks a Dickinson poem at its best when the bulk of it "is an outward gesture, that then, in the last line or two, runs back upon itself—with an ironic, perverse, failed stab at Yankee neatness."

For Dahlen, 'The doctrine of justification by faith placed the responsibility for redemption on each individual soul," for many, an intolerable burden. "There is a way in which, beginning with Luther, the Protestants steadily drained mercy from Christianity." With the day of salvation postponed, "the figure of Christ retreated" in the face of exhortations to confront God unaided. Dickinson's absolute "refusal to accept the debased God of a now liberal, prosperous America" was part and parcel of her radical subjectivity. If she was not a Puritan, she nevertheless submitted to the authority of her own soul, her withdrawal from the world her final act of critical rebellion. With reference to Dickinson, Dahlen quotes Julia Kristeva: "A woman, a daughter has nothing to laugh about when the symbolic order collapses . . ." Since the essay is so complex, deepening as it proceeds, there is no way I can do justice to its manifold richness, except to recommend it to those who can take their reality straight.

In reading Dickinson, Hayden Carruth believes it is necessary to reduce the poem to a more conventional arrangement regarding punctuation, provided he or she returns to the poem as Dickinson wrote it. An adroit, experienced reader can perform these two operations almost simultaneously. Yet he concedes that this reduction to conventional syntax and punctuation may leave us with "an insipid piece of work." Mainly because, consciously or not, she forces us "to think and imagine in feminine modes," he considers Dickinson the most significant woman in western literature after Sappho. Of her poetic gifts, foremost are her verbal resourcefulness and unexpected changes of direction.

When the tapes of Robert Creeley's lecture, "The Girl Next Door" arrived, I couldn't wait to hear them. Creeley's strong Massachusetts accent stood out. Itsy Borenstein, who was doing the transcribing, had to stop the machine every 10 or 15 seconds, so hard was it for the hands to keep pace with the voice while maintaining accuracy. Creeley's combination of slang, colloquialism, and some fairly sophisticated usage, was not always easy to follow. His Dickinson was a reasonably healthy, well-to-do young girl attending one of the best private schools in the country, easily the equivalent of a present day school like Andover or Exeter. Many of the teachers at Amherst Academy had or would teach at Amherst College. Anyone acquainted with the faculty and curriculum at Amherst Academy would not be too surprised at the extraordinary number of references to contemporary developments in geology, archaeology and biology that appear in her poems. Finally, even if she was already having her doubts on the subject of religion, she gave no particular sign of being reclusive. Toward the latter part of his talk, Creeley's voice began to drag some, as if he were a little drunk. Much fiddling with the equipment did wonders for his sobriety. In slowing down the machine in order to make things easier, we had gone a bit too far. When we had gone as far as we could, we sent a copy of our transcription to Michael Palmer, who had agreed to look it over. Palmer had been present for the lecture, in addition to being close to Creeley. His corrections made a difference.

Susan Howe's essay is full of startling details. She shows how, under the wing of her brother Austin, a budding industrialist and art collector, Emily was exposed to the most advanced contemporary art promoted by the New York dealers. Reading Ruskin, she was influenced, Howe suspects, by his evocation of Turner's imaginative vision in terms of both the form and content of her poems. Also influential were a group of American painters with a religious sense of landscape. Even the poet's handwriting was influenced by one or more of these artists. Howe gives facts and figures in dealing with the Dickinson family's role in the industrial capitalist expansion of the Civil War era. Also, she pinpoints letters and references passionately intense, directed to both sexes. Howe's paper is so far-ranging, there is no way it can be summarized.

Perhaps the most scholarly of the essays on Spicer, John Granger's study of the four dictated books suggested that his writing bore the scriptural character of a work whose profound disturbances were resolved in a second, invisible order, such as God. Of all modern authors, Spicer read most like Lorca, Yeats and Blake, "for each of whom division is the sign of profounder communion—the idea of the alien [is] itself a unity subsuming division . . ." Then the poet, through whom "Beauty wages continual war with God," composes a world from the fragments of division. According to Jack Spicer, "you see division and then know God."

Of all the Spicer essays, Burton Hatlen's was probably the clearest and best written, limited as it was to a single important book. He used Bakhtin's ideas on the dialogic character of language to show how Spicer related himself to Lorca through both his choice of poems to translate and his choice of images, not to mention the character of the letters he addressed to the dead poet. Altogether, it was a superb essay.

Bruce Boone's "Spicer's Writing in Context" was impossible to summarize and next to impossible for me to understand. Expecting more, I was disappointed. Given the dense texture of Spicer's project, Boone's point of entry, through an exploration of group paranoia, fails to take him to the center of the labyrinth and out the other side.

Gilbert Sorrentino's "chrestomathy" or album of quotations important to an understanding of Spicer, included 18 from Spicer himself, four from Maurice Blanchot, two from Foucault and Williams—a rich trove, many of the Spicer quotes familiar from other essays. On its own terms, this pastiche offers genuine value, even if Sorrentino's previous work on Spicer had led me to expect a good deal more.

From the Spicer circle, I asked George Stanley for something relating to the earlier books. What he sent me was "Diamond and Heart: The Transition in Jack Spicer's Poetry." The essay concentrated on the symbolism in those early books: the meaning of words or things like "seagull", "ocean", "sand", "room", "football", "lemon", "diamond" and "heart." Stanley underlines Spicer's injunction to "get the real into the poem" and, to stress the secondary, instrumental value of language, quotes Spicer again: "Words are what sticks to the real." Another member of the Spicer circle whom I asked to write at the suggestion of a mutual friend, Bill Moore, was Dora Fitzgerald. Her piece on "Jack As Coyote" lovingly recounted Spicer's habits and methods of teaching and indoctrinating his students along with the ways Spicer used and understood the Tarot deck.

For Ross Feld, Spicer's disgust with what he called "the big lie of the personal" was self-defeating. Partly because he was a professional linguist back in the '50's, and read Saussure even then, he was a genuine visionary, at least twenty years ahead of his time. For poetry, Spicer's critique of metaphor was radical to the point of destructiveness. Who are we, it asked, to make metaphors—who are them ourselves? While Feld saw the brilliant, breathtaking character of Spicer's project, his goal, it was easy to foresee its inevitable failure. Still, as Feld makes plain, Spicer's religious concerns were genuine. It is to Feld's credit that he was able to recognize the contradictory nature of Spicer's project and, in language he made memorable, its bearing on the rest of us. Unabashedly critical of his subject, he is even more critical of other schools of poetry such as the Objectivists and the Confessional Poets.

The Dickinson issue included two poems in her own hand to demonstrate E.D.'s unorthodox method of breaking lines. Also, a photograph of the poet's room, possibly the most famous such room in the history of poetry. There was also a selection of eleven Dickinson poems. For the Spicer section, I added a similar selection of poems, along with two nearly-finished poems of Jack Spicer. In addition, we reproduced the first page of Spicer's review of Thomas H. Johnson's three-volume edition of *The Poems of Emily Dickinson*, which originally appeared in *The Boston Public Library Quarterly* for July, 1956.

As we approached final paste-up, two distinct but related problems emerged, complicating my job. First was the necessity of reproducing two Civil War photographs from another magazine for the Dahlen essay when neither the original author nor editor could refer me to the original photographs. Even so, they wound up being reasonably well-reproduced, only to have their captions switched. The second problem involved different spacing for a number of Dickinson poems where Susan Howe considered the space between words to have been made deliberately larger or smaller. While the standard editions of E.D.'s poems do not indicate this, Howe was following Dickinson's own home-made booklets with their own spacing. Understandably, Howe was so worried that she wanted not only rough *and* final proofs but xeroxes of the final paste-ups. Initially, I erred on the side of too little space between words or surrounding a dash; later on, too much space. To complicate matters, Howe was traveling to a conference at the time, and I had to mail them express with great precision, since she was rarely more than a couple of days in one place. Alas!, while the final paste-up pleased her, she had no idea these final proofs could grow a brand new set of typos. I noticed them late in the game and managed to correct most of them but some still escaped me. Although our typesetter called it a fluke, flukes multiplied as the proofs were returned to us. Those we corrected would grow even more errors to replace the old ones, like a second set of measles after two weeks of antibiotics.

*   *   *

In fall, 1985, Kathy Allen phoned to say that the Tucson Poetry Festival wanted the 1987 Festival to honor *Ironwood*. Would I work with them? I asked for a week to think it over. My answer, when I gave it, was yes, but included a number of conditions. First was that the poets chosen should not be labeled *Ironwood* poets—they belonged to themselves and, for the most part, had enjoyed multiple sponsorship. Another thing was, I didn't want the poets to come for less than they deserved. Although the poets chosen had to be agreed to by the committee, they would need my approval as well. We wound up agreeing on Hilda Morley, Czeslaw Milosz, Linda Gregg, Michael Burkard, Steve Orlen and Alberto Ríos, although Alberto was supposed to introduce the others, having read at the first Poetry Festival. There would be an art show made up of the paintings, drawings or photographs from our covers along with two or three additional works from each artist—a terrific idea.

When the time came, the little theater in the downtown community center with its strongly-textured walls and high ceilings had enough space for visitors to stand back and take in the larger paintings. It was the perfect place for such a show. There was an exhibit with all the *Ironwood* issues through #28 side by side. The crowds were good, there was good feeling among the poets. Since Michael Burkard was unable to come, Alberto Ríos agreed to read. A panel of all the poets discussed the private and the public voice with Eugene McCarthy, the erstwhile Presidential candidate, acting as moderator. My original choice, had turned me down, understandably bothered by his not being asked to read himself. Most poets, including McCarthy, gave single one- or two-hour workshops in the morning. Milosz gave an afternoon talk on Jeffers, Lowell and Allen Ginsberg. I was asked to read on the last afternoon. The fact is, I had written more and better poems in the last year and a half than I had in over a dozen years. Since Alberto Ríos would introduce me, I asked him if he could help situate the mike for me, since my voice required it to be very close. When nothing else worked, Alberto picked up the mike with its heavy stand and held it slantwise in front of me like a guitar. It was perfect, my voice never better. I read six or seven poems, twice what I had been asked, and enjoyed a good response.

A number of our friends came from out of town for the occasion. Jim Sloan, whose watercolor had graced the cover of #24, was here from Point Reyes and brought along a six-foot log of ironwood, which was placed near the entrance. Frances Gregg, Linda's mother, came from Marin with Dale Gilson, another old friend. We had a dozen or so poets and other friends for a buffet supper before Saturday night's reading, and some of the same people later on. All in all, the festival ran smoothly and well, with a surplus of good feelings.

Of the more than 60 poets in *Ironwood 29*, only six had been asked to send poems: Carl Dennis, Laura Jensen, Czeslaw Milosz, Charlie Smith, C. K. Williams and Tess Gallagher. Whether or not Alberto Ríos, who had three fine poems in the issue, was asked, I don't remember. I had missed Carl Dennis's reading. When I heard that he had read a number of strong political poems dealing with Central America, I hastened to phone him. To my surprise, a good number remained unpublished and he mailed me six. Reading them, what impressed me was how reasonable Dennis was, rarely if ever raising his voice, inclined to put the best face on those who disagreed with him. Although at key points the poems were specific in their grievances, always Dennis held up some fuller, nobler idea of the public life, the public weal, against which current issues took on a certain perspective. Often framed in terms of early Athenian civilization, this ideal vision added resonance and philosophical depth. I took three of the six poems and placed them at the head of the issue.

Among noteworthy submissions from relative unknowns, three stood out: Richard Lyon's five poems, Elliot Figman's four, and David Kresh's seven-page "Keats's Handkerchief." It required a prolonged correspondence with Richard Lyon before I was able to get the poems I wanted. In such a young writer, what amazed me was how well he kept the tone down, giving, at the climax of his poems, great force and weight to some simple ethical precept or observation. Although their philosophy was hardly the same, it reminded me in some ways of William Bronk. Another thing that gave some of these poems their measure of success was the way some small, subtle phrase or image would, in the final stanza, trigger memory into awareness of an old, seemingly dead love affair. Clearly, Rick Lyon was someone to watch. In the tradition of Whitman, Ginsberg and Jerry Stern, Elliot Figman's poems glowed with raw, vital energy, made palpable by their close adherence to natural speech. Kresh's Keats poem drew much of its energy from one or two dominant images

endlessly transformed, as the writer gradually contracted an illness like
the one that killed John Keats.

In addition to the above, there were strong poems by David Rivard,
John Taggart, Diane Glancy, Kate Daniels, Charlie Smith, Czeslaw Milosz, Bruce Beasley and Michael Waters.

With all of these, plus a handful I haven't mentioned, there remained
the four poets whose work in the issue brought each a Pushcart Prize:
Michael Burkard ("Dim Man, Dim Child") Laura Jensen ("Cheer"), Susan Mitchell ("Leaves That Grow Inward") and Alberto Ríos ("What She
Had Believed All Her Life").

There is so much I could say about the poetry of Alberto Ríos that
needs saying in the present tense. First perhaps would be to point out
the degree of felt life that animates it, a life rooted in community. Again
and again, this community is represented as the adults or, very often,
the elders, great-aunts or grandparents. Most often these are women,
comfortable in their familiarity yet strangely "other." This connection to
woman is the deepest source of his connection to the community. Whether
mother, grandmother, great-aunt, sister or wife, for him, one feels they
are a potent source of mystery, love, and energy, the bearer as well of
family and communal values. When you think about it, it is difficult to
name even a handful of American poets, apart from women themselves,
from whom you can learn much about women beyond an obsession with
their sexuality and a perfunctory nod to their otherness. Ríos begins
with this otherness, this strangeness, and never forgets it. While this
stance is not restricted to women, it is here that he is most apt to listen
at the wall. Here he perceives various forms of female awareness, invok-
ing metaphors for them when ordinary statement will not suffice. For
him, female awareness is not necessarily centered on men, nor even
always on the body. More frequently than with men, though, the body
serves as the instrument of awareness. Obviously, the country he attempts to map is largely *terra incognita*, but his approach makes that
clear at the outset: he is exploring the darkness with a pencil-sized flash-
light. Many poems stay with the woman all the way through, others
openly operate within a man's awareness. Still others may shift back and
forth with emotion or awareness shifting and deepening in both. While
Ríos's early poems saw the world and others from a child's perspective,

his standpoint has changed as his work develops and matures. His achievement is ongoing, incomplete, a task for other male poets, particularly the younger ones, to take up for themselves. What follows is not the poem that won him a Pushcart Prize:

HE WILL NOT LEAVE A NOTE

Mariquita awoke one morning
Before the alarm of birds.
She sat up and considered
The face of the long man next to her:
Mouth open, sheet marks and hair
Obvious on his skin.
He was a shaving man, single blade
Fitting into the timeless schemes:
His face was like each of the oceans,
A measurable tide of hair
Coming up from his chest at night.
It receded by an easy magic
With the blade in the bathroom,
Signaled by a hundred-watt moon,
This hair given over to another gravity
As later she rinsed the sink. This
He called shaving, and was something
He decided early in life like his father to do.
But Mariquita thought to herself this morning
That he was only fooling himself.
Impatient boy, that he had not after all
Watched his father to the end.
The hair soon enough would recede anyway
Starting slowly with his head
At the point where he had grown tallest.
His head spoke this clue
As still in his sleep he turned his back to her
And on the back of his head she saw
The secret place, barely visible.
A clearing under the growth for night things.
For dreams to come just farther than allowed.
He had never told her about it
The same way exactly he had not said

He would be leaving her today.
But she knew. He had not said words.
Given even a hint, no rose on his lapel
The way spies find each other.
Fall was here now, and the wind was loud.
She could hear the outside plainly.
The plants would have to be brought in.
This was October, that feeling, and November.
She would wake to him again tomorrow.
And he would leave her, again, for good.
Every day he was leaving her,
But just a little at a time.
Every day he shaved off something of himself.
One day he would be altogether different.
One day she would wake, and look at
The back of a man who was not there.

Susan Mitchell's "Leaves that Grow Inward" marked a new stage in her development. So well had she mastered her craft that she could turn wholly inward without ever losing sight of the world. The results were impressive, the entire scenery of childhood unrolling in its Rilkean richness. She was able to change direction halfway through, thereby adding another dimension to an already complex poem. In taking "The Hotel by the Sea", I was adding a virtuoso piece, extraordinary in the sense of freedom it gave the reader, the sense, too, of totally letting go, yet for all that a poem that lacked the utter seriousness of the first. Perhaps this poem and the third one should have been printed separately from "Leaves that Grow Inward."

I could not finish commenting on #29 without remarking Tess Gallagher's three poems, especially "Bonfire" and "Photograph of a Lighthouse Through Fog." In these two poems, her perceptual apparatus was in perfect order, each perception leading to a further one, with the entire page available for beginning lines, extremely rare in Gallagher's work. In "Bonfire", courage and beauty go hand in hand:

So many kinds of crying. So much raw gaiety,
        variegated with glittering
                        silence. And you,

my sudden bouquet,
who came to me awkwardly at the head of the stairwell

Finally, Martha Nichols contributed an 11-page review-essay of the
Wisconsin Objectivist Lorine Niedecker's *The Granite Pail*, her selected
poems.

Our cover painting was by Alfredo Arreguin. Born in Mexico and now
living in Seattle, Arreguin was a leader in the revival of pattern painting.
He was strongly recommended by Tess Gallagher. The issue appeared
soon enough to be sold at the Tucson Poetry Festival honoring *Ironwood*. One of our best, it became scarce almost immediately when the
printers could only deliver 1000 copies.

*   *   *

During my seventeen years as editor, there have been many changes
in the world of poetry: the eclipse of surrealism, the rise and decline of
the poetry of childhood, the return of the "culture" poem and what John
Ashbery has called "the Masterpiece Theater School of poetry," the increase in line length, the decline of the simple imagist lyric, the resurrection of myth and the ancient world, the resurgence of narrative poetry, the rehabilitation of history and ideas as fit subjects for poetry, and
alternatively, the growth of new kinds of formalism—'language' writing
on the left and the revival of traditional forms, including meter and rhyme,
at the other end of the spectrum.

Still, perhaps the most important of all is the growing number of women
who write well and submit the results. Along with this, women are writing poems that take a different road from what they perceive as a male
aesthetic: machine-tooled, goal-oriented, in search of perfection. Not only
do women have their own subject matter, they view it differently. The
very structures they create are likely to differ from those of men. That
they invite their share of male imitators is a good sign.

Looking back at our first four issues, I blush at how few women were
included: 4 of 37, 5 of 35, 6 of 30, 8 of 36. True, Ai was the star of our
first two issues with the percentages of women slowly mounting. Still,
only with *Ironwood 12*, where women numbered 16 of 35, did they

begin to achieve a semblance of equality. The question of equity is what makes this change the most important one, distinguishing it from others. At this point, the percentage of female contributors tended to stabilize, fluctuating from a little above to just below 40 percent. While I recall a distinctly smaller percentage of women submitting work during our first few issues, I am not sure after that, though I'm convinced it continued to rise. As with most excluded groups, when people you know begin to be accepted for whatever right or job has been denied them, the tendency, if you have been excluded yourself, is to follow their example. For whatever reason, greater numbers of talented women began to study creative writing, going on to become poets and novelists. Women seemed to do better with the commercial presses, maybe because, once the barriers came down, profits were a more impersonal test. In a world with thousands of losers, "standards" were a lot more difficult to ascertain or measure, being more subject to abuse.

I remember how much easier it was, in the early seventies, to get a good young poet to make changes in a manuscript if the poet was a woman. In the last few years those figures have been almost reversed— the influence, I suspect, of feminist thinking. Still, these changes, while obvious, were not extreme. People resist or comply for all sorts of reasons, right or wrong. Apart from equity, the poetry scene is a whole lot richer and healthier with such a great number and variety of women making their contribution.

To the best of my knowledge, *Ironwood* was the first poetry magazine to print reviews, memoirs or essays on poetry by Mary Oppen, Kathleen Fraser, Jean Valentine, Barbara Guest, Linda Gregg and Beverly Dahlen. Also, one of the very first to print prose by Louise Glück, Tess Gallagher, Hilda Morley, Leslie Ullman and Ilona Karmel. While we printed lengthy review-essays by Hilda Morley and Martha Nichols on H.D. and Lorine Niedecker, I often preferred women to write on male writers and vice-versa. Usually, it was the writers themselves who chose their subjects. Once in a while, though, sensing an affinity, I would urge a particular poet to exercise her powers on work that was relatively unfamiliar, but with good results. To do less was to place artificial limitations on both sexes.

Our Fifteenth Anniversary Issue, *Ironwood 30*, was very nearly the final one. But for Mary's insistence that our stopping in November, 1987 would be too sudden and irresponsible, an opinion seconded by Michael Waters and Greg Orr, I would have thrown in the towel. The truth is, I was tired, terribly so, sick of the drudgery involved in getting out a poetry magazine. So, after preparing slips to let poets and readers know that I would no longer be reading new submissions, I decided in September to have one more fling at it—a double issue. It would be made up in good measure by poets I had solicited, plus whatever I had on hand by the middle of November. In addition, almost half of those solicited would be asked to recommend one or two promising poets. The results later.

While issue #30 was not remarkable for its poetry, it included some illuminating prose—essays, reviews, notebooks and memoir—as well as extraordinary poems by two relatively unknown Russians: Arkadi Dragomoshchenko and Aleksei Parshchikov. In asking to look at Lyn Hejinian's poems, several of which we printed, I learned of these translations and asked to see them. At first, she sent a Dragomoshchenko poem that ran close to 15 pages, too long for me to print without seeing the others. By the time we were done, she had sent me a larger group from which I selected four shorter poems. Then she sent an eight-page Parshchikov poem, "New Year Verses", translated by Michael Molnar, a genuine tour de force with extraordinarily long lines. Parshchikov planned his poem as a kind of mocking "song of farewell to my youth suffused by the hot surge of democracy— . . ." He saw childhood as "a reservoir of existence outside of time." As for Dragomoshchenko, his language never faltered or outran his perceptions. Listen to this, from "Footnotes":

> The taste of milk is the taste of real dust,
> "I knew your hair in the heat, I called each hair by name"
> Time flowed between the stones as hours echoed
> Dust over the roofs.
> In the hand, iron and cherries burn equally
> I knew you completely in a single word—forgotten . . .
> as if behind a skin of sun, that became the reverse side
> of touch,
> The sexless seed from which time has been subtracted.

Leading off the issue were three profoundly musical poems by Frank Stewart, the kind that stay with you long after you are safe in bed with the lights out. I have shown them to many people. Other poems that stood out for me were the two David Graham poems dealing with the nature of photography, Karen Brennan's two successful experiments, "Desire" and "In The Mirror", marking her first foray into 'language' territory, and the poems of Philip Booth, Michael Dennis Browne, George Evans, Anthony Petrosky, Nils Nelson, Gregg Orr and Lucia Perillo. Finally, Tom Andrews contributed "The Animist", "After Bobrowski" and "from A Language of Hemophilia", three spare, stripped-down experiments in perception wedded to verbal economy. How can one praise the outstanding poems and not mention Brenda Hillman's "To The Gull"? Or Ed Nobles's "Threads" and "Catholic Digest?" Or Ruth Doty's panoramic epic, "The Child Prince Myshkin"? Or Charlie Smith's two sensitive evocations of another time and place? If you make the mistake of rereading them, you wind up feeling you should have named nearly all of them. It makes one grateful this book is coming to an end. The poems will always be there, in the issues, for those who need them. Or you will see them in the authors' own books. Did I mention Eric Torgerson? Last in the issue, his four poems came closer to being first. That last spot is a place of honor. Those who have occupied it—William Meredith, Faye Kicknosway, Tess Gallagher, George Oppen, Czeslaw Milosz, Linda Gregg—their names read like a roll of honor.

At Fanny Howe's suggestion, Ilona Karmel, a survivor of the Holocaust and author of *The Estate of Memory*, sent me a long essay on Dostoyevsky's *The Brothers Karamazov*. Not something I would normally feel was appropriate, the decision expressed an earlier self along with that of the editor of a poetry magazine on its next-to-last run. Karmel's essay clarified and illumined the central issues of Dostoyevsky's masterpiece in a way I found convincing. C. D. Wright's review of Philip Booth's *Relations: Selected Poems of Philip Booth 1950–1985* shows her clearly at home with her subject, able therefore to make us feel at home as only a good Arkansas hostess can. We all have reason to be grateful to both. In his brief essay, Eric Torgerson points out the contradiction between a masterpiece of open form and what it's like reciting it after 20 years when the freshness has all but evaporated. Anthony Petrosky contributes a loving reminiscence of what it felt like to be John Logan's student, helping him as well with deciding what poems to take for *Choice*. W. S. DiPiero had sent us a selection from his recent *Notebooks* which, with only a few deletions, we printed. His selections were remarkable for their incisiveness, the ferocious intelligence at work on serious, sometimes intractable issues. Fanny Howe contributed a brief note on Edith Stein, Jew and Catholic, feminist and philosopher, who perished at Auschwitz unaware she would become the subject of so much controversy.

Our cover painting was by Jim Davis, another member of the Rancho Linda Vista commune at Oracle. Although I'd met him once or twice, I didn't really know him well. Yet I had seen his work enough for it to be unmistakable. Since coming to Arizona twenty years earlier, his vision had been consistently surrealist. At the time I was making my choice, he had shows going in Washington D.C., West Berlin and Tucson. Nobody was better at handling paint. While the narrative elements in his paintings could make it difficult for them to work as covers, El Greco Park, the one I chose, was unified by an enormous figure of El Greco himself in red cardinal's robes against a backdrop of modern Crete. Given the size and quality of the transparency, it was impossible to fully realize the original, particularly its color relationships. What remained was still enough to haunt you.

While Ed Nobles and I were writing back and forth concerning his poems, he happened to mention his friend, Li-Young Lee. Years back, when Lee was a student at the University of Arizona, I had heard him read a few of his poems. There was one, "Persimmons," that I was anxious to print, but I was too slow in asking, or else it had already been taken by another magazine. What had impressed me about "Persimmons" was how, with all the purity of a raindrop, the feeling structure of the poem embodied Lee's perceptions. For several years now, I had been trying sporadically to locate Lee and so asked Ed for his address. It was months before anyone answered Lee's phone. When I reached him late that spring, he lamented the fact that he had only a few poems, and these extremely long, none of them remotely ready to be sent anywhere. Six months later, at Thanksgiving, Lee was still mired in what was for him a new kind of poem. By now, it was too late to start thinking of #29—time to look ahead to our final issue.

Another poet from whom I had sought poems in the past was Louise

Glück. It almost happened with the Oppen issue when I asked her for an essay. As our deadline approached, she sent me a poem written several years before on George Oppen, but I was more concerned with obtaining her direct testimony about his writing. Obviously, it would have been better to have both. Still, when Glück came through with her brief but compelling essay, I felt vindicated. Not long after, she told me she was at work on a new book: a sequence in which the short poems could all be considered part of a single, longer one. She made it sound as if, were *Ironwood* or someone else to print a few of these, it would be like tearing apart a seamless garment. At some point in the process, I began to consider a special issue on Glück and broached the subject to her. She seemed embarrassed by the very idea—as if it might be bad for the soul. I could not gainsay that.

*   *   *

In late October, a few weeks before the appearance of *#30*, I began working toward *Ironwood 31/32*. As I have already suggested, I was tired, too tired to do justice to the daily flow of unsolicited poems. In order to avoid having to read each day's mail, I needed to solicit enough good poets to guarantee a 350-page issue. Such an issue would relieve Mary and me of the burden of putting together a separate spring issue. To do the job well would mean getting in touch with all kinds of poets: Language poets Gerrit Lansing, Nathaniel Mackey and Benjamin Hollander; Black Mountaineers Clayton Eshleman, Jimmy Santiago Baca and Gerald Burns; New York School veteran Barbara Guest.

That March, I had heard the Canadian b.   p. Nichol read his poems. Tall, heavyset, he used a cane to help him get around on a bum leg. In spite of his pain, he was genial and open, a man of profound learning. As a reader, he could talk as softly or as loud as the poem required, rapping on wood with his knuckles to punctuate those places where the text was marked with an asterisk. His were the first poems almost that I had accepted for the issue. Yet before we were in print, Nichol was dead, the result of an operation on his hip where, it developed, a malignant tumor had been growing for years.

Tomas Tranströmer let me have "Golden Wasp", a poem that had impressed me immensely when I heard him read it here in the spring.

While ostensibly about TV evangelists and religious fanaticism gener-
ally, the poem stays close to the poet's experience, impossible to summarize. The last three lines yield a glimpse of this dialogue between
light and darkness:

But today my sight has left me.
My blindness has gone away.
The dark bat has left my face and is scissoring in summer's bright space.

Poets I wrote to for the first time included Bernadette Mayer, John
Engels, Robert Morgan, David Ray, Jimmy Santiago Baca, Nathaniel
Mackey, Michael Ryan and Clayton Eshleman.

Of the poets I had solicited, David Ray, Jorie Graham and Carol Frost
were the first to submit work in quantity. Ray and I must have written
back and forth at least half a dozen times. I wound up with four poems,
good ones, but unrelated to each other. With Carol Frost, it required
almost as many letters, but I wound up with five poems, most of them
admirably suited to one another. Jorie Graham responded after a month
with a large envelope of poems of which I took three. Graham's poems
were exciting, intricate in their rhythms. "At The Cabaret Now" and
"From the New World" balanced two narrative lines, the poems refo-
cusing every stanza or two. Graham's poems demanded work from the
reader but repaid threefold whatever you put into them. Hers was one
of the few big talents on the American poetry scene in the service of a
higher vision, a talent that did not admire itself but remained contemporary without any sacrifice of dignity. In April, when Hilda Morley
began sending poems, I could feel the issue building at last. Morley's
five poems led her consistently into new, deeper territory.

Five long poems took up more than 50 pages between them: Kathleen
Fraser's "La La at the Cirque Fernando, Paris", Li-Young Lee's "Furious Versions", D. F. Brown's "The Other Half of Everything", Todd
Moore's "anna", from Dillinger Book VII, and Peter Dale Scott's sections from Coming to Jakarta. Fraser's poem enacted the story of a female circus acrobat from one of Degas's paintings in language that was
brilliant, memorable:

> So comes that city of papaya ceilings. I row my hair
> with arches. Soak in pulp of fruit, go straight up—

my white, cut-out boots laced high over tights.
Let paper faces swallow me, drink me slowly
from the instant I let the cape fall.

Fraser appended a matrix, using numbers 1–3 and letters A–D plus a
coda with nine separate words arranged in three columns. The words in
the matrix were the children of mother words who gave birth when the
typewriter accidentally capitalized letters in the middle of several words,
forming new, smaller ones. Fraser extended the process until she wound
up with a dozen words, which comprise the matrix. D. F. Brown's poem
came out of his Vietnam experience. While its tone was private, its form
a monologue which the reader might feel he was overhearing, most of
the poem's fragments referred back to the war and its putative causes or
forward to the confusion of aftermath, the endless, inevitable postmor-
tems, a world of fragments where nothing stays put. Li-Young Lee's
"Furious Versions" involved exile and journeys, several of them, from
China to Malaysia to Chicago, with the poet's relation to his father a
central theme. Hear what he has to say:

the taste of blood
in a kiss
someone whispering into someone's ear,
someone crying behind a door,
a clock dead at noon.
My father's hand
cupping my chin, weighing
tenderness between us, . . .

Todd Moore was attempting to do with *Dillinger* what Ed Dorn had
done 25 years ago with *Gunslinger:* to embody in myth a legend known
to millions. To do so required accessibility, a relaxed, colloquial style,
the common touch. Whether Moore possesses the requisite extra something for such a myth to acquire a permanent place in our literature is
uncertain. The jury is still out. Written in spare *terza rima*, Peter Dale
Scott's account of the CIA's successfully-engineered coup in Indonesia,
which may have killed close to a million persons, was composed from
the perspective of the decoding rooms in New York and the message
traffic between Washington, Ottawa and East Java.

In the seven weeks before I stopped reading unsolicited mail, three poems arrived from Donald Platt, a total unknown. I took two and, after writing back and forth, added another. Platt had a way of adding an extra detail to an image, as here: "master of sunlight/settled like fine, twice-sifted flour/ on the thousand leaves of the birch." It is the *twice-*sifted whose initial stress slows the line, making the difference palpable. Or again, from another poem, "The Gideon Bible": "I wonder what angels. . /have broken the cellophane wrappers/ around the plastic cups,/ rinsed the day's taste from their mouths,/ and lain down on this bed/ sagging from our thousand bodies." What made this work for me was Platt's inserting "our" in the line, "sagging from our thousand bodies." Most poets would have used the indefinite article, leaving the image impersonal, quasi-abstract. By placing himself in that bed, Platt added his own warmth and experience, along with his sense of union with the other occupants. Not "us and them" but "us".

Clayton Eshleman responded to my invitation by sending a group of poems, plus a series of prose notes subtitled "Marginalia To 'Love's Body' ". Wide-ranging, they tended to concentrate on sexuality, coitus, the dream life, with Eshleman exploring the real and literary connections between this mostly unconscious material and the everyday world of art and politics. I took the prose piece and two shorter poems which had been linked with it. When Eshleman later returned his proof with ¾ of one poem cut, I did not include it.

More than a fifth of the nearly 100 poets, American and foreign, are represented by three or more poems, nine by four or more. Of the several 'language'-related poets I had invited to participate, Susan Howe and Beverly Dahlen responded with seven- and six-page selections, Nathaniel Mackey with six pages from *Outlantish* and Charles Alexander with five poems. When I invited submissions from Gerrit Lensing, Susan Griffin, Michael Palmer and Benjamin Hollander, the first three initially accepted but proved unable to come up with any poems they felt were worthwhile. Griffin, who came down that spring with Epstein-Barr Syndrome, was concerned enough to suggest Margie Sloan, a promising young 'language' poet. The net result was three poems from Margie Sloan. I was pleased to have genuinely good work from a newcomer.

Lucille Broderson had sent poems well before I began soliciting for

#31/32. A Minnesota grandmother in her seventies, she had been writing for a few years only but the results were astonishing: poems composed around a stillness, rarely saying outright what could be suggested. There were eight poets from Tucson: Karen Brennan, Charles Alexander, Barbara Cully, Cynthia Hogue, Jane Miller, Boyer Rickel, Steve Orlen and Steve Fisher. Steve Fisher was a paroled prisoner who was back in prison by the time the issue appeared. Of the five Tucson poets in our very first issue, two, Ai and Steve Orlen, were there for the last. Other poets represented in both issues were David Ignatow and John Haines.

Among seasoned veterans who sent me work, Robert Morgan, Hugh Seidman, Stephen Dobyns and Barbara Guest stood out. I was especially pleased by contributions from Dobyns and Seidman. Barbara Guest spent the last month of the summer in Berkeley. She came one night for supper with her daughter and a copy of "The Poet Who Threw Roses", which we placed near the beginning of the issue. It was such a compelling poem to read over and over that, later, I could not help say over to myself phrases like "—her face from remoteness / divided into orchards" or "framed by lonely work." So disturbed was I by her novel, *Seeking Air*, some subtle menace there, that I found myself unable to finish it, as if the blank spaces between chapters were even more threatening. A little older than I had expected, Guest was cheerful and intelligent, with a highly-evolved sensibility. To my surprise, she had grown up on the West Coast, going east at about the same time as Marjorie Perloff. Since we knew some of the same people in Water Mill and the nearby villages, we spent some time comparing notes, filling in the gaps. It had been nearly twenty years since I had been back there.

Jean Valentine, who had become a very close friend in the last few years, had given me two exalted poems, love poems really; whether human and/or divine love the reader must judge. Among other things, I had loved Jean's poems for the way they combined intimacy and intelligence in summoning you into their depths. But these two, along with a handful of others in her newest book, *Home Deep Blue*, appeared to speak from and to a place of rapture, verging on the mystical. There were some things more important than poetry.

Louise Glück, whose work I had been seeking for several years at least, overcame her diffidence at last and sent nine or ten poems, four

of which I took. The new poems were several shades less formal, closer
to spoken English. They were all family poems. Even though the poems
largely eschewed a high style, some could still serve as parables. To
employ that much overused word, *real*, the poems were real rather than
existing in a kind of air-conditioned space devoted to poetry. The following lines, the fifth stanza of "Celestial Music," show where Glück's at
now:

In my dreams, my friend reproaches me. We're walking
on the same road, except it's winter now;
she's telling me that when you love the world you hear celestial music:
look up, she says. When I look up nothing.
Only clouds, snow, a white business in the trees
like brides leaping to a great height—
Then I'm afraid for her; I see her
caught in a net deliberately cast over the earth—

Of four sets of translations, what stood out were six of Montale by
Antony Oldknow and six more from the German of Ingeborg Bachman
by James Reidel.

When I reached Jimmy Santiago Baca, he was living in Florida, about
to move back to his native New Mexico. He sent me the entire manuscript of *Black Mesa Poems*, asking for suggestions. Of the three poems
we took, one would earn him a Pushcart Prize. James Harms sent two
poems filled with that ambiance special to L.A. and Dean Young three
lyrics furious with energy, poems with all the earmarks of our collapsing
century. It would be criminal not to mention John Haines, William Bronk,
Jack Gilbert, Linda Gregg, Michael Ryan, Jane Miller, Gerald Burns,
Sharon Olds, Chana Bloch, David Ignatow or C. D. Wright. Or the
guitar in Nils Nelson's "The Smallest Of Fires," of which the poet writes:
"He left it in the back seat of a car,/and like a child, it suffered in the
heat./ Nothing could make the blisters go away,/ but in dry weather I
cut a slice of green apple/ and leave it in the case./The wood drinks what
it needs."

Although Hass and Milosz were among the first to respond, they were
the last to send their work. The first few lines of Milosz's "Dante" show
how relentlessly specific this most enduring of modern poets can be:

To be so poor. No heaven, no abyss.
A revolving wheel of seasons.
 Men walk under the stars and disintegrate
Into ash or a stellar dust.
The molecular machines work faultlessly, self-propelled.

Here, the morning after Thanksgiving, looking over Bob Hass's four poems, my eye catches on these lines from "Natural Theology:"

which do not reflect so much as they remember.
as if the light, one will all morning, yielded to a doubleness
in things—plucked skins of turkeys in an ill-lit butcher shop
in the pitch-dark forenoon of a dreary day . . .

although the poem explores the multiplicity of landscape and weather, the fluctuations of light and the body's responses to all this, there is, Hass concludes, "one desire/ touching the many things and it is continuous."

Of the prose features, John Taggart's Oppen lecture explored the poet's use of the dash, ellipses, (the dots that indicate something missing) and gaps of white space. All are signs for silence in which "the world is stopped and illuminated, in which there can be moments of vision." These devices are inducements to "go down, to go into." The moments of silence and vision elicit wonder and terror, the tyger and the leviathan.

At the time of the second Oppen issue, I had asked Cynthia Anderson if she could put together a longer piece, with earlier versions plus notes on each poem in *Primitive*, George Oppen's last book. As good as her word, she sent us a rich manuscript. Some of the lines Oppen discarded en route to his final version were stronger than what replaced them, but that is the nature of revision, where a line too strong for its context must be sacrificed. Here, Oppen often proceeds by subtraction, although parts that survive may give birth to further perceptions, extra lines. Included are notes where the poet is speaking to himself with profound candor and great feeling.

The vivid, often startling, portrait of a servant, a family and a place contributed by Frances Mayes, was a pleasure to read and ponder.

Carl Rakosi's *Collected Poems* received an eight-page review by Charles Alexander. The issue included reviews of William Witherup's and Carol Frost's most recent collections.

Then, there was the kid from a leukemia ward—Mitch Adelman. I had liked his toughness and asked to see several poems again. Now, only a day or two after the issue went to the printer, a letter from his workshop teacher. But for a few delayed exchange ads, the issue was pasted up. Mitch had another month or two to live. I talked to his teacher and later reached Mitch. I'd come so close but this guy was going there, living his few days at a singular pitch of intensity. I explained the problem with the ads. If one or two failed to arrive soon, . . Otherwise. . The ads showed and Mitch slowly receded. Then, since the only way to squeeze him in was to move someone's second poem onto the same page as his first, that's what we did. Mary air-mailed his copy, alerting him by phone. Mitch was overjoyed. When he died six weeks later, he asked that his *Ironwood* copy be buried with him.

Our cover painting was *Oracle Hills*, a watercolor by Bruce McGrew, a tall, sensitive painter and friend of poets like Ginsberg, James Wright, and W. S. Merwin, to name only a few. The landscape situates the viewer at a good distance above and to the side of several distinct layers and kinds of landscape. As if we are climbing up and out of the world, viewing and reviewing as we go higher.

*   *   *

That is how it feels to me, this memoir, a second or overview, watching the scenery of the past unroll, issue after issue, as it moves toward a present that won't stay put. One wishes he could enter again and change some things, make them right or do them better. But it is all there—the imperfect, the errors, the occasional glimpse of perfection.

BACK ISSUE LIST

Chapbooks and all issues listed below may be purchased singly, except #1, #5, #10, #13, #15 and #17 which are available at $40 each but only in sets which include at least the first twenty issues. All prices are subject to change. Available from Michael Cuddihy, IRONWOOD, Tucson, Arizona 85717.

#1
Feb–72
Ai (4), Berry, C. K. Williams, Oppen, Schmitz, Simic, Wakoski, Haines, Meredith (6), Ignatow et al. Hall interview. Sets only

#2
Jan–73
Ai (3), Neruda (14), Hugo, Merwin, P. Levine, Peter Nelson, Lifshin, Ratner, Heather McHugh, Sonya Dorman et al. $12

#3
Dec–73
Peter Nelson, Bruce Andrews, Eskimo Poems (7), Petrosky, James Wright, Edson, Piercy, Dacey, Rogers, Follain, Eich, Machado (R. Bly). Matthews interview. $8

#4
Jan–75
Andrews (5), Benedikt, Dunn, Fraser, Hejinian, Logan, Rakosi, McPherson, J. Moore, Lippe (5), Rankin, Tarn, Stanford (7), Stafford, Petrosky (5). Levertov interview. $10

#5
Feb–75
Oppen Special. New poems (18pp.). Memoirs by Mary Oppen, Andrews, Reznikoff, Rakosi. Essays by Enslin, DuPlessis, Wakoski, Tomlinson, Fauchereau. Letters, photos. Sets only

#6
Nov–75
Scalapino (9), Taggart (17pp.), Torgersen, Weigl, Braverman, Supervielle (7), Simic, Magowan, Stanford, Strongin, Linenthal (6), Haines, Valentine. Essay on Objectivism. $10

#7–8
Dec–76
Ai (3), Amorosi, Andrews (6), Ignatow (6), Kicknosway (5), Lynn Emanuel, Mekeel McBride, Orlen, Mary Oliver, Weigl, Simic (4), Romtvedt, Steele, Greg Pape, Zawadiswky, Nils Nelson et al. Special section on Simic. $15

#9
Apr–77
Brodine, Stanford (10), Masiello (4), Hallgren, Hoover, Bronk, Lynn Sukenick, David Ray, Burkard (9), Oppen (8), Olds, Haines, Klefkorn, Dubie, Fraser, Moore, Gallagher. Orlen on Gallagher, Halperin *Anthology.*. $12

#10
Dec–77
Special James Wright issue. New poems (14pp.), essays by Orlen, DeFrees, J. Robinett, Logan, Shirley Scott, R. Bly, Hass, Phyllis Thompson, Dave Smith, Leonard Nathan, Stitt. Memoir by Carol Bly. Sets only

#11
Mar–78
Kaufman, Hampl, Skoyles, Bronk, Morley, Saner, Fraser, Masiello, Burkard, Logan, Johnson, Hoben, Amorosi, Smith, Saltman, Gregerson, Taggart on Bronk. $8

#12
Stanford (5), Oppen, Rilke, Ai, Krolow, Stern, Valentine,

Feld, Sorrentino, Elingham, George Stanley, Dora Fitzgerald and John Granger. $6

#29 Dennis, Richard Lyon, Jensen, Elliot Figman, Jill Gonet,
Apr–87 Glück, Milosz, Taggart, Izumi Shikibu (8) & Ono No Komachi (8pp.), Theresa Bacon, Beth Bentley (6pp.), Hirshfield, Rivard, Stringer, Diane Glancy, Nina Bogin, Burkard, Claudia Keelan, David Kresh (7), Daniels, Paola, Hilary Sideris, Waters, Reiss, Ríos, Beasley, Ali, S. Mitchell (7). Carruth, C. K. Williams (6), Jerry Ratch, Gallagher, B. Kelly, Reidel, Silliman, Ivan Lalic, Myung Mi Kim, and Charlie Smith. $15

#30 Arkadii Dragomoshchenko (7), Aleksei Parshchikov (9), Ruth
Nov–87 Doty (10), Petrosky, Bruce Andrews, Tom Andrews, Karen Brennan, George Evans, Kloefkorn, Jane Mead, Wong May, Frances Mayes, Nils Nelson, Perillo, Orr, Barry Spacks, Charlie Smith, Frank Stewart, Eric Torgersen, Rolly Kent, Barbara Jordan, Roberto Juarroz, Edward Nobles, David Wojahn, Michael Petit, David Graham, Lyn Hejinian, Jill Gonet. $6

#32 Long poems by Fraser, Li-Young Lee, Susan Howe, Na
Nov–88 thaniel Mackey, D. F. Brown, Todd Moore, Peter Dale Scott. Poems by Louise Glück (4), Ray (4), Frost (5), Guest, Morley (5), Ai, Valentine, Tranströmer, B. P. Nichol, Montale (6), Weigl, Specks, Hass (4), Orlen, Eshleman, Rita Gabis, Dean Young, Gregg, Gilbert, Bronk (4), James Harms, J. Graham (9), Jane Miller, Jimmy Baca, Margy Sloan, Waters, Mathis, Robert Morgan, Gerald Burns, P. Kirkpatrick, Dahlen, Dobyns (4), Karen Brennan, Haines, Ignatow Milosz, Ríos, Alexander (5), Bernadette Mayer, Hashimoto, Scates et al. $10

IRONWOOD CHAPBOOK SERIES